Cotton Mather

COTTON MATHER

The Puritan Priest

by BARRETT WENDELL

with a new introduction by Alan Heimert

A Harbinger Book

HARCOURT, BRACE & WORLD, INC.

NEW YORK AND BURLINGAME

New introduction by Alan Heimert © 1963
by Harcourt, Brace & World, Inc.
First Harbinger Books edition 1963
First published in 1891

Library of Congress Catalog Card Number: 63-12740

PRINTED IN THE UNITED STATES OF AMERICA

Contents

Introduction to the Harbinger Edition

by ALAN HEIMERT

"Two generations of Harvard scholarship," V. L. Parrington observed in the first volume of his *Main Currents of American Thought* (1926), had thus far ventured "into the thorny fields tilled by the Mathers." Always "a consciousness of dealing with Harvard worthies would seem to have laid the writers under certain inhibitions." Parrington's barb—that Harvard scholars invariably read the Puritan past "by the gentle light of filial loyalty"—was hurled most venomously at Kenneth B. Murdock, whose *Increase Mather* had appeared in 1925. But behind him, and for Parrington the primary agent of Harvard filiopietism, was Barrett Wendell and the biography of Cotton Mather published in 1891 and reprinted in 1926 by, fittingly enough, the Harvard University Press. The reason was simple: in thirty-five years nothing had challenged Wendell's *Cotton Mather* as the "standard" biography. Today, after another nearly equal period, it remains the best single-volume study. Yet its reputation continues to be clouded by the suspicion that Barrett Wendell, Harvard graduate and Harvard professor, could not possibly have been the "detached critic" that Mather, according to Parrington, demands.

Wendell, who died in 1921, was for the generation of the 1920's, like the "genteel tradition" his name recalled, a "favorite symbol of snobbery and Puritanism." The latter term had been made by critics and historians—Waldo Frank, Van Wyck Brooks, Mencken, James Truslow Adams—into "a byword for repression, icy self-righteousness, and even morbid abnormality." To those who considered D. H. Lawrence the great emancipator it mattered little that Wendell (who more than relished liquor) had passionately resisted the Prohibition that seemed a triumph of "Puritan" prudery. Had not Wendell written what all historians agreed was an "apology" for Cotton Mather, the "witch-hunter" whose very name was a synonym for all "the unlovely features" of sterile, conformist seventeenth-century New England? Furthermore, Wendell had been a self-avowed "Tory" who, in his last years, gloried in an inherited mansion which he cherished as the most authentic pre-Revolutionary residence in all America. Thus, nearly two decades after Wendell's death he would serve Van Wyck Brooks as the perfect emblem of New England's "Indian Summer"—a crusty Boston patrician whose notion of "American traditions" was "that good old families had good old glass" and Heppelwhite chairs, and "that they had been English and should have remained so."

In sum, Barrett Wendell was apparently the spokesman of a declining Boston aristocracy that in the years before World War I shut its ears to the violins tuning up elsewhere in America and chanted in unison psalms of praise to the tribal gods of the holy city. To this day one hears repeated F. L. Pattee's remark of 1924 that Wendell's *Literary History of America* (1900) should have been entitled "A Literary History of Harvard University, with Incidental Glimpses of the Minor Writers of America." The jibe rings true, of course, only if one blinks the actual text of the *Literary History*, where Wendell rebukes a "complacent Harvard man" who sneered at the Hartford Wits as the only "considerable efflorescence of Yale" with the reminder that up to the time of Dwight and Barlow no Harvard graduate "had produced literature half so good as theirs."* Moreover, Wendell, who carefully identified Jonathan Edwards with New Haven and the Connecticut Valley, declares that throughout the eighteenth century Boston did "not loom so large in the foreground" of American literature "as Massachusetts tradition would have us believe." In fact, the *Literary History* focuses until 1830 on Jefferson and Hamilton, the Philadelphia of Philip Freneau and Charles Brockden Brown, and a host of deserving Knickerbocker writers.

The next quarter-century—"The Renaissance of New England"

---

* Of course Wendell wrote without knowledge of the poems of Edward Taylor, which remained unpublished until 1937.

—occupied nearly half the pages of the *Literary History*. Wendell, complained William Dean Howells in the *North American Review*, was clearly "patronizing." But then Howells apparently was among the few to read the *Literary History* carefully; for his criticism was not that Wendell exaggerated the importance of New England but that he presumed to suggest that Longfellow and Lowell, even Emerson, seemed less than major writers if viewed from any reasonable perspective. Wendell by no means dismissed all American literature as worthless; indeed he pointed to quality long overlooked—such as Thoreau's superiority to Emerson as a hewer of "artistically beautiful" sentences and paragraphs. Moreover, he praised Poe in strains that led to a celebration of the Virginian–New Yorker as the only American writer who was "not local but surely, enduringly national." In short, there was no New England tradition left unchallenged, except the long-violated Puritan persuasion that one should not discuss the merits of the living. And even this archaic bond Wendell burst in order to declare *Huckleberry Finn* "the most admirable work of literary art yet produced on this continent." Such opinions, however shocking to a nation which ("for want of anything better to brag about," Wendell explained) had for fifty years boasted "about the letters of New England," were surely not designed to comfort those whose crabbed parochialism Wendell was presumed to embody.

It was something more than irony that Howells rose to defend the inhabitants of New England's pantheon from the defiling hands of Barrett Wendell. It is a reminder that any simple label —"witch," "puritan," or whatever—confesses the mind's impatience with complexity. Howells took Wendell to be the model of a Boston gentleman, and therefore thought it a masterstroke to expose Wendell's "lapses" into "hopelessly rustic" language. Howells made his little joke at the expense of leaving unimproved the very order of evidence to which Wendell was most attentive: socially revealing nuances of thought and expression. Privately Wendell paraded such sensitivity—often enigmatically and frivolously, seldom without sardonic exaggeration and never complacently—but he was not a "snob." In his *William Shakspere* (1894) Wendell derided those who sought a more aristocratic author for the plays: Shakespeare just "happened to be what many another man of humble origin has been before and since, —a man of genius." At the same time, however, Wendell considered it even more deplorable to charge with "snobbishness" a Shakespeare (or a Franklin) who aspired to "local dignity" and gentility. What counted for Wendell was a man's achievement, which to rightly assess one needed to know the structure and dynamic of his society.

Many Bostonians preferred to ignore the kind of wisdom vouchsafed to Wendell: for example, that the world of Gilbert Stuart, of late Federalism and early unitarianism, of the Athenaeum and the *Monthly Anthology*, was one of *arrivistes* with few ties to either the gentry or the intellectuals of pre-Revolutionary New England. To this culture Wendell traced the Emersonian Renaissance—his general subject at the moment of observing that Theodore Parker's intemperate and abusive language showed that a lower-class Yankee, "however admirable, can rarely quite outgrow all the limitations of his origin." Wendell's purpose was not to disparage the successful Parker but to suggest why the same behavior was inexcusable, and worse, unhealthy, in Wendell Phillips and Charles Sumner. Not only had these scions of high-Federalism turned upon their class, but they had done so, Wendell hinted, because piqued by the failure of mercantile Boston to accord them the status they thought theirs by right of inheritance. Wendell's perspective is worthy, if not of emulation, then at least of the attention of anyone who hopes to understand the American past—if only because it so rudely shatters the image of Barrett Wendell as one with the first families of flowering New England.

One could, of course, be beguiled by name alone, as was the western college student who in Barrett Wendell's day hopelessly confused him with Wendell Phillips. Wendell was amused, and not the least of his reasons was an inability to forget how much separated him from *the* Boston Wendells. Though born on the north side of Beacon Hill in 1855, Barrett Wendell had moved eight years later to New York, where his father's firm needed a commercial agent. Jacob Wendell had been made a junior partner only a year before Barrett's birth—no small achievement for one whose earliest memories, the son later recalled, were of "actual poverty." (A history of misguided land speculation and manufacturing ventures explains the unaltered appearance of the family home; no Wendell could afford modifications or even new furniture!) At the age of 17 Jacob Wendell had come to a Boston where, despite his name and distant kinship to such other notables as the Quincys, "he literally knew no man." There he married a young woman from the town of Quincy, whose people, the Barretts, though likewise related to many "well-to-do" Bostonians, were equally strangers to its society. So too was Barrett Wendell when in 1872 he arrived at Harvard.

His freshman year Wendell looked back on as bitterly lonely, but this he attributed to a nervous disorder that forced him to withdraw. After a little tour of France with his mother Wendell returned, now out of class, to a perhaps more difficult life, the testament of which is a play written in his senior year. Entitled "We Bostonians," the drama has as its protagonist a young New Yorker whose love for a Brahmin girl seems hopeless—his rival being a Harvard professor and her mother insistent that proper Bostonians marry only their first cousins. Then the hero thrills to the discovery that this professor, at least, is socially insignificant, and to the mother's gracious acknowledgment that some of the bluest blood in the country flows in Hudson valley "manorial" families! It was not until two years after graduation that Wendell met the first of his illustrious "distant kinsmen," the younger Holmes. He happily reported the incident to his father and thereafter developed a passion for tracing his New England connections. Yet he remained proudest of his Dutch and Huguenot ancestry—and this while living in a New England which Wendell believed so "homogenous" that any but the racially pure Yankee was obtrusive.

The classmate to whom Wendell remained closest was Theodore Roosevelt, and his favorite Harvard colleague was another New Yorker, William James. It was James who at a faculty dinner in the early 1900's, after confessing himself still something of a stranger at Harvard, pointed to Wendell as someone who seemed completely at home. The suggestion stunned Wendell, who had never felt "settled" in Cambridge. When on another occasion Roosevelt explained to Wendell that the trouble with Harvard was its incurable provinciality, Wendell sulkingly replied that he was the last person to need gratuitous enlightenment. After thirty-five years Cambridge still impressed him as "the most densely local place—in point of ideas—this side of Paradise, where the will of God unanimously prevails." Against the Cambridge platform of his day Wendell constantly played the devil's advocate, but his first target was the dogma, current in his undergraduate years, concerning the cultural inferiority of "enterprising shopmen." In the newly founded *Lampoon* he scored this article of faith—one imbibed by James and Roosevelt—as itself shoptalk, the argot of insecure persons who themselves happened to be in no "very thriving business." Twenty years later Wendell interrupted a lecture to defend businessmen as performing feats of "constructive imagination every whit as marvellous" as the work of "any artist or poet." Like his fellow mugwump William Graham Sumner, Wendell could allow neither the self-made man nor his virtues and achievements to be forgotten.

Barrett Wendell always professed a fondness—undoubtedly genuine—for his father. Yet he did not delight in Jacob Wendell's presence. Whatever the nature of the tension (and one suspects that Wendell thought himself an invalid weakling in the father's eyes), it was Barrett Wendell's explanation for his decision to work in Boston after leaving the Law School. After a brief and most unsuccessful legal apprenticeship, he awaited, even courted, parental displeasure; instead he received a warm invitation to the father's firm. But Wendell (unlike Cotton Mather) insisted on a calling of his own; in 1880 he accepted Harvard President Eliot's offer of an instructorship in English composition. Half-apologetically, half-defiantly, Wendell wrote his father of the honor and at the same time announced his intention to be married and his expectation that the teaching appointment would give him time to pursue the vocation of novelist. Jacob Wendell neither objected to his son's decision nor approved it; in 1880 and after the father's function was that of an example, however remote, of successful energy.

Within a year of embarking on his new career Barrett Wendell thought the only novel worth writing autobiographical—its title, "A Study of a Failure." Such a mood, beginning a decade after the year assigned by Henry Adams to his own, would continue to plague Wendell; but its depths were sounded in the 1880's, when Wendell composed his own epitaph: "He lacked the courage to do good or evil." He wondered aloud if anyone ever reached his age in New England "without wanting to kill himself." Evidently not, if we may credit William James's efforts, in these very years, to provide the young men of Boston and Harvard with an affirmative answer to the question, "Is Life Worth Living?" But Wendell imagined his *malaise* a personal curse, perhaps inherited from a great-grandmother who had suffered what he called an "interrupted personality." He lived in regular expectation that the "hysterical paralysis" of his freshman year would recur.

Despite all dread, Wendell wrote and published two novels. *The Duchess Emilia* (1885), which dealt with metempsychosis, created a critical ripple as a promising "Hawthornesque" romance. *Rankell's Remains* (1887), distinguished by a vivid description of the robbing of a New York merchant's grave, aroused a mild furor over Wendell's "radical" caricature of the convention that nominated Blaine. Both were soon forgotten, and in 1888 Wendell, overcome by a "damning sense of uselessness," put his writing aside and committed himself to an assistant professorship. He had come to feel that the times were out of joint— overcome with illnesses that were nearly all at bottom "hysterical." He noted the apparent success of "The Mind-Cure," but having privately confessed agnosticism, was skeptical about the metaphysics of Christian Science. Mild consolation was found in reading the literature of the Elizabethan age, so "exuberant" by contrast to his own inert and introspective generation: "one condition of sanely vigorous life is that there shall not be too much preliminary thinking." In 1890 he agreed to prepare a life of Cotton Mather.

Both Wendell's acceptance and the commission itself are at first glance puzzling. In 1890 Wendell was delivering the Lowell Lectures which, published a year later as a study of *English Composition*, would pass through some 30 editions as the fruits of his early teaching. And Cotton Mather was surely a surprising candidate in 1890 for inclusion in a series on the "Makers of America." In the Revolution, to be sure, his name and writings had been enlisted in the cause of colonial patriotism, and since then evangelical Americans had continued to cherish Mather's memory. The last of many orthodox biographies—that by the Reverend Abijah P. Marvin—was being prepared for the press as Wendell began his research. But wherever reason reigned in 1890, Cotton Mather was remembered as the agent of the "superstition and barbarism" so happily expelled from America.

Mather's place in American hagiography was inextricably involved in the emancipation of the New England mind from the rigors of Puritanism. In 1747 Dr. William Douglass, who had opposed Mather's efforts to have the people of Boston inoculated, succeeded, by belaboring in his *General History of America* all the marvels and providences related in Mather's *Magnalia Christi Americana*, in making Mather the symbol of all the rational mind held anathema. Over the next century the image was perfected until in Channing's Boston it was fashionable to revile Mather and perilous to defend him. About the best that could be said of Mather was that one of his tracts launched Franklin into rational doing-of-good. Otherwise Mather was assumed to have been a fanatic, unscrupulously and hypocritically vain, and, in the words of Jared Sparks, New England historian and Harvard president, "a credulous old fool!"

All of Mather's imperfections were adumbrated, of course, in the witchcraft frenzy, responsibility for which Robert Calef had placed on Mather's head in 1700. There it hovered until in 1867 C. W. Upham seemed to fasten blame securely with his exhaustive *Salem Witchcraft*. Orthodox historians rushed to observe that Mather had actually urged the Salem judges to beware of "spectral evidence," but no legal quibble could exonerate him of complicity in what Longfellow had called the "wickedness and crime" of 1691. Nineteenth-century America had gone be-

yond even Jefferson in certainty that the "reign of witches" represented a contest between medieval tyranny and modern liberty.
To them Salem proved that the common law was superior to
Scripture as a guarantor of individual freedom. This view, somewhat tempered, was codified in Brooks Adams' *The Emancipation of Massachusetts* (1886), where the witchcraft crisis was
seen as having shaken "to the centre" the "moral despotism" of
the Puritan clergy. And whatever the particulars, the Puritan's
very belief in the supernatural—so at war with the inductive
science that had triumphed with Darwin—seemed but an instance of the "common madness" of the seventeenth century.
1891, the second centennial of the Salem "delusion," saw in the
nation's leading intellectual journals articles (most of them accompanied by an engraving of the stern-visaged Mather) expressing gratitude for the historic victory of "reason"—with its
corollaries of science, "law, self-interest, freedom of speech and
of the press"—over Mather's Puritan delusions.

Thus stood the account when in the autumn of 1891 there
appeared Wendell's study of the "Puritan Priest"—with the proclaimed intention of proving Mather a "good man." In Boston
the biography was acclaimed by the orthodox clergy but greeted
otherwise by considerable bewilderment, especially at Harvard.
In that day, at least, few alumni were less fitting objects of
"filial loyalty" than Cotton Mather, who, among other things, had
along with his father fought to keep the college a bastion of
orthodoxy. Perhaps it was the story of this die-hard struggle
against the forces of "liberalism"—famously derided in President
Josiah Quincy's then-standard history of Harvard—that first drew
Wendell to his subject. For already in 1890 Wendell was ques-
tioning some of the innovations whereby President Eliot was
transforming Harvard into America's foremost university. Still,
Wendell's attacks on the "kindergarten" elective system, on the
"infatuation" of Radcliffe, and on "the alien tyranny" of Teutonic
graduate studies were well in the future. In 1890 Wendell,
though discontent, would not permit himself even the thought
of disloyalty to Eliot. Unless, of course, it were a gentle treason
to contrast the Mathers' "age of passionate religious enthusiasm"
favorably with the corpse-cold rationalism that had come to be

sovereign at Harvard. But all Wendell knew for certain was that he could understand Cotton Mather better than any historian who judged him from the "seclusion of Libraries." Wendell had seen Mather as he must be seen: in the midst of life.

II

Wendell's surprising portrait of Mather derived from a major literary discovery. Previously the only familiar Mather writings were those excerpted in Stedman and Hutchinson's *Anthology of American Literature* (1889-90): the *Wonders of the Invisible World* and the *Magnalia*. On the basis of these, and perhaps less, James Russell Lowell had in 1860 set down Mather as the most "pedantic" representative of a New England which had become soon after the Restoration "narrow in thought, in culture, in creed." The judgment was sustained in M. C. Tyler's study (already in 1890 a classic) of *American Literature in the Colonial Time* (1878); but Tyler had slaked his appetite for sources with Mather's published work and had not used, except for a few selections printed in 1862-63, Cotton Mather's "Diaries." Wendell, however, made a thorough search of New England libraries for these journals (he found most of them) and, more importantly, read them as they had never before been read.

The Mather diaries had been consulted by Quincy and J. G. Palfrey, author of the *Compendious History of New England* (1858-90), who found them only moderately helpful in untangling the politics of Mather's day. Antiquarians seeking light on seventeenth-century manners and customs deemed Mather's journals useless by comparison with the *Diary of Samuel Sewall*, which had been published in 1878-80 by an editor who thought Sewall depicted the olden time "as if by thousands of daguerrotypes." The very thinness of external detail in the Mather diaries was to Wendell a revelation; they had been intended not as chronicles but as records of Mather's "inner and spiritual life." Thus read, Wendell realized, "the pages no longer seem dull, but rather glow with spiritual passion"; they capture, and exhibit to the imaginative seeker, "what life meant" in an earlier and more earnest generation. Wendell was, of course, supremely qualified to appreciate the richness of Mather's inner life: he was not unfamiliar with introspection and depression. And Mather, Wendell discovered, had for each "grotesque day" of inertia enjoyed more than one of exuberantly vital activity.

In his fascination with the diaries, Wendell tended to depend for his knowledge of Mather's public utterances on the titles and infrequent synopses supplied in Sibley's *Harvard Graduates*. Challenged on this score by his classmate Lindsay Swift (the historian of Brook Farm), Wendell replied he had made "no pretense to exhaustive research." Such impressionism was consistent with Wendell's life-long distaste for "the whole dry-as-dust convention of modern scholarly apparatus." But Wendell did not delight in inaccuracy—though the citations in the *Mather* are often maddeningly incomplete; he respected the "precision" of detail provided by the "man of learning." But he also believed that the "man of letters"—in which category Wendell placed himself— performed a perhaps more important service. By viewing the past with "a fresh eye" the amateur might discern what the experts' "very familiarity would have prevented them from seeing."

The quality of Wendell's new light was revealed in a paper he wrote in the summer of 1891 on "Some Neglected Characteristics of the New England Puritans" and communicated to the American Historical Association. The early Puritans, Wendell declared, shared with all Elizabethans a "spontaneity" of temper and "enthusiasm of purpose." With such a pronouncement Wendell challenged a mythology more imposing than that of the "Blue Law" chroniclers: the even more perverse tradition, established by John Adams and reinforced by Webster and many another nineteenth-century American—that New England had been settled out of a desire for political and economic liberty. The fathers of New England, Wendell insisted, had been impelled to America "by the fervent spirit of their faith." In seizing on this most neglected of truths Wendell had entered no trivial demurrer from the emphasis on "Anglo-Saxon institutions" that in 1891 guided not only the seminars of Johns Hopkins and Columbia but the pens of such Harvard worthies as James K. Hosmer. More significantly, perhaps, Wendell was trying to escape the confining ideology that Taine and Darwin had imposed on James's *Hawthorne* and Henry Adams' *History* and, indeed, on the American mind itself: obsession with the "circumstances" surrounding and determining the life of the past.

Wendell was neither the first nor the last to resurrect what American memory periodically buries: the "passionate enthusiasm" of the Puritans. What is noteworthy is that Wendell, refreshed even as one first confronting Chapman's *Homer,* summoned the inspiring example of Puritan faith before an age that seemed as parched as any since the last days of Cotton Mather himself. So impressed was Wendell by the intense energy Mather poured into his calling that he tended in the *Mather* to identify the Puritan "spirit" with little more specific than the strenuous life. His anecdote concerning an early Puritan's prowess at football seems ready-made for use by Veblen in his commentary on leisure-class "sports." But the Puritans were for Wendell more than "bully"; what he admires is an intellectual vigor that allowed them to transcend the material facts of everyday life and to free themselves from the fell clutch of circumstance. Except for reminders that the source of this energy was Calvin's doctrine of election, Wendell does not dwell in the *Cotton Mather* on theological niceties; he summarizes the Puritan creed and defines it as essentially a form of "idealism." Quite obviously this term carried for Wendell none of the precise meaning it held for Josiah Royce, H. W. Mabie, and the others who in Wendell's time met the challenge of Darwinian fact with quasi-Platonic Hegelisms. To Wendell as to Hamlin Garland "idealism" connoted a point of view that elicits from the world not meaning but an impression and sense of inner vitality. What matters for Wendell is not what the Puritans took to be the content of the invisible spheres but the "subjective life" that made the transcendent seem so real and was in turn quickened by communion with it.

In the *Mather* Wendell over and again compares this imaginatively and intensely passionate faith with the Yankee's "rather lifeless formalism." The nineteenth century, he implies, has not only obscured the history of Puritanism but has in doing so denied itself a like creative energy. Such a characterization of the Puritan age is of a piece with William James's celebration of the Reformation and the age of Wesley as among those "great periods of revival" when man is told that the "inmost nature of reality" is congenial to human powers. Thus Wendell's *Cotton Mather* stands as a contribution to and commentary on that effort to reinvigorate New England which found ultimate expression in "The Will to Believe."

Wendell's spiritual longings led him to errant and highly personal interpretations of the colonial past. He was led astray not by his radical perception of "Elizabethan Puritanism," but by a willful belief that the very same flame burned brightly and continuously into the age of Increase and Cotton Mather. To correct Wendell it is not necessary to argue, as would Charles Francis Adams, that with the Synod of 1648 New England entered on its "glacial period." Nonetheless, American Puritanism can be seen, if followed in the course Perry Miller has so majestically traced, to have moved even in its early years toward the cooling of Reformation piety. Both logic and experience subtly rationalized New England's creed and humanized its Deity, until by Increase Mather's day American Calvinism no longer centered, as Wendell believed it did, on the fervent hope of election by a "capricious God." Such a declension Wendell ascribes only to the vaguely defined avatars of historically insurgent secularism and rationalism. In fact, at the time Cotton Mather entered on his inheritance the dominant temper of the clergy itself was what Wendell rightly sensed when he observed in 1891 that the "Yankee Puritan" was perchance "largely Jewish in blood," so "strongly Hebraic" was his character. In an era saturated by the thought of Matthew Arnold, "Hebraic" implied the very opposite of the incandescent "Hellenic" spirit which Wendell in the *Mather* effectively attributes to late-Puritan New England. The term had even more precise meaning in the seventeenth century, when Increase Mather himself had been instrumental in persuading New England of its similarities to the Jews by joining—reluctantly to be sure—the ministerial effort to sway the "chosen people" with the formula of the Old Testament covenant and its literary expression, the "jeremiad."

Such a creed, though modified already in the 1680's by Increase

Mather, conditioned Cotton Mather's responses to the witchcraft and provided the framework for the *Magnalia*. But it was not all-controlling. Wendell, like so many others, allowed the back-ward-glancing *Magnalia* to convince him that Cotton Mather strove only to perpetuate inherited ideas. A "superficial glance" at Mather's "Biblia Americana," with its evidence of interest in Newtonian science, showed Wendell that Mather was "by no means wholly a man of the past." But Wendell failed to appreciate the full significance of such works as *The Christian Philosopher*, which Woodbridge Riley in the early twentieth century called the fountainhead of both American Deism and, in its "spiritualizing" of nature, of Transcendentalism. Cotton Mather was not the last and most typical Puritan but a man of the eighteenth century, at once hailing the dawn of Reason and awaiting with even keener anticipation the noonday sun of Pietism.

Since it was Wendell's stated "business" to portray the "character" of Cotton Mather it is not surprising that the alternate historical sections of the *Mather* are thin and occasionally in error. It would be absurd to correct Wendell's every inaccuracy, for he suffered from the primitive state of scholarship in 1891. Yet it is noteworthy that even when Williston Walker's epochal *Creeds and Platforms of Congregationalism* (1893) appeared Wendell was not swerved from the conviction that the controversies in which the Mathers engaged were solely intellectual and the opposition they met and aroused only personal. Such thoughts do leap from the pages of Cotton Mather's diary, but even they disclose what all the literature of the period assumes— that the good old way was being undermined by those who preferred New England as "a plantation of trade." This is not to say that the Mathers' platform was "anti-business," for they coupled lamentation for New England's worldliness with acknowledgment of the value, if not the inherent virtue, of the world's way to wealth. But though Cotton Mather in the Revolution of 1689 effected an entente between the clergy and Boston's moderate merchants he surely understood that the gentleman-founders of the Brattle Street Church, for instance, were something more than the merely "sensible" and "unimaginative" Yankees of Wendell's description. It is interesting, to say the least, that Wendell saw ardor cooled and orthodoxy eroded not by commercial aspiration but by the vain "liberalism" of Harvard intellectuals.

Finally, Wendell conveys the impression that Increase and Cotton Mather stood sublimely alone, the ground all New England once stood on crumbling beneath their feet, and that they did so, not so much as father and son, but as "brothers," sounding a common "death-cry" of an old order whose cause both knew was lost. Actually Increase Mather was not always allied with his son, nor did the latter, particularly in the years of the father's mission to England, invariably follow the letter of paternal instructions. Nor did Increase Mather join with his son and the other Boston ministers who proposed to modify congregationalism in order to arrest the decline of Puritan orthodoxy. Indeed after 1700 Increase Mather abandoned all hope of restoring New England to its lost spiritual glory. Cotton Mather would not agree; he adjusted to change, even conceded much to it, and assumed a perhaps double responsibility for urging New England to the fulfillment of its early promise. He ended his days as something of a John the Baptist to Jonathan Edwards. But Wendell relished less a Cotton Mather who prophesied in sackcloth than one whose shoulders were easy under the mantle of Elijah.

When all this has been said, Wendell's *Cotton Mather* is remarkable for its penetration into the inner mind of its intended subject. Obviously Wendell did not scale the Delectable Mountains outlined by Kenneth Murdock when in 1929 he demanded of anyone who hoped to understand Mather a full appreciation of "the tangles of his psychological constitution." The reader must judge for himself Wendell's insight, which is seldom made explicit, except for intermittent suggestions such as that Mather's anticipations of marriage had "more than he knew to do" with his intimations of angelic and diabolical visitations. Wendell's gentle hints are probably to be preferred to the bolder, and less stimulating, assertions of later scholars that Mather was "oversexed," or a classic example of the Oedipus complex. It is no doubt wise, as Murdock warned, to await fuller knowledge before forcing Mather "into some Procrustean category of modern psychological theory." Yet Mather's personality may in the last analysis prove to have turned on what most haunted Wendell: Mather's relationship, not to his illustrious ancestors merely, but to a magisterial and all-but-immortal father. On this matter Wendell by no means uttered the last word, but he did observe that the *Magnalia*, though perhaps useless as a history of early New England, was extraordinarily revealing "psychologically," and surely he sensed as much about Cotton Mather's memoir of Increase Mather. Wendell's speculations on what the father meant to the son—in the moving chapter on the death of Increase Mather—are no mere paraphrase of the *Parentator* but a compellingly personal gloss. Whatever Wendell's source, he succeeded not merely in focusing on what may be an archetypal American relationship but in conveying a sense of its everlasting complexity.

W. C. Ford, who edited Mather's diaries, thought him perfectly representative of "a morbid condition" that prevailed throughout an "ossified" third-generation New England. Wendell had offered a more useful formula: Mather was "a conveniently exaggerated type of the characteristics that marked the society of which he formed a part." So fragmenting a culture as that of provincial New England continues to defy easy generalizations, but of this melancholy country—divided against itself, abandoning its heritage yet seeking to give the ancestral faith new meaning, Cotton Mather's troubled soul was curiously typical. His meditations and "particular faiths" were the desperate gestures of a mind straining to rekindle the ancient warmth; his "ejaculations" and other "engines of piety," devices for reviving enthusiasm in a people from which it had disappeared. Cotton Mather fondly thought himself recapturing the primitive spirit of Puritanism, but he was in fact the flower of New England's Age of the Baroque.

Though Mather was not, as Parrington would have it, "a New England flagellant," he clearly goaded himself into matching the fervor he imagined had been his ancestors' portion. But however contrived his "stimulators," they testified that he was not content with a paralyzed New England. This much Wendell appreciated, but he did not quite realize that Cotton Mather convinced himself that his father's life too had centered on "ecstatic prayers and afflations." Nor did Wendell grasp the full import of Cotton Mather's editing of his diaries: he had heightened his visions and ecstasies in the hope of leaving to his children an inspiring legacy. Perhaps because he was thus innocent did Wendell comprehend what later generations often forgot—that Cotton Mather was no tragic victim of parental discipline or unconscious rivalry but a son who, however compelled, built upon what he took to have been his father's achievements.

III

In 1891 Wendell's *Cotton Mather* was received by Americans (outside of Boston) as a refreshingly progressive and even "popular" utterance. It would be left to others to confound this judgment by attributing to Wendell agreement with every "reactionary" Puritan principle and policy. When subsequently so arraigned, Wendell insisted he had been Mather's "apologist" only in the sense that any "honest biographer" must "set forth the man of whom he writes as that man saw himself." If Wendell failed of the detachment some consider the critic's duty, he clearly often placed Mather in judgment on himself—as when the "life-long foe of witchcraft" is observed rejoicing that his prayers have been answered in the providential diseases of his enemies. And Wendell stepped before the curtain so deliberately in his summary judgment on Puritan priestcraft that a Boston clergyman thought him "unjust to the ministerial character." This indignant critic was "a very radical Unitarian divine," whose intellectual forbears were the very "liberals" whom Wendell, even as he expressed sympathy with the Mathers' warmer faith, saluted as heralds of a prized intellectual freedom. Such a constellation of paradoxes should suggest the difficulties involved in identifying past parties with their "apologists" and indicate as well the unprofitableness of easy classifications.

For the taxonomically minded there is something of a ready equivalent in the early 1890's for Wendell's strictures on the Puritan establishment. Wendell supplied it himself when as a self-proclaimed "blind Democrat" he protested in 1892 that Republican tariff policy threatened an alliance of "Commerce and State" just as oppressive as the orthodox Puritan platform. It should be noted, however, that Wendell's strident objections to the Republican party—more benighted in its defense of privilege than "the old slaveholders"—appeared in a letter justifying his "radicalism" to his father and hesitantly recommending that Jacob Wendell was perhaps shortsighted in his conservatism. Seen in this light Wendell's judgment on the "tyrannically dominant priestly class" of Puritan New England, seemingly so straightforward, reveals convolutions so intricate as to demand closer examination of the sentiment on which the *Cotton Mather* closes —Wendell's intransigently Protestant "None but God shall be our guide."

The last chapter of the *Mather* is something of a scenario for Harold Frederic's analysis of the intellectual torment of the fin-de-siècle ministry, *The Damnation of Theron Ware* (1896). Like Frederic, Wendell concerns himself with the relationship of the clergyman's ambition and desire for approval to his sense of divinely commissioned public responsibility. But Wendell's discussion of "The Puritan Priest," however keenly insightful as regards the self-delusion inherent in the will-to-power, leaves unsaid wherein such as Cotton Mather wrongly yielded to temptation or the precise nature of his overreaching. Was it in his desire to liberate the spirits of New England's people, or in his endeavor to control their wills? Obviously Cotton Mather had no notion that such a line could be drawn, and it would seem that Wendell too was unsure. His selective approbation of Puritan orthodoxy—delighting in its spontaneity while spurning its discipline—is perhaps consistent. But Wendell is at the same time uncomfortably overinsistent in his ringing declaration of eternal hostility to all forms of tyranny over the minds and spirits of men.

Wendell's exultation in the priesthood of all believers is modified, if not belied, by a note, muted but nonetheless audible, of annoyance with a New England who ungratefully rejected the guidance of its professed benefactor. Wendell cannot accept the full implications of either his creed or his analysis of magisterial pretensions. Cotton Mather, after all, strove only "to do good to mankind," and despite his feet of clay deserved better of the public. More particularly, Wendell's account of the 1690's insinuates that there was something unsavory about the impatient desertion of Mather by the very "democracy" whom he had rushed to serve (and lead) during his father's absence. Actually Cotton Mather's services were not so quickly forgotten, especially not in those nether reaches of society who expected more of the Revolution. What resentment he aroused after 1696, when it became obvious that leadership had passed from the ministry, was the consequence of his inability to adjust swiftly enough to changing popular moods and interest and of a confusion, not unique with Cotton Mather, of power with prerogative.

If Mather was, as Wendell believed, an "earthly failure," it was not for want of effort to place a guiding hand, not merely on New England's intellectual life and institutions, but on the multitude. He continually re-assessed the popular mind and devised ever-changing techniques for reaching and affecting it; and thus Mather, far from being forsaken of mankind, attained by the end of his career an influence in many respects greater than at any time since the new charter. Something of how this latter-day ascendancy was achieved emerges from the pages of what Thomas Prince called Mather's "extraordinary lustre of pious and useful" sermons. These Wendell might profitably have read —had he not, like Henry James and the rest of tone-deaf post-Civil War New England, considered oratory an antique, if not despicable, art form. Wendell's failure to do so, like his view of Mather as a silent, solitary, and imperious intellectual, was not unrelated to the fact that within a few years of the *Mather* Wendell found himself appalled by "the primeval utterances of Mr. William Jennings Bryan." Much as Henry Adams after the defeat of Liberal Republicanism had given America over to the inexorable laws of history which he would seek to comprehend but not presume to manipulate, so too had Wendell registered disappointment with the impact of his literary contribution to the Mugwump movement. His initial reaction was not to damn the public for failing to hearken to its true counsellors; rather Wendell despaired that no communication whatever could overcome popular lethargy.

In the *Cotton Mather* the popular offense is, if anything, a too-slow and irresolute fulfillment of "the democratic spirit of Protestantism." In Wendell's telling, Mather's sceptre is not usurped; the attrition of priestly authority is the result of apathy. But Wendell refuses to draw the conclusion, ironic if nothing else, implicit in this history; the personal blessings of liberty and vitality, he persists in believing, are not incompatible. Nor does Wendell consider the possibility that if enthusiasm were revived in Mather's New England the "theocrat" might be restored to his throne by a grateful populace. Or worse. For was not such a perilous balance struck the last time, according to Wendell, in the revolt against Andros? And was it not fortunate that the "democracy" was then guided by someone this side of God?

Wendell's incautious faith resembles nothing so much as the political creed incidental to William James's speculations of the late 1880's. He hoped for a national hero—and for a while thought Grover Cleveland the man—who, by his personal example, would somehow release the energies of all men. James could not conceive that such a national savior might by his authority restrain individuality or that it might be violated by a vitalized populace. Thus James, looking to the past, and fixing his eyes on the same "great man" to whom Cotton Mather in 1713 musingly referred as "my admirable *Cromwel*," saw him only as one of those "kindred spirits" by communion with which each individual could unlock and fortify "what creative energy might lie in his own soul." Such a Cromwell, seen apart from the circumstances of bloody war and the Protectorate, was one of those distillations of history which James allowed every man according to his needs —in happy indifference to the uses others might make of a different selective reading of the past. In 1889 James could not foresee Teddy Roosevelt charging San Juan Hill or standing at Armageddon in the Progressive convention of 1912—or the American people's energies channeled into the deplorably non-individualistic armies of union labor. Nor had Edwards, when in 1740 he recalled Cromwell as a nonpareil of Christian zeal, known all that would be made of the Puritan general in the Revolution or the Age of Jackson. But he at least understood that the Oliverian "spirit" was not wholly separable from rather strong notions concerning the Christian commonwealth. Mather too had a substantial, if somewhat incoherent, program for directing human energies into what he defined as the welfare of the community. Wendell touched on this aspect of Mather's mind when he compared him to such "emotional people"—abolitionists and the partisans of Edward Bellamy's utopian socialists—as in the nineteenth century envisioned a good society. So bemused was Wendell by Mather's felicitous personal faith, however, that he failed to note that among Mather's numerous public services was the first American proposal for an inflated currency.

In 1893 Wendell would be surprised to discover his country cursed by an overemotional "democracy" which, he suddenly realized, threatened to substitute a multitude of "damnable tyrants" for a few. A year later he was berating himself for having failed to realize that even Republican corruption was preferable to the democratic excesses seemingly unleashed by naïve gestures toward reform. It is tempting to trace the need for such self-criticism to the rise of Populism, particularly as in 1892 Wendell had justified his Democratic allegiance in part by a forecast that Republican obstinacy would provoke more radical unrest. But Wendell himself associated his public anxieties with a profound change in mood—with the onset of a "temper doubtful, reactionary," which, he bitterly lamented, was attended by a concurrent loss of confidence in his own creative powers. Populism was but the occasion for a manifestation of what was patently an exhaustion of the energies Wendell thought revived by his study of Puritan New England. Indeed over even the ebullient *Cotton Mather* had been cast the shadow of the coming failure of nerve which, in the presence of threats to the integrity of his being, produced Wendell's own panic of '93.

Wendell's account of the witchcraft in the *Mather* was hailed by several reviewers as consistent with avant-garde thought and with the "chances of the next century's demonstrations." The allusion was, of course, to the occultism that began to entrance America in the 1880's and spawned in the decade following the

Cotton Mather, along with increasing interest in spiritualism, Theosophy, and Christian Science, fantasies such as that of Frank Norris, who in *The Octopus* set forth a model of supernatural intercourse. These bizarre faiths bespoke a longing for personal release from confining matter; but also probably occult in inspiration was Bellamy's *Looking Backward.* Visionary "idealism," as the career of Hamlin Garland attests, was ever a potential inspiration of schemes for reorganizing an oppressive or atomizing society. Indeed a history of the American mind in the 1890's might be written in terms of its movement between visions of personal consolation and of the great community and of what particular order of "animism," as Veblen would call it, appealed most strongly at various moments to each social class. Suffice it to note that in the early 1890's "personal and romantic" mysticism was more prevalent among the "mass," whose wisdom, William James complained, "college-bred gentry" denied themselves by deriding popular hostility to positive science and "mechanical rationalism." A decade later psychic phenomena were no longer the diversion of the multitude, but of those more leisurely souls who sought comfort in an age of technology and amidst a multitude bent on social justice.

In 1906 a great-grandson and namesake of President Quincy would entertain the Massachusetts Historical Society with the prediction that in the new century man would be "brought into organic touch" with the supernatural. Thus, he declared, would be vindicated the Cotton Mather whose courting of the invisible world Barrett Wendell had so prophetically defended. Actually Wendell's commentary on witchcraft had been ambiguous enough that one contemporary reviewer of the *Mather* thought Wendell "a master of paradoxy." Wendell pleads for a reconsideration of the verdict passed on Mather by a victorious future, but he also uses the Salem frenzy as an occasion for raising unexpected caveats against Puritan enthusiasm itself. So severe are his strictures on the dangers of introspection, lack of deliberation, and straining after the transcendent that one is almost inclined to acquiesce in Lindsay Swift's detection of Wendell's "courteously conveyed but not expressed conviction" that Mather was the irresponsible victim of vain hallucinations. But Wendell does not, finally, repudiate emotional religion; nor does he find Mather alone culpable in 1691.

Wendell's solemn verdict is that all New England—including the "witches"—reverted to "mental and moral depths from which humanity has taken countless centuries to arise." These puzzling remarks on the evolution of consciousness were, Swift complained in *The Nation,* far too "personal" to be set before the public. Presumably Swift had in mind what his friend Wendell was to confess in a paper read in early 1892 to Salem's Essex Institute: "Were the Salem Witches Guiltless?" There Wendell recounted his own recent dalliances with the occult—among them spiritualism, which he concluded was not (as the "Mind-Cure" once had seemed) conceivably an augury of mastery over hysteria but a cruel exploitation of family heartbreak. The last and most interesting of his experiments was with automatic writing, which had been advertised as a means of releasing dormant literary creativity. Instead the venture produced in Wendell an "irritable nervous condition"; his spirit was not freed but "demoralized" by a loss of "self-control" to some "outside" force. Thus it was, according to Wendell, that when he came in the spring of 1891 to read W. E. Woodward's *Records of the Salem Witchcraft* (1864-65) it slowly dawned on him that he had "known in the flesh" the very sense of "possession" that attended the "grotesque tragedy" of 1691.

Acute sensitivity to coercions of his will was but the lesser half of the special wisdom dispensed by Wendell at Salem. He went on to explain why he was more than ever "disposed so heartily to dissent from the rationalistic view" of the witchcraft crisis. Hesitantly, but all the more hauntingly, Wendell expressed a "growing doubt whether there be not in all this"—witchcraft and modern occultism alike—"more than fraud and worse." Was there not probably at work in the universe some "mysterious thing"— "subtly evil beyond words"—lying in wait to ensnare the impatient seeker after spiritual deliverance? Such a judgment, stated far less equivocally than in the *Mather,* helps to explain the tempered esteem for enthusiasm in the second half of the biography and ever afterward in Wendell's life. He was among the first to assent to the central proposition of *The Varieties of*

Religious Experience (1902): mysticism is psychologically gratifying and therefore existentially if not metaphysically true. But
Wendell would not turn down the light to give miracle a chance
if it meant encouraging the power of blackness, which he, like
Hawthorne, insisted must be taken seriously. He continued to
affirm that Cotton Mather was not mistaken in having felt himself surrounded by "unknown regions"—for whether they "really
exist is not to the point; they certainly seem to." But he parted
company with Mather (and Hawthorne) in denying that whoever would see God must risk communion with the Devil.

Despite his own experience, Wendell considered such a fall as
that of 1691 to have been fortunate only in having erected, at
the outset of American history, a monument to human frailty.
Salem warned all who came after of the primal sin: "despairing
of Heaven," the witches had "leagued themselves before their
time with Hell." But this was not for Wendell the whole of the
crime of 1691. The sorcerers, as Mather had understood, pretended to the priestly function and did so, Wendell intimates,
because the old theology no longer provided satisfaction. For
Wendell as for George Bancroft Salem represented an anguished
clutching after some semblance of spiritual freedom. But Wendell, the "blind Democrat," cannot approve. For were not even
those who moved to suppress the witches themselves nearly
drawn into the devil's covenant and guilty of seeding what, if unchecked, would have become in effect an "epidemic" of sedition?

It may well be that Wendell had entered so deeply into
Mather's mind that he came to share his thoughts. More provoca-
tive still is the possibility that something of the crisis of 1691
was reproduced in the social and intellectual life of Wendell's
own day. In the *Mather* Wendell follows his subject in believing
that the appearance of the witches threatened to dash the fair
"prospects of Christ's kingdom" that opened with the new charter
government. It is more than likely, however, that the agitation
over witchcraft was a symptom of confusion and disaffection
when the revolution failed to fulfill popular expectations. At first
Mather tried to harmonize New England against the devil's
challenge, but when the emotions began to forebode social up-
heaval, he drew back, suspecting that the accusers were more

devilish than the "respectable" people they had finally come to accuse. Thereafter he would stimulate enthusiasm only within the healthier confines of church and closet. In 1893 Wendell underwent a remarkably similar revolution: reviewing the American past he expressed admiration for the continuing "spontaneity" of American writers; as for the republic, however, its noblest heritage from the seventeenth century was "the system by which our national life must stand or fail"—the common law of England. Americans (as distinguished, one surmises, from Protestants) were blessed in having "no earthly authority" beyond this legal order. And perhaps not even this restraint was recognized; the American democrat, Wendell complained, considered inequality of any sort "a phase of evil." The dilemmas of the *Mather* had been resolved by Wendell placing himself squarely on what he believed was the side of the angels. Convinced in 1893 that "democracy at heart must always be the sworn foe of excellence," Wendell had arrived by a tortuous path to the classic judgment that Salem somehow typified the majority's intimidation of the individual.

IV

This and other questions raised by the *Mather* led Wendell into the examination of the American grain that would occupy him over a quarter century. His essays on neglected Puritan traits and Salem he included in his *Stelligeri and Other Essays Concerning America* (1893), a volume which, in turn, was prolegomenon to the more comprehensive *Literary History*. The latter was not a history of American literature but, as Brander Matthews noted at the time, "an avowed study of the American character." Wendell's organizing theme was the persistence of an "Elizabethan strain" in the American temper long after it had been expelled from Old England with the death of Cromwell. The "spontaneity and enthusiasm of earlier days" surfaced throughout the population in the Great Awakening, triumphed with the Revolution, and thereafter kept the "native American" character so "explosive" that its historical affinities were with the French of 1789. In such a perspective the rage of 1691 was no aberration; for the awakened masses of 1740 followed the pattern of Salem in censoring their fellows and even in seeking to check their freedom. So too, Wendell discovered, during the Revolution and the so-called philanthropic crusade against slavery, and indeed whenever enthusiasm was transformed into democratic despotism.

Yet neither the *Literary History* nor the *Stelligeri* was a simple anti-Populist tract. The latter, Wendell's epitaph for a New England from which the glory had departed, was revealingly ambivalent. Wendell traced his sense that the region was "fast vanishing into provincial insecurity" to a chance encounter in early 1893 with the funeral of Phillips Brooks. Suddenly aware that New England now had "no figures of eminence left," Wendell was moved to both sadness and pride. So affected was Wendell by the death of one whom he considered the avatar of Boston's benumbing rationalism that it might seem his heartstrings were simply attuned to the adversity of whatever passing order. But witness Wendell's tortured impressions of the World's Columbian Exposition, which he deemed an appropriate epilogue for the threnodic *Stelligeri*. What struck him above all else at Chicago was the healthy vitality of the West—at once exhilarating and menacing, but above all contrasting sharply with an inert New England from whom sovereignty was being taken. The fault, as Wendell saw it, lay not in an insurgent West, nor even in a stagnant present-day New England, but in what held the Yankee's will unmoved and immovable—the dead hand of the past. In the *Literary History* Wendell sang a longer farewell to New England's greatness; but however moved to compassion, he could never be brought to forgiveness. Wendell was not an elegiac local colorist, but a Jeremiah come to judgment—and on fathers whose betrayal was to pass on god-like but delusive dreams. Wendell envied Emerson and Parker, for he always considered history's truly "great moments" those "when energy, which has been confined by tradition," burst the outward bonds. But he detested them for having denied the same opportunity to later generations; they had built not an indestructible shay but one so flimsy there was nothing to destroy.

Increasingly Wendell became the outspoken champion of such

parties of the past as had been throttled by a vigorous Yankeedom: the Tories, "good men and true," and the followers of the venerable Calhoun. Wendell deplored his participation in the prejudices of these lost causes, but because he at the time also chose to proclaim himself "the last of the Calvinists" he helped affix to that creed as to himself an all-but-permanent label of "reactionary." His conversion to Calvinism had begun in the *annus mirabilis* of the Chicago Exposition, where the dynamo symbolically taught Henry Adams that the unity of faith had been superseded by the chaos of science and where Turner announced the lamentable disappearance of the frontier. In 1893 Wendell offered his own more apocalyptic interpretation of the nation's entrance on an era of dense population: "the gloomier dogmas that the Calvinist fathers brought from wicked, overcrowded England seem after all nearer the truth visible to our own eyes." Often as Wendell applied these doctrines to a "concentrated" and increasingly industrial America he sounded like a belated but sharpened echo of William Graham Sumner, or John Adams, or even Malthus, but he did not intend his "Calvinism" as a contribution to political theory. When he did so pose, as in the confessedly amateurish *The Privileged Classes* (1908), even Wendell's best friends considered him "more opinionated than wise"—perhaps because Wendell was never quite sure whether anarchism or socialism was the gravest political danger and therefore vacillated frantically between Rooseveltian nationalism and Wilsonian freedom. In every case, however—whether as a Mahan-like prophet who thought American independence "in some sense tragic" or as the hawker of a jingoism akin to that of Brooks Adams—Wendell believed himself primarily the nation's spiritual counsellor. When he confided to William James, "I love the memory of Cotton Mather," it was in the understandable conviction that America would have been better prepared to meet both the "chaos" and the "pressures" of the twentieth century had Channing and Emerson never lived.

"Calvinism," in sum, served Wendell as a severely chastened version of Henry James's critique of pre-Civil War American innocence. Highest on Wendell's list of all the "serenely optimistic" but outmoded dogmas of the quiet past was the "assumption of human perfectability." For the persistence of this fallacy Wendell liked to blame his early sponsor, Charles William Eliot. But behind him, Wendell acknowledged, was the theology of nineteenth-century Boston and Harvard. And Unitarianism was but the archetypal expression of an American mind beguiled by a unique "inexperience" that tended throughout a continent to "prove human nature on the whole well-disposed." The United States, Wendell argued, was becoming just like the rest of the world and would have to abandon the notion that truth alone would "make life better and better." Perfection could not be engineered by imperfect men.

But even as Wendell challenged America's "deep belief in the ultimate excellence of human nature" he conceded that Calvin's insistence on the "lasting realities of sin and evil" was unpalatable as his own steady diet. Such a spirit was foreign to that of the *Mather*. Where Wendell, despite his assent to Mather's semi-provincial attribution of the witchcraft to the barbarous wilderness, could not agree with Thomas Hutchinson, James Russell Lowell, and all else who explained Salem by New England's "remoteness from the main highways of the world's thought." Rather Wendell found within the colonial people the spiritual strength to overcome whatever circumstances. From this position Wendell clearly retreated in the 1890's, influenced more than possibly by his colleague, N. S. Shaler, whose *Nature and Man in America* (1891) had postulated a future in which man's dependence on his environment would be "insuperable." In the *Literary History* Wendell would describe seventeenth-century exuberance, as it lingered in the American temper, as evidence of prolonged adolescence and intolerable nostalgia for the bygone days when both body and spirit could "move freely." Yet only four years later, in *The Literary Temper of the Seventeenth Century*, Wendell was celebrating the American's enduring "exuberance." In innocent, "youthful" America, he declared in 1909 (the very year Wendell decided *The Education of Henry Adams* should be read as merely personal reminiscence), were the only people with sufficient inherited vitality to contend with the "infinitely accelerating force" that pressed on mankind in the new "ethnologic era" of applied science. In his latter days Wendell often quoted Increase Mather's doleful expectation that there would be "no settled Good Times" before the Second Coming. But Wendell did not echo his source by predicting that America would then be Hell; rather he expressed confidence that the American people, its vast majority "excellently sound at heart," was the last best hope of earth.

Wendell's muted optimism was the result of his efforts to explain "The Effects of Calvinism on American Nationality" at the Sorbonne in 1904. America's Puritan heritage, he concluded, was not a merely enthusiastic bent but one tempered by a "saving faith in order." This trait, "so deeply ingrained in the American character," Wendell attributed in his *Liberty, Union, and Democracy* (1906) to the "neglected" Calvinistic doctrine of election —which he now decided underlay the "saving grace" of the American democrat: "a tacit recognition that excellence is admirable." If pride and envy were inherent in the American Way of Life, so too was their means of redemption; all history proved that Americans, in their utterances and their conduct, rejected the "wild melody" of Whitmanesque egalitarianism as the "least native" of New World aspirations.

By imputing to the American character a conviction that we "must always have our betters" Wendell testified, paradoxically enough, to his own liberation from formalism. He could not number himself among the elect who were privileged to lead; so Barrett Wendell acknowledged his common humanity:

Our betters are hard to find, no doubt, and hard to recognize; and the Lord may have sown them anywhere. But He has surely sown them somewhere among us.

Only Cotton Mather, it seemed, had no problem in finding these elusive "betters." His father, as Wendell had affirmed even as he wrote of the son, was "the greatest of the native American Puritans." But Wendell, who was not so blessed, spent a lifetime challenging the credentials of all whom, had there been any certain value, he would have been obliged to follow.

Out of Wendell's torment had arisen the nightmare prospect that closed the *Literary History*—of a twentieth-century Armageddon between an "authority" that might again try to "strangle" man's aspirations and a democracy barbarously yawping its rejection of all inherited standards. Out of it also, however, emerged a realization that the struggle was not between society's marshaled classes but within every man. In the pages of the *Literary History* appears a Calvinism that is not a creed, but a source of metaphor by which Wendell, as if with a two-edged sword, seeks to convey his understanding of human nature. In what is easily his most fascinating study, an analysis of the elder Holmes, Wendell writes of a "spectre" which ever rises from "his subconscious" to horrify and torture the Autocrat. This "inhuman vision" was, of course, the faith of Abiel Holmes, a father whose Calvinism the son over and again sought to repress by assailing with wit and logic its pitiful nineteenth-century relics. What Wendell had explored, in his amateur way, was a darkness from whose power no mind is wholly and forever free.

When Wendell's student and friend, Robert Herrick, complained that "Puritanism" flowed as an "ancestral blight" through his veins, Wendell understood. Perhaps he did not object because he believed anxiety a source of creation, even, perhaps, as Hawthorne and Parkman had shown, of atonement for a writer's more complacent contemporaries. There is no record, unfortunately, of Wendell's response to *The Wine of the Puritans* (1909), in which Van Wyck Brooks, recently a Harvard student, indicted the seventeenth century for America's hostility to art, pleasure, and all that is not "economically necessary." But what Wendell generally advised was avoidance of the path that for him had led only part way out of the shadows—that of casting into the dungheap whatever for the moment seemed useless or burdensome in one's heritage. Not only Jefferson and Emerson, Wendell insisted, but Cotton Mather, "bigoted, fantastic," was the "countryman of Franklin, of Washington" and—all "must surely admit" —"of Lincoln, of ourselves." Thus it little availed to call him (as Parrington would) "the last and most disagreeable embodiment of Genevan theology"—or so Wendell suggested in his final admonition to those who abused Mather, nearly two centuries after his death, "as if he were a living political opponent." It was not

by symbol and incantation, but through self-knowledge, that a
people could exorcise the darker aspects of its nature.

v

Wendell's appreciation of Puritanism had little perceptible effect on those who in afteryears searched for the roots of American culture. Only in what they thought should be rejected of the
American past did they pay tribute to Wendell's achievement—
one likewise attested by the complaint made in a recent survey
of colonial scholarship: "Puritan historiography in America has
been too exclusively intellectual." It was Wendell who first and
most unqualifiedly insisted that "things" were of less importance
than how they "presented themselves to human intelligence" and
the history of the American mind more interesting than its "material and intellectual progress." In the larger sense surely Wendell made only the most modest of contributions to that revolution against Darwinian formalism which began with Lester
Ward's *The Psychic Factors of Civilization* (1892). But it may
well be that Wendell did, as one of his students asserted, almost
single-handedly force American scholars to see that *ideas* were
the "determining factor in American history."

If Wendell dwelt on the New England mind, it was because he
believed that the contours of American thought, everywhere
roughly similar, were in no other literature revealed quite so
graphically. Certainly he made no extravagant claim for the literary merit of Mather or any other writer of colonial New England. His appreciation of the *Magnalia* was previously unmatched
except perhaps for Fitz-Greene Halleck's unpublished poetic
tribute to its balanced character-portraits, but Wendell also declared flatly that the student of "real literature" was wasting
"precious time" in studying any of the "scribblings" of Americans
before 1800. Wendell could not agree, however, with those who
dismissed the *Magnalia* as "so much dust and rubbish" or with
Howells, who declared Franklin the only colonial writer "whom
lovers of literature can wish to know." What critics such as John
Macy (who in 1913 held Edwards a "dreadful bore" undeserv-

ing of a place in the same volume with such a "genius" as James Whitcomb Riley) failed according to Wendell to understand is that "literature" offers more than one order of enjoyment or enlightenment.

"There are few more wonderful experiences," Wendell explained in 1908,

than that which will come to you if you have patience to pore over some musty, crabbed Puritan sermon until the words begin to swim, and their meaning to fade even beyond its harsh obscurities, and, of a sudden, you are aware that this is only another daring, futile, fleeting effort to express in the passing terms of earth an ecstatic sense of the eternal mysteries above.

As Wendell himself developed ever-greater patience, he came to care for literature, first of all, not as an "aesthetic" fact, but as "an expression of the meaning of life." But beyond even this, Wendell concluded that literature is the "most interesting, and most significant, when we consider it as the unconscious expression of national temper." Viewed this way there was *no* author one could not wish to know. Wendell's last major statement on American literature was a sympathetic introduction to an anthology of *Cowboy Songs* edited in 1910 by his student John A. Lomax.

Toward the end of his career Wendell devoted his major energies to the lectures out of which came *The Traditions of European Literature, from Homer to Dante* (1920). This study was the final embodiment of the creed he offered humane students of the past: one knows literature only when he feels that authors "could never have been what they were but for the historical forces that surged about them," and if one tries to think of social and political movements as "voiceless"—apart from literary expression—he will find they "instantly begin to lose something of the vitality which now makes them undying." Literature and history were not "completely independent," nor did the larger profit lie in considering Milton and the English Civil War separately, or Sidney Lanier and the American, or Dickens and the Reform Bill, or Shakespeare and the Great Migration. What Wendell conceived as the proper and most fruitful study he set forth in a review of Edward Eggleston's *The Transit of Civilization* (1901):

The historian of a past civilization must somehow bring himself into imaginative sympathy with the human spirit of the times with which he deals, until he understands not only bare facts but also how those facts made the living men feel who knew them in the flesh.

Even as Wendell penned this sentence, however, he conceded his approach to the past held little appeal to a scholarly world in which the "man of letters," already a survival from a "past epoch," would "soon be extinct." Though he believed his teaching had kept open a way for a new Harvard "in the Cimmerian midnight" of Eliot's specialized university, Wendell soon after the inauguration of President Lowell requested an early retirement.

At Wendell's death the waves of critical novelty were cresting in T. S. Eliot and the newest viewpoint of historians was that of the investigator of social life and institutions. Wendell's one surviving monument was Harvard's undergraduate honors field of History and Literature, which he had served as its first chairman. But Wendell's larger legacy was shared by many, among them Horace Kallen, whose first study of the national spirit was dedicated to the teacher and close friend who had encouraged unorthodox speculation on the meaning of America. Nor is it likely that today any who seriously study American civilization will share either the disdain of the Harvard professor of history who in 1891 dismissed the *Cotton Mather* as "nothing but literature" or the disappointment of the critic who in the same year complained he had expected more extensive commentary on Mather's "literary" qualities. It is now possible to appreciate how very modern was Barrett Wendell's "apology" for the Puritan priest.

Note

Whoever finds anything in this little book must share my gratitude to the possessors of Cotton Mather's manuscripts, who have so generously put them at my disposal. To the Massachusetts Historical Society, the American Antiquarian Society, the Congregational Library, and Mrs. Skinner of Chicago, our most earnest thanks are due.

I heartily regret that I have not been permitted to examine the exhaustive life of Cotton Mather left in manuscript by the late Rev. Mr. Marvin, of Lancaster, Massachusetts.

Cotton Mather

I. *Introduction.*

Two hundred years ago there was living in Boston a man whose name is still remembered. Few nowadays know why we have heard of Cotton Mather; but even in this last decade of the nineteenth century few Yankees do not know his name. My object is to tell what manner of man he was, what manner of world he lived in, why—with all the oddities and failings that are to us so grotesque —he seems well worth remembering. For this Cotton Mather was of those who take life in earnest; and the life he took in earnest was, throughout the sixty-five years he passed on earth, the life of that New England which we who come of it like to believe the source of what is best in our own America. If, for a while, we can make ourselves see life as he saw it, we shall have done what I have in view.

Cotton Mather's diaries, together with his published works, express his views of life with rare completeness. So far as may be, then, I shall tell his story in his own words. In so doing, I shall doubtless expose myself to little less than the contempt of many serious students of Colonial history. The man's veracity has been seriously questioned; and one can see why. In the first place, he was the champion of a cause that, even in his own time, was hopelessly lost,—the cause of the old hierarchy of New England, that once hoped to govern the Western world in accordance with no laws but those of God and Calvin; and not the least tragic fate of men whose cause is hopelessly lost is that victorious posterity rarely appreciates how they can have been honest. Again, Cotton Mather was a priest, and in this world priests are generally accepted in one of two ways: whoever will not bow to their authority is lost in horror of their priestcraft.

Finally, Cotton Mather was a man of such passion as rarely
worries a human being from the cradle to the grave: throughout
his life his emotions swept him into ecstasies which he found
sometimes divine, sometimes diabolical; and, having a ready
tongue and pen, he gave utterance to many hasty things not always consistent with fact or with each other. Wherefore such of
posterity as have not loved his memory have inclined now and
again to call him by a name he would probably have been the
first to use in their place,—a very great liar.

To me he seems otherwise. The better I know him, the more
firmly I believe that from beginning to end he meant to be honest.
Beyond doubt, like emotional people about us,—abolitionists,
nationalists, what not,—he often saw things not as they were but
as he would have had them. What counted for him was God's
own work, what counted against him the Devil's; and God's work,
of course, was all good, and the Devil's refreshingly free from any
redeeming trait. But I do not believe that he often wrote or spoke
a word that he disbelieved when it was written or spoken. He
writes as follows in the Magnalia:—

I have not commended any person, but when I have really judged,
not only that he *deserved* it, but also that it would be a benefit unto
posterity to know wherein he deserved it; . . . yett I have left unmentioned some censurable occurrences in the story of our Colonies,
as things no less unuseful than improper to be raised out of the grave,
wherein Oblivion hath now buried them.

If we cannot accept him, then, as a veracious historian of all
that went on before him, it is rather that his eyes were blinded
than that his pen put down what he knew was error. And we may
accept him, I believe more and more, as a singularly veracious
historian of himself, who shows us year after year not exactly
what things were, but exactly what he felt God bade him believe
them.

In the chapters that follow, I shall try first to give some account of the race he sprang from, and of the place and the period
in which he found himself. Then I shall try to tell, from his own
point of view, the story of his own career. And I shall be sorry if
I do not make it seem that there is still good ground for believing
that it was a good man they buried on Copp's Hill one February
day in the year 1728.

II. *The Puritan Fathers: Cotton and Mather.*

1585-1662 To understand the founders of New England we must recall more than tradition has preserved. All the world knows that to a rare degree the settlers of Plymouth and of Massachusetts alike were men of character. Cromwell himself is no bad type of them. Among the descendants of one of the emigrant ministers, indeed, a tradition is preserved that Cromwell, at the height of his power, once said that he had been more afraid of their ancestor at football than of "armies in the field." One may almost say that all the notables during the first generation of New England were men who might have played at football with Cromwell, and who, if they had, would probably have kept his hands full. All the world knows, too, that these men came hither to found a state where for once the laws of God and of man should coincide. But in the course of two centuries the world has forgotten that their conception of the laws of God was very different from what prevails nowadays. Yet to understand the Puritans at all we must in a general way understand their creed.

To the time of the Reformation, England, with the rest of Europe, had virtually accepted the doctrines of Christianity as expounded by the Catholic Church. The Reformation and the Renaissance, affecting England together, produced there a new state of religious thought, which was greatly fostered by the political accidents of the time. Under Queen Elizabeth the first duty of Englishmen was to fight Spain; and Spain was the head and front of the powers that professed allegiance to the Church of Rome. Protestantism, in that sense of the word which means repudiation of Rome, was the spirit that must be nurtured. Bibles in the English language were chained to public reading-desks in the churches; so were great folios of Foxe's Book of Martyrs: whoever could read might go and read the truth. The truth they read was not favorable to ecclesiastical authority. When the danger of Spanish aggression was passed, the Church of England found that in fostering patriotic Protestantism it had permanently strengthened a class of people not free-thinking enough to discard religious authority, but firmly resolved to accept no other authority than Scripture. The Scriptural creed thus developed in England, but formulated most definitely at Geneva, was the creed of the founders of New England.

Stripped of subtlety and technicality, it may perhaps be stated as follows:[1] In the beginning God created man, responsible to Him, with perfect freedom of will. Adam, in the fall, exerted his will in opposition to the will of God: thereby Adam and all his posterity merited eternal punishment. As a mark of that punishment they lost the power of exerting the will in harmony with the will of God, without losing their hereditary responsibility to Him. But God, in His infinite mercy, was pleased to mitigate His justice. Through the mediation of Christ, certain human beings, chosen at God's pleasure, might be relieved of the just penalty of sin, and received into everlasting salvation. These were the elect: none others could be saved, nor could any acts of the elect impair their salvation. Now there were no outward and visible marks by which the elect might be known: there was a fair chance, then, that any human being to whom the Gospel was brought might be of the number. The thing that most vitally concerned every man, then, was to discover whether he were elect, and so free from the just penalty of sin, ancestral and personal. The test of election was ability to exert the will in true harmony with the will of God,—a proof of emancipation from the hereditary curse of the children of Adam: whoever could ever do right, and want to, had a fair ground for hope that he should be saved. But even the elect were infected with the hereditary sin of humanity; and, besides, no wile of the Devil was more frequent than that which deceived men into believing themselves regenerate when in truth they were not. The task of assuring one's self of election, then, could end only with life,—a life of passion-

[1] Magnalia, V. I.

ate aspirations, ecstatic enthusiasms, profound discouragements. Above all, men must never forget that the true will of God was revealed, directly or by implication, only and wholly in Scripture: incessant study of Scripture, then, was the sole means by which any man could assure himself that his will was really exerting itself, through the mediatory power of Christ, in true harmony with the will of God.

Such, if I read the Magnalia aright, was the creed of the fathers of New England, at least as Cotton Mather understood it. To live in accordance with this, they crossed the Atlantic. To lead unmolested their lives in accordance with this, they confined the franchise to actual communicants, and dealt so summarily with whoever proclaimed other opinions,—Mrs. Hutchinson, Roger Williams, and the crazy fanatics whom they called Quakers. To preserve this unaltered, they founded Harvard College. In obedience to the implications of this, they rated far above other men the official ministers of the Gospel.

Cotton Mather sprang from a race of these ministers. His very name combined two of those most distinguished among the emigrant clergy of Massachusetts. In his chief book, the Magnalia, he has written the lives of his grandparents. And these lives, combining the historical and the domestic traditions amid which he grew to manhood, deserve our attention, if we would understand the life he strove to live throughout in accordance with these traditions.

Among the ministers who came from England in the full flush of their powers, none was more eminent than John Cotton.[2] Born at the town of Derby in 1585, the son of a pious and industrious lawyer, he was sent at the age of thirteen to Trinity College, Cambridge. Early chosen a fellow of Emanuel, he distinguished himself by

"an University sermon, wherein, aiming more to preach *self* than *Christ*, he used such florid strains, as extremely recommended him unto *the most*, who relished the *wisdom of words* above the *words of wisdom*: though the pompous eloquence of that sermon afterwards gave such a distaste unto his own *renewed soul*, that with a sacred indignation he threw his notes into the fire." For at this time, "such was the secret enmity & prejudice of an *unregenerate soul* against *real*

[2] Magnalia, III. I. 1.

holiness, & such the *torment* which our Lord's *witnesses* give to the consciences of the *earthly-minded,* that when he heard the bell toll for the funeral of Mr. Perkins, his mind secretly rejoiced in his deliverance from that powerful ministry, by which his conscience had been so oft beleagured: the remembrance of which being afterwards did break his heart exceedingly." Converted by the preaching of a certain Dr. Sibs, he signalized his regeneration by preaching at St. Maries a sermon so plain in substance and diction that "the vain wits of the University . . . discovered their vexation . . . by their not *humming,*[3] as according to their sinful & absurd custom they had formerly done. . . . Nevertheless, the satisfaction which he enjoyed in his own faithful soul, abundantly compensated unto him the loss of any human favour or honour."

Shortly after this he was invited to become the minister of Boston, in Lincolnshire, where, in spite of the Bishop's opposition, he was settled at the celebrated church of St. Botolph for twenty years. Throughout this period his non-conformity steadily increased: his conscience bade him discard every rite and vestment for which he could not find authority in Scripture. At length, neither his learning, nor his character, nor the moral excellence of his work, nor the friends he had made among those in power, could save him from the consequences of a charge, brought by "a debauched fellow in the town," that the magistrates under his cure did not kneel at the sacrament. The debauched fellow, in fulfilment of a prediction of "the renowned Mr. John Rogers of Dedham,"

quickly after this, died of the *plague,* under an *hedge,* in Yorkshire; and it was a long time ere any one could be found that would bury him. *This 't is to turn persecutor.*

But Cotton was driven into hiding.

Doubtful whether to remain in Boston, preaching in private, he consulted an elderly divine, who gave the opinion

"That the removing of a minister was like the draining of a fishpond: the good fish will follow the water, but eels, & other baggage fish, will stick in the mud." Which things, when Mr. Cotton heard, he was not a little confirmed in his inclination to leave the land.

---

³ Cf. page 9.

So he ultimately came to New England in a ship which brought two other notable ministers,—Hooker and Stone. It was pleasantly said at the time that this ship brought New England "three great necessities: *Cotton* for their *clothing*, *Hooker* for their *fishing*, and *Stone* for their *building*." Among them the three managed to solace the voyage by a daily sermon; and in favorable weather by three sermons a day. Hooker and Stone became the ministers of Hartford: Cotton remained in

"New-Boston, which in a few years, by the smile of God, . . . came to exceed Old Boston in everything that renders a town considerable." On his arrival "he found the whole country in a perplexed & a divided state, as to their *civil constitution*"; and being requested to suggest convenient laws "from the laws wherewith God governed his ancient people," he recommended among other things "that none should be *electors*, nor *elected*, . . . except such as were *visible subjects* of our Lord Jesus Christ, personally *confederated* in our churches. In these & many other ways, he propounded unto them an endeavour after a *theocracy*, as near as might be, to that which was the glory of Israel."

This theocracy came near getting him into trouble. In spite of the passionate defence of Cotton Mather, there is little room for doubt that he was almost perverted by the heresies of Mrs. Hutchinson; but he retraced his steps in time, learning for once in his life to conform.

Nineteen years & odd months he spent in this place, doing of *good* publickly & privately, unto all sorts of men, as it became "a good man full of faith, & of the Holy Ghost." Here in an expository way, he went over the Old Testament once, & a second time as far as the thirtieth chapter of Isaiah; & the whole New Testament once, & a second time as far as the eleventh chapter to the Hebrews. Upon the Lords-days & lecture-days, he preached thorow the Acts of the Apostles; the prophesies of Haggai & Zechariah, the books of Ezra, the Revelation, Ecclesiastes, Canticles, second & third Epistles of John, the Epistle to Titus, both Epistles to Timothy, the Epistle to the Romans, with innumerable other scriptures on incidental occasions.

At last, in 1652, going to preach at Cambridge, he caught cold; his voice failed in the midst of his sermon. It had been

his declared wish "That he might not outlive his work!" . . . he had rather *be dead* than *live dead*. . . . On the eighteenth of November he took in course, for his text, the four last verses of the second Epistle of Timothy,[4] giving this reason for his insisting on so many verses at once, "Because else (he said) I shall not live to make an end of this Epistle"; but he chiefly insisted on those words, "Grace be with you all." Upon the Lord's day following he preached his last sermon on Joh. i. 14,[5] about that 'glory of the Lord Jesus Christ,' from the *faith* to the *sight* whereof he was now hastening.

In a day of secret humiliation and prayer, he took solemn leave of "that *study* which had been *perfumed* with many such days before." As he lay sick, friends came to take leave of him.

When his colleague, Mr. Wilson, took his leave . . . with a wish that God would lift up the "light of his countenance" upon him, he instantly replied, "God hath done it already, brother!" He then called for his children, with whom he left the gracious *covenant* of God, as their never-failing portion: & now desired that he might be left *private* the rest of his minutes, for the more freedom of his applications unto the Lord. So lying *speechless* a few hours, he breathed his blessed soul into the hands of his heavenly Lord, on the twenty-third of December, 1652, entring on the sixty-eighth year of his own age: & on the day— yea, at the *hour*—of his constant weekly labours in the lecture, wherein he had been so long serviceable, even to all the churches of New-England.

Cotton was

"an indefatigable student," who "judged ordinarily that more benefit was obtained . . . by conversing with the *dead* [in *books*] than with the *living* [in *talks*]. . . . He was an early riser, taking the morning for the Muses; & in his latter days forbearing a supper, he turned his former supping time into a reading, a thinking, a praying-time. Twelve hours a day he commonly studied, & would call that *a scholar's day*." He read, wrote, and spoke Hebrew, Greek, and Latin. "For his *logic* he was completely furnished therewith to encounter the subtilest adversary of the truth." As for theology, even his "incomparable mod-

---

[4] "Salute Prisca and Aquila, and the household of Onesiphorus. Erastus abode at Corinth: but Trophimus have I left at Miletum sick. Do thy diligence to come before winter. Eubulus greeteth thee, and Pudens, and Linus, and Claudia, and all the brethren. The Lord Jesus Christ be with thy spirit. Grace be with you. Amen."

[5] "And the Word was made flesh, and dwelt among us, (and we beheld his glory, the glory as of the only begotten of the Father,) full of grace and truth."

esty" could not prevent his telling a private friend, "That he knew
not of any difficult place in all the whole Bible, which he had not
weighed, some what unto satisfaction. . . . And being asked, why in
his latter days he indulged *nocturnal studies* more than formerly, he
pleasantly replied, "Because I love to sweeten my mouth with a piece
of Calvin before I go to sleep."

Two or three anecdotes, preserved by Cotton Mather, show
that he had a vein of humour. On one occasion,

"an humourous & imperious brother" complained to him "that his ministry was become generally either dark or flat: whereto this meek man,
very mildly & gravely, made only this answer: 'Both, brother, it may
be, both: let me have your prayers that it may be otherwise.'" Again,
"a company of vain, wicked men, having inflamed their blood in a
tavern at Boston, & seeing that reverend, meek, & holy minister of
Christ . . . coming along the street, one of them tells his companion,
'I'll go,' saith he, '& put a trick on old Cotton.' Down he goes, & cross-
ing his way, whispers these words into his ear: 'Cotton,' said he, 'thou
art an old fool.' Mr. Cotton replied, 'I confess I am so: the Lord make
both me & thee wiser than we are, even wise unto salvation.'" One
can see why "the keeper of the inn where he did use to lodge, when
he came to Derby, would profanely say to his companions, that he
wished Mr. Cotton were gone out of his house; for 'he was not able
to swear while that man was under his roof.'"

In family devotions he was very short, accounting "that it was
a thing inconvenient many ways to be tedious in family duties."
But his Sabbath-keeping was something marvellous.

"The Sabbath he began the evening before: & I suppose," adds Cotton Mather, " 't was from his reason and practice that the Christians of
New England have generally done so too.[6] When that evening arrived,
he was usually larger in his exposition in his family than at other times:
he then catechised his children & servants, & prayed with them, &
sang a psalm; from thence he retired unto study & secret prayer, till
the time of his going unto his repose. The next morning, after his
usual family worship, he betook himself to the devotion of his retire-
ments, & so unto the publick. From thence towards noon, he repaired
again to the like devotions, not permitting the interruption of any
other dinner, than that of a small repast carried up unto him. Then to
the publick once more; from whence returning, his first work was
closet-prayer, then prayer with repetitions of the sermons in the family.

---

[6] Cf. page 33.

After supper, he still sang a psalm; which he would conclude with up-
lifted eyes & hands, uttering this doxology—'Blessed be God in Christ
our Saviour!' Last of all, just before his going to sleep, he would
once again go into his prayerful study, & there briefly recommend all
to that God, whom he served with a pure conscience."

Such was John Cotton, at least as Cotton Mather believed him.
He left a widow. The mothers of New England were not fond of
widowhood. Before long, she became the second wife of the
Reverend Richard Mather, minister of Dorchester.

This Richard Mather[7] was born in Lancashire, in 1596. His
parents, though in reduced circumstances, gave him a liberal
education. At fifteen he went as schoolmaster to Toxteth Park,
near Liverpool, where the

difference between his own walk & the most exact, watchful, fruitful,
& prayerful conversation of some in the family . . . where he so-
journed, . . . caused many sad fears to arise in his own soul that he
was himself *out of the way.* . . . But . . . about the eighteenth year
of his age, the good Spirit of God healed his broken heart, by pouring thereinto the evangelical consolations of "His great & precious
promises."

A little later he went to Oxford; and in 1618 he returned to
Toxteth as minister. When the Bishop of Chester ordained him,
the prelate startled him by requesting a private interview.

Mr. Mather was now jealous that some informations might have
been exhibited against him for his Puritanism; instead of which, when
the Bishop had him alone, what he said unto him was, "I have an
earnest request unto you, sir, & you must not deny me: 't is that you
would pray for me; for I know (said he) the prayers of men that fear
God will avail much & you I believe are such a one."

At Toxteth Richard Mather preached fifteen years. In his
private manuscripts he wrote thus of the trial by which he was
finally suspended for non-conformity:—

"In the passages of that day I have this to bless the name of God
for, that the terrour of their threatening words, of their pursevants, &
of the rest of their pomp, did not terrifie my mind, but that I could
stand before them without being daunted in the least manner, but
answered for my self such words of truth & soberness as the Lord put

[7] Magnalia, III. II. xx.

into my mouth, not being afraid of their faces at all: which supporting
& comforting presence of the Lord, I count not much less mercy, than
if I had been altogether preserved out of their hands."—"But all
means," adds Cotton Mather, "used afterwards to get off this unhappy
suspension were ineffectual; for when the visitors had been informed
that he had been a minister *fifteen* years, and, all that while never
wore a *surpliss,* one of them swore, 'It had been better for him that
he had gotten seven bastards!' "

Once suspended, his thoughts turned to New England.

He drew up some arguments for his removal thither, which arguments were, indeed, the very reasons that moved the first fathers of
New-England unto that unparallelled undertaking of transporting their
families with themselves, over the Atlantic ocean:

    I. A removal from a *corrupt* church to a *purer.*

    II. A removal from a place where the truth & professors of it are
persecuted, unto a place of more *quiet* & *safety.*

    III. A removal from a place where all the *ordinances* of God cannot
be enjoyed, unto a place where they *may.*

    IV. A removal from a church where the *discipline* of the Lord
Jesus Christ is wanting, unto a church where it may be practised.

    V. A removal from a place, where the ministers of God are un-
justly inhibited from the execution of their functions, to a place where
they may more freely execute the same.

    VI. A removal from a place, where there are fearful signs of *desola-
tion,* to a place where one may have well grounded hope of God's
protection.

So in 1635, after a stormy voyage, he came to Boston. The first
church founded in Dorchester had followed its minister to Connecticut. Within a year, Richard Mather had gathered there a
new church, where

he continued, a blessing unto all the churches in this wilderness until
his dying day, even for near upon four and thirty years together. . . .
He never changed his habitation after this till he went unto the "house
eternal in the heavens"; albeit his old people of Toxteth vehemently
solicited his return unto them when the troublesome Hierarchy in
England was deposed.

In 1669 he died of the stone, "wherein, according to Solomon's
expression of it, 'the wheel was broken at the cistern.' "

As he judged that a preacher of the gospel *should* be, he *was* a very hard *student:* yea, so intent was he upon his beloved studies, that the morning before he died, he importuned the friends that watched with him to help him into the room, where he thought his usual *works* & *books* expected him; to satisfie his importunity they began to lead him thither; but finding himself unable to get out of his lodging-room, he said, "I see I am not able; I have not been in my study several days; & is it not a lamentable thing, that I should lose so much time?"

His temperament was sombre, self-conscious.

He was for some years exercised with . . . uncertainties about his everlasting happiness. . . . In those *dark hours* . . . a *glorious light* rose unto him . . . which I find in his private papers thus expressed: "My heart relented with tears at this prayer, that God would not deny me an heart to bless him, & not blaspheme him, that is so holy, just, and good; though I should be excluded from his presence, & go down into everlasting darkness & discomfort." On his death-bed, "though he lay in a mortal extremity of pain, he never shrieked, he rarely groaned, with it; & when he was able, he took delight in reading Dr. Goodwin's discourse about patience, in which book he read until the very day of his death. When they asked 'how he did?' his usual answer was, 'Far from well, yet far better than mine iniquities deserve.'"

His last recorded words were a solemn charge to his son as to who might properly be admitted to baptism,—a question then seriously disturbing the churches of New England. The only bright touch in Cotton Mather's picture of him is that which tells how, one Saturday evening in 1661, two of his sons, both ministers, arrived at about the same time,—one from England, one from

a Remote place where he was now Stationed in the Country; And the Comforted Old Patriarch, sat shining like the Sun in *Gemini,* & hearing his two Sons, in his own Pulpit entertain the People of GOD, with Performances, that made all People Proclaim him, An Happy Father.[8]

Richard Mather's first wife[9] was

Mrs. *Katharine Holt;* a Gentlewoman Honourable for her *Descent;* but much more so, for her *Virtue.* . . . She sometimes told her Son, while he was yet scarce more than an *Infant,* but very much her *Darling,* That she desired of the Glorious GOD only two things on his behalf;

[8] Parentator, p. 23.   [9] Ibid., pp. 3-5.

the one was, The *Grace* to Fear & Love GOD; the other was, the *Learning* that might Accomplish him to do Service for GOD. . . . Among her Instructions, it is to be *Remembred* that she mightily inculcated the Lesson of *Diligence* upon him, & often put him in Mind of that Word, *Seest thou a Man Diligent in his Business: He shall* STAND BEFORE KINGS. . . . When he was about Fifteen Years Old, she Died Marvellously Triumphing over the *Fear of Death*, which thro' *all her Life* she had been Afraid of.

If a pretty late Abortion might have Passed for a *Birth*, it might have been said of this Gentlewoman, she was a Mother of *Seven Sons*. . . . *Four* proved Useful, & Faithful, & Famous Ministers of the Gospel. INCREASE was the *Youngest* of them; Whom his Father called so . . . because of the never-to-be-forgotten *Increase*, of every sort, wherewith GOD favoured the country, about the time of his Nativity. . . . Had he been Indisputably a *seventh son*, yet he would not have Countenanced the Foolish, Profane, Magical Whimsey of the silly People which furnishes the *seventh Son*, with I know not what *uncommon Powers*; 'T was among the *Vulgar Errors* always derided with him. However, we shall hear of *Strange Things* done by him, & for him.

Born at Dorchester in June, 1639, Increase Mather,[10] to use his own words,

Swam quietly in a Stream of Impiety & Carnal Security for many Years together, till it pleased the Lord in the year 1654, in Mercy to Visit me with a sore Disease, which was Apprehended to be the Stone.

The serious frame of mind thus induced resulted in his conversion. In 1656 he took his first degree at Harvard College,

At which time the Præsident,[11] who was deep in the Dark Principles with which the *Stagyrite* has for so many Ages Tyrannized over Human Understanding, upon a Dislike of the *Ramæan* Strains in which our Young Disputant was carrying on his Thesis, would have cut him Short; but Mr. *Mitchel* Publickly Interposed, *Pergat, Quæso, nam doctissime disputat.*[12]

In 1657,

on his *Birth-Day*, he Preached his *First Sermon*, at a Village belonging to Dorchester. And on the next Lord's-Day he Preached in his

---

[10] Throughout my account of Increase Mather, I follow Cotton Mather's "Parentator."
[11] Charles Chauncy, who was inclined to Baptist heresies.
[12] "Let him go on, I beg, for he is arguing like a great scholar."

Fathers Pulpit, . . . When the whole Auditory were greatly Affected
with the *Light* & *Flame*, in which the Rare Youth Appear'd unto
them: Especially was his Father so, who could scarce Pronounce the
Blessing, for the Tears which from the *Blessing* he had himself now
so Sensibly Received, he was thrown into.

A month later, young Increase Mather sailed for England,
whence he presently went to Dublin, where his brother Samuel
was settled as a minister. The next year he proceeded Master of
Arts at Trinity College, where

the Scholars were so Pleased with the Wit & Sense & Polite Learning
brilliant in his Exercises, that they Publickly *Hummed* [13] him; which
being a Complement that he had never heard Paid unto any one before, at first had like to have given too much Surprise unto him.

Declining a fellowship, he preached for one winter in Devon-
shire; and in 1659 became chaplain to the garrison of Guernsey.
But the Restoration was upon him. In 1660, finding that he must
"either conform to the Revived Superstitions in the Church of
England, or leave the Island," he gave up his charge. Refusing a
living in the Established Church, disappointed in a chance to
travel on the Continent, his thoughts turned homeward. "In fine,
all things Conspired for the moving of the *Star*, to illuminate the
Western Hæmisphere."

In June, 1661, he sailed from Weymouth; in August he came to
his "comforted old patriarch" of a father at Dorchester, who had
now for six years been the husband of John Cotton's widow.
The following winter Increase Mather passed in preaching alter-
nately for his father and "to the New Church in the North-part
of Boston." In the course of the year, Mrs. Mather's daughter,
Maria Cotton, conquered his affections.

On March 6, 1662, he Came into the Married State; Espousing the
only Daughter, of the celebrated Mr. *John Cotton;* in Honour to whom
he did . . . call his First born son by the Name of Cotton.

Of such parentage, whose story I have told chiefly in his own
words, Cotton Mather was born, in Boston, on the 12th of February, 1662-3.

[13] Cf. page 8. A capital example this of Cotton Mather's "inconsistency."

III. *The Youth of Cotton Mather.*

1662-1678 At this time the Plymouth Colony was about forty years old, the Charter of Massachusetts about thirty. Their story has been told again and again. Founded shortly before Laud became Archbishop of Canterbury, the Colonies were first strengthened by such emigration as was stimulated by the persecutions in England, and then confirmed in their strength by the independent responsibility thrust upon them by the civil wars, which kept the attention of England centred on herself. During the Commonwealth, home matters were too important to permit much attention in England to subjects beyond the Atlantic; for the rest, these professed a faith and a policy not very different from those which for twelve years prevailed in the mother country.

What that faith was, we have seen; and in some degree what that policy was, too. It was based on a hope that the government of the visible world might, by the grace of God, be brought into harmony with the system by which God governed the invisible. At the outset the Puritans were met by a difficulty they never quite realized. The government of God, as they understood it, was the reverse of democratic. But the very fact that drove them to a wilderness for the founding of their system was the assumption at home of divinely autocratic power by kings and bishops for whose claims they could find no authority in Scripture. On Scripture only they were determined to rest; but who should interpret Scripture? "All things in Scripture," they themselves professed, "are not alike plain in themselves, nor alike clear unto all." [1] Clearly no bishops, no ecclesiastical tradition, could do

[1] *Magnalia*, V. I. i. vii.

their business; they must fall back on active ministers of the
Gospel. But whence came the authority of these ministers, which
might be held final? Again, only from Scripture, or from such
occasional presences of God as we shall see revealing themselves
in the ministrations of the Mathers. And who should designate
the Scripturally authorized interpreters of the Scripture on which
all authority must ultimately rest? Scripture, unhappily, contained no prophetic catalogue of its proper exponents. They fell
back on the visible members of churches, on those of themselves
whose public profession of religious experience had proved, as
far as earthly processes could prove, their regeneration. The elect
of God became the electors of God's chosen. In other words, their
system at once claimed autocratic power, temporal and spiritual,
and yet rested its claim on something remarkably like the consent
of the governed. They strove to establish a thing that can never
exist,—a Protestant priesthood.

The democratic spirit implied in all Protestantism, in all revolution, was greatly strengthened by the political circumstances in
which they found themselves. Under the first Charter of Massachusetts, virtually that of a trading corporation, the freemen
elected the magistrates. And though for more than a generation
the theocratic principles of John Cotton prevailed, and none were
freemen but the members of churches, there was neither among
the churches nor among their members that heavenly unanimity
which alone could prevent voters from now and then—and more
and more—voting as they pleased. "The will of man," their creed
admitted, "is made perfectly and immutably free to good alone
in the state of glory only." [2] In the first thirty years of their life
in America, the theocratic spirit was strong enough to establish
the terms of the franchise, to banish Roger Williams and Mrs.
Hutchinson, to hang the Quakers; the democratic meanwhile had
established and maintained civil order, and had been forced by
the presence of Indians and other harassing neighbours into
strengthening demonstrations of military power, as well as into
that confederacy of New England whose memory is dear to
lovers of Union. The democratic spirit, I take it, made Sir Henry
Vane Governor in 1637; a year or two later, the theocratic drove
him in disgust from the Colony. It was the growth of the demo-

[2] Magnalia, V. I. i. ix.

cratic that stopped the hanging of Quakers before Cotton Mather was born.

In 1660, Charles II. came to the throne of his father. Massachusetts had grown unaccustomed to paying much attention to what went on in England. She sent him a complimentary address; but it was more than a year before she was brought to the point of officially proclaiming him sovereign. Theocracy and democracy, priesthood and protestantism, agreed in profound disinclination to be meddled with. Together they met in peaceable but dogged resistance to the effort of royal commissioners to assert in New England a power superior to that of the Charter. In their common cause their mutual antagonism was forgotten. What is more, the two spirits were not sharply distinguished: both were inherent in the original constitution of the Colonies. Theoretically, pretty much everybody believed at once in the divine authority of the clergy, and in the right of godly men to say who should preach to them and who govern them.

It was at this time that Cotton Mather came into the world. Little record is preserved of his childhood; but he was of a temperament at once so sensitive and so precocious that we must consider the aspects of life that first presented themselves to him.

For above a year, Increase Mather hesitated to accept the charge of the Second Church in Boston, having

some Views . . . of greater service elsewhere. At last, the Brethren of the Church kept a *Day of Supplications* unto Him who has all Hearts in His Hands, to pray that GOD would Incline him and Perswade him, to Accept the Invitation which they had given him. From *This Day,* he felt another *Biass* on his mind, and soon Complied with their Desires; and on *May* 27, 1664, he did with a great Solemnity, wherein his Father publickly gave him his *Charge,* Accept the *Pastoral Care* of the Flock; with which, (Them and Their Children,) he *Continued Serving the Lord, with many Tears and Temptations, and keeping back nothing that was Profitable for them,* for more than Threescore Years together.

Early in his work he was assailed by Satanic temptations to doubt the existence of God: these he overcame, not by reasoning,—"it puts too much Respect upon a *Devil,* to Argue and Parley with him, on a Point which the *Devil* himself *Believes and Trembles at,*"—but by "flat contradiction," fortified by the re-

flection that, since some of his prayers had been answered, there
must evidently be a God to answer them. Failing in this direct
attack, the Devil betook himself to the hearts of the parish, which
he so hardened as to keep Increase Mather's salary for some
years decidedly below his expenses. Amid the heavy debts that
naturally followed, the good man had recourse to prayer, sometimes tempered with thanksgivings for such blessings as he was
graciously permitted to enjoy. After a while, the church paid
him well, to the very end of his life,—a consummation which
Cotton Mather attributes chiefly to these prayers. In fact, the
form which the answer to these prayers probably took was a
growing and well grounded conviction on the part of the members of the Second Church that unawares, in calling to their
ministry a promising young man, they had secured to themselves
the ablest and most eminent minister in America.

An indefatigable worker he seems to have been. His diary
records devices for saving and employing every moment, and for
maintaining incessant seriousness of heart. And in 1669, when his
father died, and his brother Eleazar, of whose death he had supernatural warning, he broke down. The mood in which, some
months later, he recovered, is best phrased in his own diary, for
the 11th of June, 1670:—

The Threefold Wish of the Chief of Sinners. I *Wish!* I *Wish!* I
Wish! 1. That I may do some *Special Services* for my dear GOD in
JESUS CHRIST before I leave this World. 2. I would fain *Leave Something* behind me, that may be doing of Good upon *Earth,* after I
shall be in *Heaven.* 3. After I have finished my *Doing Work,* I would
fain *Suffer* for the Sake of my dear GOD, and for JESUS CHRIST.[3]

In 1674, "observing the *Sins of the Times,* & therewith Discern-
ing the *Signs of the Times,*" he preached a prophetic sermon on
the text, "The Day of Trouble is near." The next two years were
the most dreadful in the history of New England. The Colonies,
which since the discomfiture of the royal commissioners had been
disturbed by no more insidious tests of their civil strength than
discussions about baptism, and the intrigues concerning the
presidency of Harvard College that broke the heart of Leonard
Hoar, were plunged into the horrors of King Philip's war. Palfrey

[3] Cf. pages 35-36.

tells in detail the story of that helpless struggle of the native savages, and of the organized military power which at last exterminated them with no foreign aid. Sewall's Diary gives glimpses of the ghastly news of massacre that now and again found its way to Boston. But neither Palfrey nor Sewall emphasizes the sentiments concerning the Indians that pervade the long accounts of the struggle which form an interesting part of Cotton Mather's "Magnalia." In the view of the Puritans, the Indians were the wretched remnant of a race seduced to the Western Hemisphere by the Devil himself, that he might rule them undisturbed by the rising light of the Gospel. The landing of the Pilgrims was an invasion of the Devil's own territory; the missionary work of Eliot and the Mayhews was a direct storming of his strongholds, almost unprecedented in his experience. The outbreak of the Indians was his natural retort; every arrow, every bullet, every war-song and magic chant, of the expiring natives of New England was a missile aimed by Satan himself against the power of Christ. The laity met the attack with gunpowder; the clergy were no less active with prayer. To which should be attributed the final victory,—a victory not so much over Philip and his followers as over Philip's Satanic master,—opinions may differ. But Increase Mather was not disposed to undervalue his petitions to the Lord: his estimate of them was confirmed by a singular experience in August, 1676.

"He had for diverse *Lords-Days*," writes Cotton Mather, "made the Death of that Miserable King, a Petition which in his *Public Prayers* he somewhat Enlarged upon. But on one Lords-Day he quite forgot it; for which *Forgetfulness* I well *Remember*, that I heard him wondring at, and Blaming of, himself in the Evening. However, he was more Satisfied, when a few Hours after, there came to Town the Tidings, That before *That* Lords-Day, the *Thing was Accomplished*."—"I will not *Theologize*," writes Cotton Mather a little later, "much less will I *Philosophize*, upon the Original and Operation of those *Præsagious Impressions* about *Future Events*, which are often Produced in Minds, which by *Piety* and *Purity* and *Contemplation*, and a Prayerful and Careful walk with GOD, are made more susceptible of them. I am only to Observe that this *Holy Man of* GOD was no stranger to them."

He was no stranger, either, to ecstasies of an even more mysterious kind.

"As I was Praying," he wrote in 1672, "my Heart was exceedingly Melted, and methoughts, saw GOD before my Eyes in an Inexpressible Manner, so that I was Afraid I should have fallen into a Trance in my Study."—"In his latter years," writes Cotton Mather, "he did not Record so many of these *Heavenly Afflations,* because they grew so frequent with him. And he also found . . . that the Flights of a Soul rapt up into a more Intimate Conversation with Heaven, are such as *cannot be exactly Remembred* with the Happy Partakers of them."

Such was the career of Cotton Mather's father during the first sixteen years of the boy's life. During these years must have been founded and confirmed the passionate personal affection that marked their relations throughout life. Increase Mather, I take it, was of a temper whose affections were most conciliated by enthusiastic acquiescence. Cotton Mather never observed any other law of God quite so faithfully as the Fifth Commandment. And the father he delighted to honour, the father who handed down traditions of ancestors equally honourable, was at the same time clothed with the divine authority of the ministry, to all appearances specially favoured by God, and revered by the public both personally and in his official capacity as minister of the Second Church and Fellow of Harvard College. Under these circumstances, nothing could have made a stronger or more lasting impression on the boy's mind than the example and the teachings of his father. How that example impressed him, his accounts of his father and his grandparents show. Exactly what those teachings were is not recorded. Two or three records of domestic life at this time, however, may help us guess what Increase Mather's teachings must have been.

To understand these records nowadays, we must recall afresh the creed that at almost every moment made the concerns of another world than this the chief reality in the minds of the Puritans. It was our duty, they held, to live for the glory of God; only by so living, with all our hearts, could we assure ourselves of the election which alone could save us from the eternal penalty of Adam's sin and our own. The first thing for us to learn was acquiescence in the will of God,—in His eternal justice, His unmerited and for all we could see capricious grace; without such acquiescence our wills must inevitably exert themselves in unregenerate baseness. At worst we could be no worse off than

our damnable deserts; and if at any time we had the ineffable
joy to find ourselves elect, nothing could more exquisitely torture
us than the memory of early godlessness. As soon as children
could talk, then, they were set to a process of deliberate introspection, whose mark is left in the constitutional melancholy and
the frequent insanity of their descendants.

In the light of these facts, two entries in Sewall's Diary are
even more significant than grotesque.

"Nov. 6," 1692, runs the first, "Joseph[4] threw a knop of Brass and
hit his Sister Betty on the forhead so as to make it bleed and swell;
upon which, and for his playing at Prayer-time, and eating when Return Thanks, I whipd him pretty smartly. When I first went in (call'd
by his Grandmother) he sought to shadow and hide himself from me
behind the head of the Cradle: which gave me the sorrowful remembrance of Adam's carriage."

The second is for January 13, 1695-6:—

When I came in, past 7 at night, my wife met me in the Entry and
told me Betty[5] had surprised them. . . . It seems Betty Sewall had
given some signs of dejection and sorrow; but a little after diñer she
burst out into an amazing cry, which caus'd all the family to cry too;
Her Mother ask'd the reason; she gave none; at last said she was afraid
she should goe to Hell, her sins were not pardon'd. She was first
wounded by my reading a Sermon of Mr. Norton's, about the 5th of Jan.
Text Jno. 7. 34, Ye shall seek me and shall not find me. And those words
in the Sermon, Jno. 8. 21, Ye shall seek me and shall die in your sins,
ran in her mind, and terrified her greatly. And staying at home Jan.
12, she read out of Mr. Cotton Mather—Why hath Satan filled thy
heart, which increas'd her Fear. Her Mother ask'd her whether she
pray'd. She answer'd, Yes; but feared her prayers were not heard because her Sins not pardon'd. Mr. Willard,[6] though sent for timelyer,
. . . came not till after I came home. He discoursed with Betty who
could not give a distinct account, but was confused as his phrase was,
and as had experienced in himself. Mr. Willard pray'd excellently.
The Lord bring Light and Comfort out of this dark and dreadful
Cloud, and Grant that Christ's being formed in my dear child, may
be the issue of these painfull pangs.

A familiar example of infant piety, from the Magnalia,[7] shows
what elect children were expected to be.

[4] Born 15 August, 1688.   [5] Born 29 December, 1681.
[6] Minister of the Old South Church.   [7] VI. VII., Appendix.

Anne Greenough . . . left the world when she was but about five
years old, and yet gave astonishing discoveries of a regard unto God,
and Christ, and her own soul, before she went away. When she heard
any thing about the Lord Jesus Christ, she would be strangely transported, and ravished in her spirit at it; and had an unspeakable delight
in catechizing. She would put strange questions about eternal things,
and make answers her self that were extreamly pertinent. Once particularly she asked, "Are we not dead in sin?" and presently added,
"But I will take this way: the Lord Jesus Christ shall make me alive."
She was very frequent and constant in secret prayer, and could not
with any patience be interrupted in it. She told her gracious mother,
"that she there prayed for her!" and was covetous of being with her
mother, when she imagin'd such duties to be going forward. When she
fell sick at last of a consumption, she would not by sports be diverted
from the thoughts of death, wherein she took such pleasure that she
did not care to hear any thing else. And if she were asked "whether
she were ready to die?" she would still cheerfully reply, "Ay, by all
means, that I may go to the Lord Jesus Christ."

Such domestic influences as these surrounded Cotton Mather's
childhood. The Boston in which they flourished was between
thirty and forty years old. From a bare peninsula of such gravelly
hills as one may still see about the harbour, it had become a
flourishing seaport, in aspect not unlike the older parts of New-
buryport or Portsmouth to-day. The population of Massachusetts
in 1665 was, according to Palfrey, about twenty-five thousand, of
whom a large minority resided in the capital. New England, in
short, was becoming too important to be much longer abandoned
to its own devices. By far the most vivid pictures of the social
life of the time are in Sewall's Diary. People were forced by
public opinion to the willing performance of their several duties:
they attended to their business, they took conscientious interest
and part in politics, they went to church as often as possible,—
which was at least three times a week,—and their most edifying
festivals were the frequent funerals incident to the physical hardship of the period. Perhaps the most suggestive fact concerning
their extreme simplicity of manners is, that young people of the
better sort habitually went into domestic service. The Sewalls
were people of consideration; but in 1676 Sewall's sister Jane
came from Newbury to live with Mrs. Usher; and, finding that
this lady had supplied herself with help, went to live at Sewall's

"Father Hull's," who wanted a maid, and discovered that it was
hard to find a good one.[8] At this time Seth Shove, a minister's
son, and later a minister himself, was also living at Mr.
Hull's, where on the day of his arrival a neighbour, mistaking him in the
dark for a stray dog, had knocked him over the head,—a circumstance which led Sewall to fear that "the Devil seemed to be
angry at the child's coming to dwell here." [9] And a little earlier
Sewall gives a very curious account of the spiritual experience
of one Tim Dwight, son of a gentleman in Dedham, and likewise
apprenticed to Father Hull.[10] Just after prayers one day, Tim fell
in a swoon, and, recovering, in a most incoherent condition
lamented that his day of grace was out. Sewall reproached him,
saying that "'t was sin for any one to conclude themselves
Reprobate." But Tim was not to be comforted.

"Notwithstanding all this semblance of compunction," adds Sewall,
"'t is to be feared that his trouble arose from a maid whom he passionately loved: for that when Mr. Dwight and his master had agreed to
let him goe to her, he eftsoons grew well." A fortnight later, Sewall
"spake to Tim of this, asked him whether his convictions were off.
He answered, no. I told him how dangerous it was to make the convictions wrought by God's spirit a stalking horse to any other thing.
Broke off, he being called away."

In such a society, and among such domestic influences as we
have seen, Cotton Mather grew up. Late in life, he wrote for his
son Samuel some account of his early years.[11]

I desire to bewayl unto the very *end* of my Life, the early Ebullitions of *Original Sin*, which appeared at the very Beginning of it.
Indeed your Grandfather, tho' he were a wise and strict parent, would
from the observation of some Dispositions in me, comfort himself with
an Opinion of my being *Sanctified by the Holy Spirit of God in my
very infancy*. But he knew not how vile I was, he saw not the instances of my *going astray*, even while I was yet an infant. However,
there were *some good things* in my childhood, in which I wish *my
child* may *do better* than I. I began to *pray*, even when I began to
speak. I learned myself to *write* before my going to school for it. I used
secret prayer, not confining myself to *Forms* in it: and yett I composed
Forms of *prayer* for my school-mates (I suppose when I was about

[8] Sewall's Diary, I. 34, 35.   [9] Ibid., 30.   [10] Ibid., 15, 16.
[11] Paterna. MS. in the library of the late Judge Skinner, of Chicago.

seven or eight years old), and obliged them to *pray*. Before I could *write Sermons* in the public Assemblies I commonly *wrote* what I remembered when I came home. I rebuked my play mates for their wicked *words* and *ways;* and sometimes I suffered from them, the persecution of not only *Scoffs* but *Blows* also, for my Rebukes, which when somebody told your Grandfather, I remember he seemed very *glad*, yea, almost *proud* of my Affronts, and I then wondered at it, tho' afterwards I better understood his Heavenly principles.

The principal schoolmaster of this godly youth was the celebrated Ezekiel Cheever, to whose memory Cotton Mather paid a heartfelt tribute:

'Tis Corlett's praise and Cheever's, we must own,
That thou, New England, art not Scythia grown.[12]

Sewall gives a graphic account of the last days of this famous pedagogue,[13] ending with this sketch of his life:—

He was born January 25, 1614. Came over to N. E. 1637, to Boston: To New-Haven 1638. Married in the Fall and began to teach School; which Work he was constant in till now. First, at New-Haven, then at Ipswich; then at Charlestown; then at Boston, whither he came 1670. So that he has Laboured in that Calling Skillfully, diligently, constantly, Religiously, Seventy years. A rare Instance of Piety, Health, Strength, Serviceableness. The Wellfare of the Province was much upon his Spirit. He abominated Perriwigs.[14]

What Cotton Mather studied, and how he comported himself under this master, appears from the manuscript he left his son.[15]

One special Fault of my childhood (against which I would have you *my son* be cautioned) was idleness. And one thing that occasioned me very much *idle time*, was the Distance of my Father's Habitation from the *School;* which caused him out of compassion for my Tender and Weakly constitution to keep me at home in the *Winter*. However I then much employed myself in *Church History;* and when *Summer*

---

[12] Corderius Americanus (1708).   [13] Diary, II. 230, 231 (August, 1708).
[14] This was always a serious matter with Sewall: "Friday, Nov. 6 [1685]. Having occasion . . . to go to Mr. Hayward, the Publick Notary's House, I speak to him about his cutting off his Hair, and wearing a Perriwig of contrary Colour: mention the words of our Saviour, Can ye not make an Hair white or black. . . . He alledges, the Doctor advised him to it." Diary, I. 102. And cf. II. 36, 37.
[15] Paterna.

arrived I so plied my Business, that thro' the Blessing of God upon my endeavours, at the Age of little more than *eleven years* I had composed many *Latin* exercises, both in prose and verse, and could speak *Latin* so readily, that I could write notes of sermons of the English preacher, in it. I had conversed with *Cato, Corderius, Terence, Tully, Ovid,* and *Virgil.* I had made *Epistles* and *Themes;* presenting my first Theme to my Master, without his requiring or expecting as yett any such thing of me; whereupon he complimented me *Laudabilis Diligentia tua.*[16] I had gone through a great part of the New Testament in *Greek,* I had read considerably in *Socrates* and *Homer,* and I had made some entrance in my *Hebrew* grammar. And I think before I came to Fourteen, I composed Hebrew exercises and *Ran* thro' the other Sciences, that *Academical Students* ordinarily fall upon.

At twelve he had been admitted to Harvard College. What the College was then like may be guessed from the "Laws, Liberties, and Orders" printed in the Appendix to Quincy's History of Harvard University.[17] In brief, the students had to observe rules of pious decorum inconceivable in the nineteenth century, and ultimately to prove their fitness for the bachelor's degree by showing that they could "read the original of the Old and New Testament into the Latin tongue, and resolve them logically." To be sure, human depravity had so manifested itself among undergraduates as early as 1659 that the authorities of the College thought proper to authorize the town watch to keep order in the college yard. But in general whoever looks through the pages of Sibley's "Harvard Graduates" must feel sure that during the first half-century of its existence Harvard College to a rare degree fulfilled the purpose for which it was founded, and gave the Colonies a notably vigourous, learned, devoted ministry. In the "Magnalia"[18] Cotton Mather gives a catalogue of the Congregational ministers officiating in New England in 1696; he names one hundred and twenty-one; of these only eleven were not graduates of Harvard.

Of his academic studies, Cotton Mather writes thus:

I composed *Systems* both of *Logick* and Physick, in *Catachisms* of my own, which have since been used by many others. I went over the use of the *Globes,* and proceeded in *Arithmetic* as far as was ordinary. I made *Theses,* and Antitheses upon the main *Questions* that lay be-

[16] "Your diligence is praiseworthy."   [17] Vol. I. p. 515.   [18] I. VII.

fore me. For my *Declamations* I ordinarily took some Article of *Natural Philosophy* for my subject, by which contrivances I did Kill two birds with one Stone. Hundreds of books I read over, and I kept a Diary of my studies. *My son* I would not have mentioned these things, but that I may provoke *your* emulation.[19]

Meanwhile his spiritual life had been growing.

"I can't certainly remember," he writes,[19] (having by an unhappy casualty[20] lost some of my records) when it was that I began to keep *Days of Prayer with Fasting* alone by myself. But I think it was when I was about *fourteen* years old. And I remember well That I made *Mr. Scudder's Christian's Walk* my Directory in those Duties."

He notes that he was melancholy, and thought he had every distemper he read of. His self-consciousness was enhanced by what often afflicts people of active mind,—an impediment of speech.[21] He "had great benefit from a Society of Young Men, who met every *Evening* after the Lord's Day for the Services of Religion." Two other small facts about his undergraduate career are recorded in the Mather Papers: he sent to his uncle abroad a carefully drawn map of the region, wherein his uncle was surprised to find that the Blue Hills were not, as he remembered them, north of Boston; and during some vacations he was invited to act as tutor to some kinsmen older than he. At sixteen, he became a member of the Second Church.

Slight enough these facts; but they should help us to imagine what manner of boy it was who in 1678 presented himself for the bachelor's degree. At that time he was the youngest who had ever applied for it at Harvard; to this day but two have applied younger.[22] And this is what President Urian Oakes said to him in his Commencement oration:—

Alter vero Cottonus Matherus nuncupatur. Quantum Nomen! Erravi, fateor, Auditores; dicissem etenim, quanta Nomina! Nihil ego de Reverendo PATRE, Academiæ Curatore vigilantissimo, municipii Academici socio primario, dicam; quoniam coram et in os laudare nolim; sed si Pietatem, Eruditionem, Ingenium elegans, Judicium Solidum, Prudentiam et Gravitatem AVORUM Reverendissimorum JOANNIS COTTONI et RICHARDI MATHERI, referat et representet, omne tulisse Punc-

[19] Paterna.   [20] See page 200.   [21] S. Mather, Life of Cotton Mather.
[22] Paul Dudley, 1690, and Andrew Preston Peabody, 1826. Sibley, III. 6.

tum dici poterit; nec despero futurum, ut in hoc juvene Cottonus atq: Matherus tam re quam Nomine coalescant et reviviscant.[23]

[28] Sibley, III. 6, 7.—"The next is named Cotton Mather. How notable a name! I am wrong, my friends; I should rather have said what notable names! I will say nothing of his reverend father, the most watchful of guardians, the most distinguished Fellow of the College: I dare not praise him here, to his very face. But if this youth bring back into being the piety, the learning, the elegant accomplishment, the sound sense, the prudence, and the gravity of his very reverend grandfathers, John Cotton and Richard Mather, he may be said to have done his highest duty. Nor is my hope small that in this youth Cotton and Mather shall, in fact as well as in name, join together and once more appear in life."

IV. *The Fall of the Charter.*
—The Beginning of
Cotton Mather's Ministry.

1678-1686 The next eight years were among the most critical in the history of Massachusetts. From the settlement the Colony had been governed under a royal charter, granted to the Governor and Company of Massachusetts Bay in 1629. Under this, as we have seen, none but church-members had been freemen. Church-members had elected all political officers; they had established their own system of law; on their actions, and on their actions alone, rested everything in the rapidly strengthening community; not so much as the title to an acre of land came from any other source. The relation of the Colony to the Crown, in short, was comprised in the fact that the Crown had originally granted the Charter. As we have seen, the disturbed condition of England during the Civil Wars and the Commonwealth conspired with the original insignificance of the Colony to allow it virtual independence; and its political history is that of a conflict between the theocratic and the democratic spirits inherent in its original constitution.

A new factor had now appeared, however. Theoretically, New England, in virtue of its discovery by the Cabots, was the private property of the sovereign. Only the voluntary act of the sovereign, in the Charter, gave the colonists any rights at all; their position resembled that of tenants on a private estate. And from the beginning the Charter had been contested by some gentlemen, who maintained that it was in violation of previous royal grants to them. Under Charles II. this attack was renewed, partly perhaps because New England was growing too prosperous to be let alone. During King Philip's War there came to Boston for the first time Edward Randolph, agent of the Lords of Trade, with a royal letter requiring the Governor and Assistants of Massachu-

setts at once to send representatives to England, there to answer
the claims of those who contested the Charter. The contest thus
begun lasted till 1684. Massachusetts fought to the death, but no
diplomacy could save her. What is more, a party appeared in the
Colony itself which favoured submission to royal authority. This
party seems to have been built up chiefly by the exertions of
Randolph, who constantly went back and forth from England,
and achieved a popular detestation not yet quite forgotten. At
the head of the Royalists was Joseph Dudley, son of Thomas
Dudley, second Governor of the Colony. In 1684 came the end:
the Court of Chancery vacated the Charter of Massachusetts.
Without a government, without a single legal right, the Colony
lay at the mercy of the Crown. It was the intention of Charles II.
to send over as governor, vested with absolute authority, that
Colonel Percy Kirk whose "Lambs" a few months later did such
notable work in suppressing the traces of Monmouth's rebellion.[1]
But before anything definite was done, Charles was dead, James
on the throne, Monmouth in arms, and Kirk busy cutting unde-
fended throats. Meanwhile, in Massachusetts, one more election
was held under the forms of the vacated charter: the last
Governor elected by the people was Simon Bradstreet, who was
likewise the last survivor of the magistrates who nearly sixty
years before had founded the government now at an end.

With these facts in view, certain dry notes in Sewall's Diary[2]
grow dramatic. He tells how, on the 14th of May, 1686, the Rose
frigate arrived at Nantasket; how Randolph came to town by
eight in the morning, and took coach for Roxbury, where Dudley
lived; and how, with other magistrates, he himself was summoned to see the judgment against the Charter with the Broad
Seal of England affixed. He tells how, on the following Sunday,
Randolph came to the Old South Church, where Mr. Willard in
his prayer made no mention of Governor or government; but
spoke as if all were changed or changing. He tells how next day
the General Court assembled, and how Joseph Dudley, temporarily made President of New England, exhibited the condemnation of the Charter and his own commission under the Broad Seal
of England; how the old magistrates began to make some formal

[1] See Macaulay's History of England, Chapter V.   [2] Vol. I. pp. 137-40.

answer, and how Dudley said he could not acknowledge them as a court nor in any way capitulate with them; and how, when Dudley was gone, a sorrowful group of the old magistrates decided that there was no room for a protest: "The foundations being gone what can the Righteous do?" He tells how Increase Mather with other ministers vainly strove to persuade Dudley not to accept the presidency. And finally comes this note:—

> Friday, May 21, 1686. The Magistrates and Deputies goe to the Governour's. . . . Mr. Nowell prayed that God would pardon each Magistrate and Deputies Sin. Thanked God for our hithertos of Mercy 56 years, in which time sad Calamities elsewhere, as Massacre Piedmont; thanked God for what we might expect from sundry of those now set over us. I moved to sing, so sang the 17. and 18. verses of Habbakkuk.[3] The Adjournment . . . was declared by the weeping Marshall-General. Many Tears Shed in Prayer and at Parting.

This dry note marks the end of the pristine government of Massachusetts. From that day to this church and state have been finally separate there. Until the American Revolution, the people never had a word in the choice of another Governor. The dream of the Puritans—the dream of a state governed only by the dictates of Scripture—had passed, with other dreams of men, into the region of things that may not be.

For seven months Joseph Dudley was President of the provincial government of New England. On Sunday, May 30, Sewall notes that he sang

> "the 141 Psalm . . . exceedingly suited to the day. Wherein there is to be worship according to the Church of England, as 't is called, in the Town House, by countenance of Authority."

In August, he had grave doubts as to whether he could conscientiously serve in the militia under a flag in which the cross was replaced; in November, he finally resigned his commission as Captain of the South Company. On Saturday, September 25, the Queen's birthday had been celebrated with drums, bonfires, and

---

[3] Hab. iii. 17, 18. "Although the fig tree shall not blossom, neither shall fruit be in the vines; the labour of the olive shall fail, and the fields shall yield no meat; the flock shall be cut off from the fold, and there shall be no herd in the stalls: yet I will rejoice in the Lord, I will joy in the God of my salvation."

huzzas. Next day, "Mr. Willard expresses great grief in 's Prayer for the Profanation of the Sabbath last night."

On Sunday, December 19, while Sewall was reading to his family an exposition of Habakkuk, he heard a great gun or two which made him think Sir Edmund[4] might be come. Sure enough he was, "in a Scarlet Coat laced." That day the President went to hear Mr. Willard, who "said he was fully persuaded and confident God would not forget the Faith of those who came first to New England, but would remember their Posterity with kindness." Between sermons the President went down the harbour to welcome Sir Edmund. The next afternoon Andros landed in state, and was escorted by the eight companies to the Town-House. Here his commission was read, declaring his power to suspend councillors and to appoint others, and vesting the legislative power in him and his Council. Then he took the oath of allegiance, and stood by with his hat on while eight councillors were sworn. The same day he demanded accommodation in one of the meeting-houses for the services of the Church of England. This was too much for the Puritans. At a meeting of the ministers and four of each congregation, it was agreed that they could not with a good conscience consent that their meeting-houses be made use of for the Common Prayer worship; and "Mr. Mather[5] and Willard thorowly discoursed his Excellency about the Meeting-Houses in great plaiñess." So for a while Sir Edmund was content to worship at the Town-House. But Sewall notes, on January 25, that "this day is kept for St. Paul, and the bell was rung in the Morning, to call persons to Service. The Governour (I am told) was there"; and on January 31 there was a similar service "respecting the beheading Charles the First."

Meanwhile there had been minor symptoms of the change that was coming to New England. As early as November, 1685,

"the Ministers Come to the Court and complain against a Dancing Master who seeks to set up here and hath mixt Dances, and his time of Meeting is Lecture-Day; and 't is reported he should say that by one Play he could teach more Divinity than Mr. Willard or the Old Testament. . . . Mr. Mather[5] struck at the Root, speaking against mixt Dances." Early in September, 1686, "Mr. Shrimpton . . . and others come in a Coach from Roxbury about 9 aclock or past, singing

---

[4] Andros, the Governor appointed by James II. [5] Increase.

as they come, being inflamed with Drink: At Justice Morgan's they
stop and drink Healths, curse, swear, talk profanely and baudily to
the great disturbance of the Town and grief of good people. Such high-
handed wickedness has hardly been heard of before in Boston." And
though on Christmas day shops were "open generally and persons
about their occasions," there was a sad affair on Shrove Tuesday:
"Joseph Maylem carries a Cock at his back, with a Bell in 's hand, in
the Main Street; several follow him blindfold, and under pretence of
striking him or 's Cock, with great cart-whips strike passengers, and
make great disturbance."

During these eight years the career of Increase Mather was
steadily advancing. No figure was more conspicuous among those
who resisted the change. We have seen how he vainly tried to
dissuade Joseph Dudley from accepting the presidency of New
England, and how he told Sir Edmund "in great plainness" that
the meeting-houses of Boston should not be used for the rites of
the Established Church. But we must turn to Cotton Mather for
a full account of his life, public and private.[6] In 1679 Increase
Mather was among the leaders of that Synod which assembled
to consider "What are the Evils that have Provoked the Lord to
bring his judgments on New England? and what is to be done
so that these Evils may be Reformed?" A general revival followed,
in which the earnest work of the preachers resulted in many
renewed covenants with the Lord. A year later, on the verge of
a severe illness, he was called to preside at a second meeting of
the Synod, which formulated the elaborate Confession of Faith
printed in the "Magnalia."[7] He "kept them so close to their
Business that in *Two Days* they dispatch'd it: and he also Composed the *Præface* to the *Confession.* On this he immediately took
to his Bed under a dangerous fever." But, in accordance with
many prayers of many good people, he recovered; and preached
his first sermon on the text, "To me to Live is CHRIST." At the
death of Urian Oakes, in 1681, he acted for a while as President
of Harvard College. Four years later, after the death of John
Rogers, he finally accepted the presidency.

It was in 1683 that the demand came from Charles II. that
Massachusetts should "make a *full Submission and entire Resignation* of their Charter to his pleasure." At a meeting of the free-

[6] Parentator, Arts. XVIII-XXII.   [7] V. I.

men of Boston, Increase Mather was invited to give them his thoughts on the *Case of Conscience* before them.

"I verily Believe," he said, "We shall Sin against the GOD of Heaven if we vote an Affirmative. . . . Nor would it be *Wisdom* for us to Comply. We know, *David* made a Wise Choice, when he chose to fall into the *Hands of GOD* rather than into the *Hands of Men*. If we make a *full Submission and entire Resignation* to Pleasure, we shall fall into the *Hands of Men* Immediately. But if we do it not, we still keep ourselves in the *Hands of GOD;* we trust ourselves with His Providence: and who knows, what GOD may do for us?"—"Upon this pungent Speech," writes Cotton Mather, "many of the Freemen fell into Tears; and there was a General Acclamation, *We thank you, Syr! We thank you, Syr!* The Question was upon the Vote carried in the Negative, *Nemine Contradicente.* And this Act of Boston had a great influence upon all the Country."

The next year came one of the most critical incidents of Increase Mather's life. A letter signed with his initials and addressed to a friend in Holland was intercepted and brought to the notice of the authorities in England. It contained sentiments which, if not treasonable, were in the highest degree offensive to the King. Nothing could more seriously affect his public influence abroad. The Mathers always declared this letter a forgery, which they attributed to Edward Randolph; their enemies, then and now, have pronounced the letter genuine and the defence a lie. The question of veracity can never, perhaps, be satisfactorily settled. But a note on the subject from Increase Mather's diary seems to me honest:—

The Lord has had respect unto all the WISHES Written down before Him; on Jun. 11, 1670 [8]—Yea he had so far Gratified my Desire of *Suffering for Him,* that my Name hath been cast forth as Vile, and Wicked Men in *England, Scotland, Ireland, Barbadoes,* and the Leeward Islands, and elsewhere, have been *Speaking all manner of Evil of me falsely.* And the Ground of these my *Sufferings* has been, because I have desired to Approve myself faithful unto the Lord JESUS, and unto His Kingdom and Interest.

A less depressing experience came on the 6th of February, 1685; at this time Kirk was expected as governor.

[8] Cf. page 20.

"THIS DAY," wrote Increase Mather, "as I was Praying to GOD for the Deliverance of *New-England,* I was very much Moved and Melted before the Lord, so that for some time I was not able to speak a word. But then, I could not but say, *GOD will deliver* New-England! *GOD will deliver* New-England! *God will deliver* New-England! So I rose from my knees, with much Comfort and Assurance, that GOD had heard me. These things, I hope, were from the Spirit of GOD. Before I Prayed, I was very sad, and much dejected in my Spirit; but after I had Prayed, I was very Cheerful and joyful; I will then *Wait* for the *Salvation of GOD!*"

Sure enough, Kirk never came to Massachusetts.

It is during these eight years that we begin to have definite accounts of Cotton Mather's private life. Twenty-four of his diaries are preserved; and of these, four fall within this period.[9] The diaries always begin on his birthday; and as he begins the year, after the old fashion, on the 1st of March, the first three weeks of each volume bear date of the year before the rest of it. By far the greater part of the entries concern his spiritual experiences; yet among them are notes of other matters sufficient to give us a pretty vivid notion of what manner of life he led. It is characteristic of Cotton Mather that, until 1711, none of the diaries are original copies. For some years he took the trouble to copy from his records such as he deemed worth preserving, and then to destroy the notes. But the presumption of error which this process raises is greatly weakened in my mind by the fact that his diaries, after he gave up the practice of revision, show no change in the general character of the entries; and this is particularly true of one volume, which his third wife, who was occasionally insane, stole, and hid before it was finished, and which, apparently, he never saw again.

Until 1681 I find nothing concerning him beyond what his son tells.[10] Suffering from an impediment of speech, he at first believed himself unfitted for the ministry, and studied medicine; but, following the advice of a friend to "oblige himself to a *dilated Deliberation* in speaking," he "procured with Divine Help an happy delivery." On August 22, 1680, he preached in his

[9] Those for 1681, 1683, 1685, and 1686; all in the possession of the Massachusetts Historical Society.
[10] S. Mather, Life of Cotton Mather, 26, 27.

grandfather's church, at Dorchester, his first sermon, in which, "because of the Calling he had relinquished, he did . . . consider our blessed Saviour as the glorious *Physician of Souls;* chusing those words for his first Text in Luke iv. 18. *He hath sent me to heal the broken-hearted.*" Just six months later he was unanimously invited to assist his father at the Second Church.

This was his occupation during 1681, the year covered by his first extant diary. The notes in this concern little but spiritual experiences. The first is a long devotional passage, full of good resolutions, "penned by *Cotton Mather,* a Feeble and worthless, yett [Lord by THY GRACE] desirous to approve himself a Sincere & Faithful Servant of Jesus Christ." On the following Sabbath,

"The Singular Assistencies which the God of Heaven gave unto mee, in my public ministrations . . . were such as caused me to draw up this conclusion: *I believe I shall have a Glorious Presence of God with me through my whole Ministry.*" And about this time he was gratified by a subscription of seventy pounds, "for my Encouragement in my public service the ensuing year."

On the 13th of March, "in the Assurances, the glorious and Ravishing Assurances of the Divine Love, my joyes were almost insupportable." On the 19th, he was depressed; on the 3d of April, he was again ecstatic; on the 8th, he suffered from a "silence of God" in prayer-time—a punishment for "an Idle Fraud of soul"; on the 10th, he recovered his poise of temper: "If it be thy Will," he wrote, "I would *live,* to do some Special Service for thee, before I shall go hence and bee no more seen." I cite this experience in some detail, because its course and period of emotional action and reaction is typical of what followed him throughout life. In March he was

"taken with a violent *pain,* . . . which looked like a messenger of Death. Here I am," he wrote; "Afflict mee; Do what thou wilt with mee; Kill mee; for thy Grace hath made mee willing to Dy: *Only, Only, Only,* Help mee to Delight in thee, and to glorify thy dearest Name."

Two months later, he had a toothache, which induced two reflections:—

I. Have I not sinned with my *Teeth?* . . . By sinful, Graceless, excessive Eating. And by Evil *Speeches,* for there are *Liberal Dentals* used in them. II. This is an old Malady, from which I have yett been free, for a considerable while. Lett me ask then: Have not I of late given way to some old Iniquity?

The iniquity which troubled him most seems to have been the one he mentions most definitely in October.

I desire to walk Humbly before the Lord, all my Dayes, in the Remembrance of the Lothsome Corruptions, which my Soul has been from my Youth polluted withal. *Lord, Wherewithal shall a young man cleanse his way?* Altho' I have been kept from such Out-breakings of Sin, in Actions towards others, as have undone many in the world, yett I have certainly been one of the Filthiest Creatures upon Earth.

Another besetting sin was revealed to him in June. A good woman told him how one of his sermons had convinced her that she had fallen into the sin of pride. Reflecting that pride is "the sin of young ministers," he straightway discovered it in himself. A day of passionate prayer followed, which the Lord was pleased to reward with "glorious Assurances that Hee would never Leave the Work which Hee had begun in my soul." A week later came a day of secret Thanksgiving. *"Oh Lord,"* he wrote, *"Not unto mee, Not unto mee, but unto thy Name is All, All, All the Glory due;* and thou shalt have it. There shall *Hallelujahs* be sung to thee forever and ever"—for the "great works" which Cotton Mather, thus freed from the sin of pride, shall accomplish. But before he closes this grotesque day, he earnestly thanks God, too, for "the Life and Health of my dear Father, whom I may reckon among the Richest of my Enjoyments."

Meanwhile, several of his experiences had been comforting. In May, a man whom he had warned of Divine displeasure for not joining a church, fell off a roof,

and received a Blow, whereof he Lay, for some while, as Dead. But coming to himself one of the first things he thought on, was what I had said unto him; under the sense whereof, hee quickly went and joined himself unto the *South* church.

In October, he preached in the pulpit of his Grandfather Cotton,

with a very singular Assistance of the Lord. Yea, such was his powerful presence with mee, that some afterwards declared their melted and Broken Hearts could hardly forbear crying out in the Assembly.

About the same time, he fixed on certain habits of devotion which he found permanently edifying: one was

"to start the day with a Scripture . . . which might be of some special consequence to my everlasting Interests"; and his first meditation was on Zech. 13. 1,[11] "cast into Three Observations. The *Blood* of the Lord Jesus Christ is fitly compared unto a *Fountain*. This is an *Open Fountain*. And, the End of it is, for the *Washing away* of Sin, which is Uncleanness."

A little earlier he had had a still more comforting experience:—

As I was in Meditation . . . *How I might glorify God?* I happened to Look thro' the window upon the Heavens; and this Thought was after a most powerful and Refreshing manner cast into my mind, Surely, If the Lord intended not forever to glorify mee in Heaven, Hee would never have put it into my Heart, that I should seek to Glorify Him on Earth.

But perhaps his most characteristic experience in 1681 was this:—

I bought a Spanish Indian; and bestowed him for a Servant on my Father. This Thing I would not Remember . . . but only because I would observe whether I do not hereafter see some Special and Signal Return of this Action. . . . I am secretly persuaded, *That I shall do so!*

In the course of his life he had a great many secret persuasions and particular faiths: this is the first he records. In the "Magnalia" he defines them:—

Good men, that labour & abound in prayer to the great God, sometimes arrive to the assurance of a *particular faith* for the good success of their prayer. . . . Many a real Christian . . . is a stranger to . . . this thing; . . . it is here & there a Christian, whom the sovereign grace of Heaven does favour with the consolations of a particular faith. . . . The *wondrous meltings*, the *mighty wrestlings*, the *quiet waitings*, & the *holy resolves*, that are characters of a particular faith, which is no delusion, are the works of the Holy Spirit, wherein his holy angels may be instruments.[12]

[11] "In that day there shall be a fountain opened to the house of David and to the inhabitants of Jerusalem for sin and for uncleanness."
[12] IV. II. I. § 6.

A particular faith which proved no delusion, then, was above
most things else an assurance of election: it was, as it were, a
momentary sharing of the foresight of God. To justify his faith
about the Spanish Indian, Cotton Mather had to wait sixteen
years: then a knight whom he had laid under many obligations
bestowed a Spanish Indian on him.[13]

The actual facts he noted this year are few. On August 9th,

I took my Second Degree, proceeding Master of Arts. My Father
was *president*, so that from his Hand I Received my Degree. Tis when
I am gott almost Half a year beyond *Eighteen* in my age. And all the
circumstances of my Commencement were ordered by a very sensibly
kind providence of God. My *Thesis* was, *Puncta Hebraica sunt Originis
Divinæ.*[14]

In October he was active in forwarding a plan, objected to by
some as superstitious, that devout people should devote a given
hour every Monday to prayer for persecuted churches abroad. In
November he declined a call to New Haven. Towards the end of
December, he was elected pastor of the Second Church, with a
salary of seventy pounds. In February, 1682, he again refused
a call to New Haven.

My Reason was, because the Church of *North Boston* would have
entertained uncomfortable Dissatisfactions at my Father, if after so
many Important *Votes* of Theirs for my Settlement here, he had anyway permitted my Removal from them.

He remained minister of the North Church all his life.

Horae plusquam amoenae, nunquam rediturae,[15]

is the motto of his diary for 1683. From now on, each of his
diaries bears some motto on the outer leaf; and begins with a
devout and generally searching birthday meditation. Towards
the middle of the year he copied one of his original notes which
shows the course of his daily life:—

28 d. 6 m. Legi Exod. 34, 35, 36 | Oravi | Examinavi adolescentes
| Legi Cartesium | Legi Commentatores in Joh. 6. 37 | Jentacul |
Paravi concionem | Orationi interfui Domestica | Audivi pupillos

[13] S. Mather, Life, etc., p. 12.   [14] Hebrew vowel points are of divine origin.
[15] "More than delightful hours, never to return."

Recitantes | Legi Salmon pharmacop: | pransus sum | Visitavi plures Amicos | Legi Varia | Paravi concionem | Audivi pupillos Recitantes | Meditat: On, *the exceeding Willingness of the Lord Jesus Christ to Do good unto them that come unto Him.* And, I Resolve As to be Encouraged in my Addresses unto the Lord Jesus for His Mercy from the Thoughts of his mercifulness, then also the Endeavor that I may be Like unto Him in Humble and Ready *Helpfulness* to others | Oravi | Coenavi | paravi Concionem | Orationi interfui Domestica.[16]

He made, and often put in practice, any number of good resolutions: some concerning other people, as to encourage rich gentlemen to support a country minister, and to pay an old hawker to distribute good books; some more personal, as to govern his speech carefully, to close visits with some suitable text of Scripture, and to contrive "what Noble Attainments I should be continually purposing of." In pursuance of this last, he writes:—

"While I was lying on my Couch in the Dusk of the Evening I extempore composed the following Hymn, which I then sang unto the Lord." A typical stanza runs:

> I will not any Creature *Love*
> But in the *Love* of Thee Above . . .

I designed rather pietie than poetrie in these lines.

He comments on them in three closely written pages.

He hit upon a device of fining himself for any misconduct:—

Thus I Laid a penalty for some while upon myself, That if in Joining with the *prayers* of another, I did Lett more than one entire Sentence pass me, at any Time, without annexing some Ejaculation pertinent thereunto, I would forfeit a piece of money to be given unto the poor. And I found this effect of it, that in a Week or Two, I had Little occasion to Lay my *penalty;* for I found my Distractions in my Duties, which had been my plague, most wonderfully cured.

During an evening walk, when he

had such a prospect of our Neighbourhood as gave mee to see that God had cast my Lot, in a place exceedingly *populous,* I found my

---

[16] Read Exodus, etc.: Prayed: Examined the children: read Descartes: read commentators, etc.: breakfasted: prepared sermon: took part in family prayer: heard pupils recite: read Salmon on medicine: dined: visited many friends: read various books: prepared sermon: heard pupils recite: meditated, etc.: prayed: supped: prepared sermon: took part in family prayer.

Heart, after a more than ordinary manner melted in Desires after the Conversion and Salvation of the Souls in this place. And my soul was afterwards exceedingly Transported, in prayers for such a Mercy.

Praying over a friend critically ill,

"the good man felt, as it were, a Load or Cloud, beginning to Roll off his Spirits; and from that Instant, unto his own admiration, he began to Recover. . . . Oh! my Soul, why dost thou forgett such Benefits!" In July, "Overlooking the addresses of persons to join unto the church, I found over *Thirty Seals* of my ministry in this place. . . . From whence I may form a *probable computation* of many Scores, that have here and elsewhere been thereby helped in their acquaintance with the Lord. Blessed be God." At a young people's thanksgiving late in the year, "the Lord helped mee to preach unto them almost Three Hours (tho' I had Little more than One Hour's Time to prepare for it). . . . And a good Day it was!"

Two little incidents this year impressed him much. His father admiring his watch, he gave it to him; shortly afterwards a gentleman from whom he "had no reason to expect such a visit" gave him a better one: an experience which induced a resolution to stir up dutifulness to parents in himself and others. And a gentleman imported a seal for him, which was lost in a fire, but subsequently found in the ruins.

"I prayed herewithal," he writes, "That by no *Fire*, neither the *Fire* of *Lust* here, nor the *Fire* of *Hell* hereafter I might miss of the promise which the Blood of the Lord Jesus Christ hath sealed."

Far edifying as this year was, it was not without sorrows. His baby sister Katharine died. And in July comes a note that shows a more intimate trouble:—

Using a sacred *meditations* (with mixed *Supplications*) at my waking minutes every morning in my *Bed*, and in this Course going over many portions of the *Scriptures* a *Verse* at a Time, the Thought of Isaac having his happy Consort brought unto him *when* and *where* he was engaged in his Holy Meditations, came sometimes into my mind, and I had sometimes a strange persuasion, That there would a Time come, when I should have my Bed Blessed with such a Consort given unto mee, as Isaac, the Servant of the Lord, was favoured withal.

In December he found Satan buffeting him with unclean temptations.

"Besides my . . . usual . . . Devotions," he writes, "I did this Day write after this manner, That I may pluck out my Right Eye, and cutt off my Right Hand. . . . Oh! Blessed Saviour, Save me from the horrible pitt."

He prayed and fasted assiduously; but a month later the same "Sorrowful and Horrible Vexation" tormented him again. About the same time an elderly minister violated the Seventh Commandment: Cotton Mather fasted and prayed more than ever.

I likewise carried the wounded minister in my prayers unto the Lord for all reasonable mercies.

At the very end of the year, he began to fear that he had carried his mortification of the flesh so far as to violate the Sixth Commandment:—

'T is well, if I escape a Consumption. . . . What! Are my Duties now but Murders? Lord, pardon mee and pitty mee, for the sake of Jesus Christ!

The record of the year closes with a long list of the ejaculatory prayers he accustomed himself to utter on all occasions: a typical one is this:—

On the Gentlewoman that carv'd for the Guests: "Lord, . . . Carve a rich Portion of thy Graces and Comforts to that Person!" [17]

He was the grandson of John Cotton and Richard Mather, the son of Increase Mather, sprung from a race of the chosen vessels of God, himself a chosen vessel; and he was just twenty-one years old.

The diary for 1685 finds him approaching ordination. In April there was some trouble about it, which led him to pray that if his life were a real prejudice to God, or a necessary occasion of strife and sin, he might be taken out of the world. But the "design of Satan" was frustrated by "a most uniting work of God upon the Spirits of the people." From the 22d of April to the 3d of May he was in a state of sustained ecstasy; on the 4th of May came reaction, and on that day he wrote and signed his formal covenant with God:—

"I renounce all the Vanities and Cursed Idols & Evil Courses of this World," it runs. "I engage That I will ever have the Great God my

[17] S. Mather, Life, p. 107.

Best Good, my Last *End,* and my only *Lord.* That I will ever bee
Rendering of Acknowledgments unto the Lord *Jesus Christ* in all the
Relations which Hee bears unto mee. That I will ever bee studying
what is my *Dutie* in these things; and wherein I find myself to fall
short, I will ever make it my *grief,* my *Shame,* and for *pardon* betake
myself unto the *Blood of the Everlasting Covenant.* Now, Humbly Imploring the *Grace* of the *Mediator,* to bee *Sufficient* for mee, I do as a
further Solemnitie, hereunto *subscribe* my Name with both *Hand* and
Heart."

His signature to this document is more than twice the usual size.

On the 13th of May he was finally ordained, in a frame of
mind adequately expressed by his covenant. Sewall was present.

"Mr. Cotton Mather is ordained Pastor by his Father," he writes,[18]
"who said, My son Cotton Mather, and in 's sermon spake of Aaron's
Garments being put on Eleazar, intimating he knew not but that
God might now call him out of the World. Mr. Eliot[19] gave the Right
Hand of Fellowship, calling him a Lover of Jesus Christ."

Samuel Mather adds a characteristic trait:—

A truly primitive Ordination! which he never . . . scrupled the
Validity of. After a curious Examination of most of the *Fathers* in the
three first *Centuries,* he was verily perswaded that *every one* of them
had been perverted and abused by designing Men to serve their own
Ends, especially in the Instance of *Ordination.*[20]

Ten days later, Sewall notes a "private Fast," which gives a
glimpse of the manners of the time:—

The Magistrates . . . with their wives here. Mr. Eliot prayed, Mr.
Willard preached. I am afraid of Thy judgments.—Text Mother gave.
Mr. Allen prayed; cessation half an hour. Mr. Cotton Mather prayed;
Mr. Mather preached, Ps. 79. 9.[21] Mr. Moodey prayed about an hour
and half; Sung the 79th Psalm from the 8th to the End; distributed
some Biskets, & Beer, Cider, Wine. The Lord hear in Heaven his
dwelling place.

How busy Cotton Mather was this year appears from a note
he made in December:—

---

[18] Diary, I. 76.   [19] The Apostle to the Indians. See Magnalia, III. III.
[20] Life, p. 18.
[21] "Help us, O God of our salvation, for the glory of thy name: and deliver
us, and purge away our sins, for thy name's sake."

The Last Week of the month I *preached* on Lords-Day, Monday, Tuesday, Wednesday, Thursday in the same week. Yea, several weeks I have in *one week* preached *five times;* and once I preached *five times* in *Two Days* which came together.

In the course of the year he preached above a hundred carefully written sermons. At the same time he was constantly engaged in parish visiting; and, besides starting an elaborate method of Bible reading, and pursuing his studies, and devoting many days to prayer and thanksgiving, he had a number of pupils. And not content with teaching these, he

did successively use to send for them, *one by one,* into his Study, and there in the most moving, soft, obliging, and yet most solemn and lively manner discourse with them about their own *everlasting Interests;* and he would then bestow some good Books on them to further the Work of GOD . . . upon their Spirits: And . . . in every Recitation he would . . . make an Occasion to let fall some Sentence, which might have a tendency to promote *the Fear of GOD* in their Souls.[22]

His private devotions meanwhile were more prolonged and more ecstatic than ever; his emotional condition throughout the year was more and more overwrought. And for this there were several reasons: besides being constantly impressed with the solemnity of the ordination which made him at last a fully equipped minister of the Gospel, and an Overseer of Harvard College, he suffered, as did Massachusetts, from not a few buffets of Satan. In August, his supplications were

especially to seek for the guidance and Blessing of God in what concerns the change of my condition in the world, from Single to married; whereto I have now many invitations.

In October, a similar state of mind recurred, slightly complicated by the fact that, like his father, he was quite willing to die for the salvation of any soul. Early in November, he was more concerned about matrimony than ever: he wanted to do God's will; if celibacy were God's will, he accepted it; but he vowed that, if God would permit him to marry, he would always keep two annual thanksgivings with his wife. Late in January came another fast, very similar, more intense. Meanwhile the scope and

[22] S. Mather, *Life,* p. 40.

variety of his good resolutions, of his thanksgivings, of his self-searching meditations, are bewildering. And he had not a few assurances of Divine presence with him.

The most remarkable of these was apparently connected in his mind with those public affairs which this year were so troublesome. Some of his records concern these. In May, when James II. was proclaimed, two friends happened in as he was busy with a private fast.

"I preached unto my Two Friends," he writes, "Three Sermons each of them about an Hour Long apeece, on a Text, which was the very first, that on the opening of my Bible for a subject of Meditation, came to sight: namely Psal. 109. 19. 20,[23] which proved wonderfully suitable."

All three resolved to do special services for Christ, if He would relieve His people from the distresses now upon them. In September, the "calamities & confusions of the English Nation" caused him to be called daily an hour earlier than usual, that he might "Retire for *Sighs*, and *prayers*, and *psalms*, to bee employed for the distressed churches of God": within a fortnight after tidings of the Lord's victory, he vowed he would keep a special day of thanksgiving, and ponder other acknowledgments. Late in January comes the following retrospective note:—

The Glorious Assurances which I have enjoyed and uttered, very many times, for now some years together, about the Lords Appearing to deliver His people from Impending Desolations are now answered. That monster Kirk, who was coming to *N. England* with a Regiment of *Red Coats,* to sacrifice the best Lives among us, is diverted from coming hither, by the happy Death of that greater Monster, K. *Charles* II. And with K. James II. Things are operating towards such a Liberty for the *Dissenters* as may for aught I know bring the *Resurrection of the Lord's witnesses:* it being just three years and a half since their Congregations were all Dissipated, and a *Thanksgiving* celebrated thro' a wicked nation for it. Wherefore Lett me now procure as many *Dayes of praise* as I can among the meetings with whom I have had so many *Dayes of prayer* on these occasions.

[23] "Let it be unto him as the garment which covereth him, and for a girdle wherewith he is girded continually. Let this be the reward of mine adversaries from the Lord, and of them that speak evil against my soul."

This entry bears no date. The one before it, dated January 27, relates a prolonged thanksgiving, which closes with a consideration of what services Cotton Mather shall render to the Lord for His mercies to himself and to New England: in particular, he concludes, he should "immediately procure some Testimony, against some Common and growing Evils, which offend him in the land." A note of Sewall's throws some light on this entry and the next:—

Jan. 20th. . . . Cousin Fissenden tells me there is a Maid at Woburn who 't is feared is Possessed by an evil Spirit.

On the 6th of February, 1685-6, Cotton Mather wrote as follows:—

It will cost mee very Bitter Toyle and paines yett perhaps I may bee very serviceable in it: If I procure to myself an Exact Account of those *Evil Humours,* which the place is at any Time under the observeable Dominion of. And, whereas those *Divels* may bee *cast out* by *Fasting and prayer,* sett apart (first) a Day of *Secret prayers* with *Fasting* on the occasion of each of them: to *Deprecate* my own guiltiness therein, and *supplicate* for such Effusions of the Spirit from on High, as may Redress, Remove, and Banish such *Distempers from the place.*

We have seen enough of Cotton Mather now, I think, to understand at once the tremendous reality to him, and the bearing on what we have just read and on what is coming, of the record I shall copy next. It bears no date; it is written on the inner side of the cover—the first leaf—of the diary for 1685:—

Res Mirabilis et Memoranda. Post Fusas, Maximis cum Ardoribus, Jejunisqu: *Preces,* apparuit ANGELUS, qui *Vultum* habuit solis instar Meridiani micantem: Caetera *Humanum,* at prorsus *imberbem: Caput* magnificâ Tiarâ obvolutum: In Humeris, *Alas: Vestes* deinceps Candidas et Splendidas: *Togam* nempe Talarem: et *Zonam* circa Lumbos, Orientalium cingulis non absimilem. Dixitqu: hic *Angelus,* à Domino JESU, se missum, ut Responsa cujusdam Juvenis precibus, articulatim afferat, referatqu: Quamplurima retulit hic *Angelus,* quae hic Scribere non fas est. Verum inter alia memoratu digna; Futurum Hujusce Juvenis Fatum optime posse exprimi, asseruit in illis Vatis Ezekielis verbis. Ezek. 31: 3, 4, 5, 7, and 9. *Behold hee was a Cedar in Lebanon, with fair branches, and with a Shadowing Shrowd and of an High Stature, and his Top was among the Thick Boughs. The waters*

*made him great, the Deep Sett him up on High with her Rivers run-
ning about his plants. His Heighth was Exalted above all the Trees
of the Field, and his Boughs were multiplied, and his Branches became
Long, because of the Multitude of Waters when he shott forth. Thus
was hee fair in his Greatness, in the Length of his Branches, for his
Root was by the Great Waters. Nor was any Tree in the Garden of
God like unto him in his Beauty. I have made him fair by the multitude of his Branches, so that all the Trees of Eden, that were in the
Garden of God, Envied him.* Atqu: particulariter clausulas de *Rationis*
ejus extendendis, exposuit hic *Angelus*, de *Libris* ab hoc Juvene com-
ponendis, et non tantùm in *Americâ*, sed etiam in Europâ, publicandis.
Additqu: peculiares quasdam praedictiones, et pro Tali ac Tanto
peccatore, valdè mirabiles, de *Operibus Insignibus*, quae pro Ecclesiâ
Christi in *Revolutionibus* jam Appropinquantibus, Hic Juvenis olim
facturus est. *Domine Jesu!* Quid sibi vult haec res tam Extraordinaria?
A *Diabolicis Illusionibus*, obsecro te, Servum Tuum Indignissimum,
ut Liberes et Defendas! [24]

Thus we find him at the close of his twenty-third year: the
youth in whom Cotton and Mather have joined and shown themselves once more in life; a minister so busy that it is still a marvel
how he found time for half the things he did; torn by emotions
that he believed to come now from God, now from Satan,—never
from anything less; bound by covenant to do great works for
the God who had answered his prayers for New England; assured by a celestial visitant that his works shall be fruitful; and

[24] "A strange and memorable thing. After outpourings of prayer, with the
utmost fervour and fasting, there appeared an Angel, whose face shone
like the noonday sun. His features were as those of a man, and beardless;
his head was encircled by a splendid tiara; on his shoulders were wings; his
garments were white and shining; his robe reached to his ankles; and about
his loins was a belt not unlike the girdles of the peoples of the East. And
this Angel said that he was sent by the Lord Jesus to bear a clear answer
to the prayers of a certain youth, and to bear back his words in reply. Many
things this Angel said which it is not fit to set down here. But among other
things not to be forgotten he declared that the fate of this youth should be
to find full expression for what in him was best: and this he said in the
words of the prophet Ezekiel, etc. . . . And in particular this Angel spoke
of the influence his reason should have, and of the books this youth should
write and publish, not only in America, but in Europe. And he added
certain special prophecies of the great works this youth should do for the
Church of Christ in the revolutions that are now at hand. Lord Jesus! What
is the meaning of this marvel? From the wiles of the Devil, I beseech thee,
deliver and defend Thy most unworthy servant."

with his thoughts directed by a chance that might well seem
providential to those visitations of the Devil—so strangely akin
to his own visitations from heaven—that the doctors of his time
called witchcraft. He was very anxious to be married, too; a fact
which probably had more than he knew to do with his state of
mind.

For the year 1686, troublous enough to New England, was a
much more peaceful one for him. Almost his first note tells how
he paid one of his first visits to a young gentlewoman, the daughter of worthy and pious parents in Charlestown, "unto an Acquaintance with whom the wonderful providence of God, in
Answer to many prayers directed" him. This was Abigail, daughter of the Honourable Colonel Phillips. He writes at some length
his notions of how godly his wooing ought to be. He notes how
one Sunday he stayed at home from Charlestown, to preach, after
the custom of the time, to a criminal,[25] who was to be executed
during the week, and was formally brought into church to hear
his last sermon; and how, as a reward, this sermon was published.
Cotton Mather never lost the passion for seeing himself in print;
and this was apparently the first book he acknowledged: it was
reprinted, with an appendix containing an account of his talk
with Morgan on the way to execution. He notes later how he
examined himself, and made sure that he really preferred Jesus
to anything else, how he prayed for a comfortable habitation,
how he refrained from asking the church to raise his salary, how
older ministers asked him to join their prayer-meeting and met
in his study. Then he tells how a young minister has been disciplined for some fall from grace, and prays that, if similar treat-
ment of him may do God good, he may be similarly treated:
"Here I am," he writes, "Do with me as Thou wilt." He notes
how his heart goes out toward neighbours who have a low opinion of him; he prays that he may not be a vessel of dishonour;
and that he may be very careful of other people's reputations.
In short, he shows himself as thoroughly in love as an honest
Puritan could be.

The 4th of May was his wedding-day. He got up early, to
ponder; but in spite of his pondering he reached Charlestown

[25] James Morgan. See Sewall's Diary, I. 111, 124-26; Magnalia, VI. VI. App.
(VII.).

ahead of time. So he repaired to the garden with his Bible, and read the second chapter of John,[26] fetching "one observation and one supplication out of every verse in that story." Then the appointed time came, and "the good providence of God" caused his wedding "to be attended with many circumstances of respect and Honour, above most that have ever been in these parts of the world." Next Sunday he preached at Charlestown; the next, at Boston, on Divine Delights, stoutly asserting that after all the Bible was the most delightful thing in his experience. This was on the very Sunday when Mr. Willard "prayed not for the Governour";[27] next day Joseph Dudley assumed the Presidency.

For several months Cotton Mather lived with his father-in-law, serene in mood and noting various promises in Scripture which we should remember daily.

"The methods of Religion," he writes, "which the Spirit of the Lord has heretofore taught me, were the most that now, for some considerable while, I contented myself withal. And I wish that thro' my slothful and carnal Disposition, some of *these* also had not begun to wither with me."

At length he moved to Boston, where he took

An *House* wherein my Father Lived in the years 1677 and 1681 and wherein my more *Childish Age* made many Hundreds of prayers unto the God of Heaven. I could not but observe the providence of God, in Ordering my *Comforts* now, in those very Rooms where I had many years before sought him with my prayers.

A year before, Mr. Shepard[28] of Charlestown, being ill, had asked Cotton Mather to preach for him. "As for you, Syr," he had said after church, "I beg the Lord to bee with you unto the end of the world." That very night, to the consternation of all his friends, Mr. Shepard had died. In September, 1686, Cotton Mather had a startling dream: he dreamt he saw Mr. Shepard, whom he knew to have been dead for above a year.

"On that account," he writes, "I was contriving to slip out of the Room; whereupon he nimbly coming up with mee, took me by the Hand, and said, *Syr, you need not be so shie of mee, for you shall quickly be as I am, and where I am.*"

[26] The wedding at Cana.   [27] Cf. page 31.   [28] See Magnalia, IV. IX.

A short fit of illness followed, in which Cotton Mather felt "the Foretastes and Earnests of *Life Eternal*."

He recovered in a somewhat disturbed spiritual condition; he had an excessive ecstasy, which made him resolve to be particular about the spiritual welfare of his dear consort and her father. He started some Sunday evening prayer-meetings, which outgrew his house, and which, for want of a colleague, he had finally to give up by reason of their very success. His last note for the year tells of a thanksgiving: he went, he writes,

from Room to Room in my house, Deliberately Looking upon the Distinct parcels of the Estate whereof I am now become the Owner, or as I would rather say, the Steward. And with a Ravished Soul, I gave Every Thing back to God, variously contriving and so Declaring How All that I have should bee made serviceable unto his glory.

He formed numerous good designs this day, too: one was to be kind to the French refugees, but to stir them up about Sabbath-keeping; another was to start certain gentlemen and certain religious families in prayer-meetings. And he recorded two distinct resolutions:—

I. The *common-prayer worship* now being sett up in this country I would procure and assist the publication of a Discourse written by my Father that shall enlighten the Rising Generation in the unlawfulness of that Worship, and Antidote them against Apostasy from the principles of the First Settlement. II. And I would prosecute the publication of the Like *Testimony* against several other superstitions that are now creeping in upon the *Rising generation*.

Sir Edmund was Governor now, Joseph Maylem was making merry on Shrove Tuesday, and there were people abroad possessed of evil spirits. No one knew quite what was coming. "And thus," closes the record, "the Good Hand of God brings mee to the end of my Twenty Fourth year."

v. *The Revolution of 1689*
and the New Charter.

1686-1692 Sir Edmund Andros, the new Governor, who came over vested with the absolute authority secured to James II. by the vacating of the Charter, was a gentleman of Guernsey, whose youth had been passed in attendance on the King's aunt, the Queen of Bohemia. From 1666 to 1680 he had served in America, for the last six years of that period as Governor of New York. In this capacity he had come into collision with the authorities of Connecticut, who had disputed his claim to the country between the Connecticut River and the Hudson. And what happened then was enough to impress him and the people of New England with sentiments of mutual disgust. In point of fact, he seems to have been an honest gentleman, a good churchman, a man of the world, and a governor of no small ability.[1] But no temperament and no policy could have been much more foreign than his to the curious society, half theocratic, half democratic, that he came to govern with an authority more arbitrary than has ever been assumed in New England, before or since. It is no wonder that, to theocrats and democrats alike, he seemed the incarnation of political villainy, that in common opposition to him the theocratic spirit and the democratic forgot for a while any differences of their own, and that the unanimous tradition of America has preserved his memory to the present day as that of a very bad man indeed.

His jurisdiction was not confined to Massachusetts, but comprised the whole of New England. Boston, to be sure, by far the most important town in America, was his capital; but here he exerted a power which extended from Canada to the Hudson.

[1] See Andros Tracts, I. Memoir of Sir Edmund Andros.

Putting aside the charges of extortion and corruption and treasonable plotting with Indians,—probably honestly made, but certainly insufficiently supported by any extant evidence,—we may
perhaps reduce the grave phases of what is still called his tyranny
to three: an effort to establish the Church of England; the assumption of the power of taxation without the consent of the
people; and the laying down of the principle, that all titles to
land had been vacated along with the Charter, and so that whoever wanted a sound title must get his claim confirmed by Sir
Edmund, and pay for it. When certain people pleaded the privileges of Englishmen, they were told that these things would not
follow them to the ends of the earth, and that they had no more
privileges left them but that they were not bought and sold for
slaves. And this I see no reason to doubt that Sir Edmund very
honestly believed. "In short," says Cotton Mather,[2] "all was done
that might be expected from a *Kirk*, Except the *Bloody Part*. But
that was coming on."

In all probability, the Mathers, along with most good people of New England, honestly thought their heads in danger.
That they really were, there is no evidence at all. But it is
no wonder that so complete an overturn of the government
set all manner of wild fancies afloat. Increase Mather opposed
Andros in every possible way, and meantime betook himself to
prayer for good tidings out of England.

"I sought unto GOD," he writes, early in 1687, "in secret with
Tears that He would send Reviving News out of *England: And* I
could not but Believe that He will do so."

He had not long to wait. In April, 1687, James II. issued his
Declaration of Indulgence.[3] Really designed, of course, to relieve
the Catholics, this proclaimed liberty of conscience, suspending
all laws against non-conformity, and authorizing all British subjects to meet and serve God in their own way. How grateful it
was to Dissenters, Cotton Mather's own words characteristically
express:—

It brought them out of their Graves: And if it assumed an Illegal
Power of *Dispensing with Laws*, yet in Relation to *Them*, it only dis-

[2] Parentator, XXIII.   [3] See Sewall's Letter-Book, I. 52, note.

pensed with the Execution of such Infamous *Laws* as were *ipso facto*
Null and Void before: *Laws* contrary to the *Laws* of GOD, and the
Rights and *Claims* of Human Nature.

The ministers of New England were for a public thanksgiving,
which Sir Edmund forbade, with threats of military force. On the
motion of Increase Mather, the churches of New England drew
up an address of thanks to the King. This it was thought best to
intrust to some "*Well-qualified Person,*" who "might, by the Help
of such *Protestant Dissenters* as the King began upon *Political
Views* to cast a fair Aspect upon, Obtain some Relief to the
Growing Distresses of the Country: and Mr. *Mather* was the
Person that was pitch'd upon." He referred the question of his
going to his church: "They that at another time would have almost as soon parted with their Eyes as have parted with him now
were willing to it: *They Unanimously Consented.*" Randolph
made an effort to stop him by bringing against him an action for
libel, based on a letter in which Mather had intimated a belief
that Randolph had forged the treasonable document signed with
his initials in 1683.[4] But Mather, having once been released by
a jury, avoided a second arrest by slipping out of his house in
disguise, and remaining for a little while in hiding at Colonel
Phillips's, in Charlestown. On the 7th of April, 1688, he managed
to board a ship, well down the harbour, and so bore away for
England. On the 6th of May he landed at Weymouth. His church
was left in charge of his son Cotton. Harvard College, of which
he had been President since 1685, was left in the hands of
Leverett and Brattle, resident tutors, and Fellows of the Corporation.

The story of Increase Mather's mission in England is told at
length in the "Parentator," and has been admirably illustrated by
the "Andros Tracts." Taken from the midst of the petty colonial
society of whose limits we should by this time have a pretty
thorough notion; placed in the midst of the turmoil, the bustle,
the intrigue, of a great capital and a corrupt court: taken from
the post of an eminent leader in matters ecclesiastical and political alike; placed where at best he was one of a multitude,
struggling and plotting for the notice and the favour of the great,

[4] Cf. page 35.

Increase Mather proved himself no common man. Hitherto, at least in the "Parentator," on which I have chiefly relied for my impressions of him, he has appeared as an honest, godly Puritan minister, doing his best to maintain the principles that are already becoming traditions. Now, without sacrificing a shade of his principle, without giving up those ecstatic prayers and afflations which whoever would understand the passionate enthusiasm of old Puritanism must always keep in mind, he shows himself able, in a rare degree, to conduct the affairs of men. In brief, his task was to persuade a Catholic King, full of belief in the Divine authority of his absolute power, to restore, of his free will, the vacated Charter of Massachusetts. On the 30th of May he presented the Addresses of Thanks to James II., thus for the first time fulfilling his mother's prophecy.[5] Two days later he had another audience wtih the King, who listened kindly to his complaints of the conduct of Andros. It was James's purpose, Cotton Mather thinks,[6] to set up the Roman Catholic religion in America. It was Mather's purpose to secure a restoration of the theocratic democracy of the fathers, and incidentally to procure for Harvard College a royal charter which should permanently secure it to the Calvinistic dissenters who had founded and cherished it. These purposes agreed in not being exactly those of poor Sir Edmund. James spoke kindly, but did nothing; Mather worked vigorously, using every influence he could command.

On the 22d of November, 1688, Sewall sailed from Boston, partly for the purpose of joining Mather in London. His notes of the voyage are pretty full.

"Friday, Dec. 21," runs one, "I lay a [wager] with Mr. Newgate that shall not see any part of Great Britain by next Saterday senight sunset. Stakes are in Dr. Clark's hand." He won his bet. Still at sea, on "Sabbath, Dec. 30th. Spake with a ship. Tells us he spake with an English Man from Galloway, last Friday, who said that the King was dead, and that the Prince of Aurang had taken England, Landing six weeks agoe in Tor Bay. Last night I dreamed of military matters."

A fortnight more the voyage lasted, and each vessel they spoke gave some new version of the great news. In point of fact, William had landed on the 5th of November, James had fled from

[5] Cf. pages 14-15.   [6] Parentator, XXV.

London on the 23d of December: and on "Sabbath, Jan. 13th," when Sewall finally went ashore at Dover, to "hear 2 Sermons from Isaiah, 66.9," [7] the Revolution was accomplished. Two weeks later, William and Mary were proclaimed.

On the 4th of April, 1689, a young man named John Winslow arrived in Boston from the island of Nevis, with a copy of the Declaration issued by the Prince of Orange on his landing in England. Sir Edmund, hearing the news, sent for him, and tried to silence him by threats and promises; failing, he committed him to prison "for bringing traitorous and treasonable libels and papers of news." But it was no use. The people of Massachusetts were ripe for revolution. Palfrey tells the story very graphically.[8] On the 18th of April, Boston rose in arms, seized the chief magistrates, besieged Sir Edmund in the Castle, dismantled the Rose frigate, and took possession of the government in the name of "His Highness" (the Prince of Orange) and "the English Parliament." To appreciate the full boldness of this bloodless revolution, we must remember that no rumor of the Prince's fortunes had reached New England, and that every man of those who put themselves at the head of the movement knew that, if, as might well be, James had prevailed in England, their action would probably cost them their heads. For all this, the magistrates who had last served under the vacated Charter resumed the power provisionally. Samuel Mather[9] says that they did it lest inaction on their part should result in bloody work by less prudent leaders. It was their fortune to be justified by what had happened abroad. On the 26th of May, a ship arrived with orders to proclaim William and Mary; on the 29th, they were proclaimed. And Sir Edmund, with Joseph Dudley and the rest of his crew, as Cotton Mather called them, were fast prisoners in Boston Castle. And absolute authority in New England had seen its last day.

The next service that Increase Mather[10] did for New England was—at least for his contemporaries—perhaps the most notable

---

[7] Shall I bring to the birth, and not cause to bring forth? saith the Lord: Shall I cause to bring forth, and shut the womb? saith thy God."

[8] Book III. Chapter XV.

[9] Life of Cotton Mather, II. 2. 2. This passage is probably the most valuable historically in the lifeless book.

[10] For all facts about Increase Mather in the rest of this chapter, see Parentator, XXVI., XXVII.

of all. On the accession of William and Mary, a circular letter
was drawn up to all the Colonies, confirming the old governors
until further order. Had this been sent to New England, it would
have reinstated Sir Edmund; and how that hot-tempered gentleman might have conducted himself towards his enemies nobody
knows. By some means, Mather succeeded in stopping it, and
in leaving authority temporarily in the hands of the provisional
government. In the end, Sir Edmund and his crew were shipped
to England for trial. Far from condemnation, they were received
there with favour. Sir Edmund was soon made Governor of Virginia; Joseph Dudley was made Chief Justice of New York, and
later Lieutenant Governor of the Isle of Wight; later still he became a member of Parliament. But New England saw Sir
Edmund no more: as for poor Randolph, all we hear further
of him is that he died in Virginia, so miserably that only two or
three negroes attended his funeral; [11] and Dudley for the moment
had his hands agreeably full abroad. There is good reason, I
think, to believe that this peaceable issue of what might have
been a very tragic matter was due chiefly to Mather's diplomacy.

There were now high hopes in New England that the Charters
would be restored. To prove their loyalty, the Colonies fitted
out an expedition against Port Royal, and temporarily annexed
to the British dominions the country that is now Nova Scotia. Encouraged by this, they followed it by a still more formidable expedition against Quebec, under the command, like the former, of
the redoubtable Sir William Phipps. But this armament came to
grief in the St. Lawrence, going far to unmake the favourable
impression established by the previous success. And the country
was generally in a disturbed condition, doubtful as to what form
its government might take, harassed on its borders by French and
Indians, and infested along the coast by the pirates whose traditional hoards still excite the interest of credulous treasure-seekers.
It is to this epoch, though not precisely to this moment, that we
owe the fame of Captain Kidd.

In England, meanwhile, Increase Mather—preaching, praying,
making the best of his way among what Dissenters were in favour
at court—was doing his utmost to secure the restoration of the
Charters. He waited on the King more than once, to be received

[11] Parentator, XXIV.

with marked, though guarded civility. He waited on the Queen, when the King was gone to Holland, and, pressing the claims of the New England Dissenters, heard from her lips what Cotton Mather calls a "Divine Sentence": "I wish all good men were of one mind; however, in the mean time I would have them live peaceably, and love one another." But all he could do brought his business little further. William of Orange was a good Calvinist, but no Republican: he was willing enough to say civil things to New England, but by no means disposed to make a prosperous part of his dominions virtually independent. The longer Mather waited, the clearer it became to him, if not to his colleagues in the mission, that the best he could do for Massachusetts was to secure for it the best Charter he could induce the King to sign. The old Charter was hopelessly lost.

Such was the state of affairs at the beginning of the year 1692, —the next for which Cotton Mather's diary is preserved.[12] What impressions I have of his personal career for these five years, then, I gather from outside sources. In the first place, we shall do well to remember the situation in which he found himself at the age of twenty-five. Full of traditional belief in the Divine authority of his professional work, he was left, by the absence of his father on the most important public business ever yet confided to a native of New England, in full charge of one of the greatest churches in America. There is no reason to doubt that, according to the standard of his time, he was a scholar unapproached by any one of his age: that is, he had read more books than anybody else, he was reading more day by day, and he was already launched in that career of authorship which made him at last the most voluminous of American writers. And the state of public affairs, bringing theocracy and democracy for the moment into complete accord, and throwing political as well as spiritual leadership once more—and for the last time—chiefly into the hands of the clergy, gave his words and actions such public authority as he never enjoyed again. All the while, too, there is every reason to believe that his ecstatic prayers and fastings kept him in

[12] In possession of the American Antiquarian Society. Occasional citations in print seem to show that some of the intermediate diaries may be preserved. But I have not come across them.

what he never doubted was direct communication with the angels of God.

Sewall's Diary gives a few glimpses of his public preaching, and of pastoral visits all the more notable for the fact that Sewall was a member, not of Mather's church, but of Mr. Willard's, the Old South. One of his sermons, in 1687, taught Sewall a practical lesson of which he made immediate use.

"Went to Roxbury," runs Sewall's note,[13] "and heard Mr. Cotton Mather preach from Colos. 4. 5, Redeeming the Time.[14] Shew'd that should improve Season for doing and receiving good whatsoever it cost us. His Excellency[15] was on the Neck, as came by, call'd Him in and gave Him a glass of Beer and Claret and deliver'd a Petition respecting the Narraganset Lands."

Three years later, Sewall heard another of his sermons with less satisfaction.

"March 19, 1690," he writes, "Mr. C. Mather preaches the lecture from Mat. 24, and appoint his portion with the Hypocrites.[16] In his proem said, *Totus mundus agit histrionem*.[17] Said one sign of a hypocrit was for a man to strain at a Gnat and swallow a Camel. Sign in 's Throat discovered him; To be zealous against an iñocent fashion, taken up and used by the best of men; and yet make no Conscience of being guilty of great Immoralities. Tis supposed means wearing of Perriwigs:[18] said would deny themselves in any thing but parting with an oportunity to do God service; that so might not offend good Christians. Meaning, I suppose, was fain to wear a Perriwig for his health. I expected not to hear a vindication of Perriwigs in Boston Pulpit by Mr. Mather; however, not from that Text. The Lord give me a good heart and help to know, and not only to know but also to doe his Will; that my Heart and Head may be his."

Of Cotton Mather's domestic life, meanwhile, I find but two or three stray notes. Three daughters were born to him before

[13] Diary, I. 181.
[14] "Walk in wisdom towards them that are without, redeeming the time."
[15] Andros.
[16] Matt. 24. 51. "[The lord of that servant] shall cut him asunder, and appoint him his portion with the hypocrites: there shall be weeping and gnashing of teeth."
[17] Everybody plays a part.
[18] Cf. page 26. In his only existing portrait, Cotton Mather wears a remarkably full wig.

1693; and one of them died. In 1688, he was much excited by a
case of witchcraft in Boston, and for a while had one of the
possessed girls in his own house. The same year his brother
Nathaniel died,—a very godly youth, who, if we may trust the
account of him which Cotton Mather published,[19] systematically
studied and worried himself to death. One of his notes, which
Cotton Mather quotes, gives a curious insight into his character.
He is lamenting, in terms which suggest all manner of misdeed,
the sins of his boyhood.

"Of the manifold sins which then I was guilty of," he goes on,
"none so sticks upon me as that, being very young, I was *whitling* on
the Sabbath-day; and for fear of being seen, I did it behind the door.
A great reproach of God! a specimen of that *atheism* that I brought
into the world with me."

Samuel Mather[20] is the chief authority concerning the part
Cotton Mather played in the Revolution of 1689. Before the
outbreak, he says, "the principal Gentlemen of *Boston* met with
Mr. Mather to consult what was best to be done: and they all
agreed, if possible, that they would extinguish all Essays in our
People to an *Insurrection*." In case of an outbreak, however, they
determined to prevent undue violence by putting themselves at
the head of it. "And a Declaration was prepared accordingly." [21]
At a public meeting of the inhabitants of Boston, shortly before
the outbreak, Cotton Mather succeeded in calming the people by
an "affectionate and moving Speech . . . at which many fell into
Tears and the whole Body . . . present immediately united in
the Methods of Peace Mr. Mather proposed unto them." In spite
of this he was to have been committed to prison for his politics
on the very day when the insurrection broke out: on that day and
the exciting ones that followed, he devoted all his energies, with
success, to hindering "the Peoples proceeding any further than
to reserve the Criminals for the Justice of the *English* Parliament." On the whole, Samuel Mather's last remark on this subject
is the most notable.

"Upon Discoursing with him of the Affairs," it runs, "he has told
me that he always pressed *Peace* and *Love* and *Submission* unto a

[19] Magnalia, IV. X.   [20] Life, II. 2. 2.
[21] See Andros Tracts, I. 20. This paper has been attributed to Cotton Mather.

legal Government, tho' he suffered from some tumultuous People, by
doing so; and upon the whole, has asserted unto me his *Innocency*
and Freedom from all *known Iniquity* in that time, but declared his
Resolution, from the View he had of the fickle Humors of the Populace, that he would chuse to be concern'd with them as little as possible for the future."

Apart from this, I get my chief impression of him during this
interval from the list of his works in Sibley's "Harvard Graduates." Indeed, there are but two definite facts that I have noted
from any other authority. One is, that on the 12th of June, 1690,
he was elected a Fellow of Harvard College.[22] I doubt if the
Corporation has ever had a younger member.[23] The other is,
that in November of the same year, when there was a dispute
between hot-tempered Sir William Phipps and his prisoner, M. de
Meneval, the captured Governor of Port Royal, concerning certain moneys on which Sir William had laid hand, "Mr. Moody
and Mr. Mather . . . had very sharp discourse; Mr. Mather very
angrily said that they who did such things as suffering Sir William to be corrected by Meneval were Frenchmen, or the people
would say they were, etc." [24] Cotton Mather had a temper of his
own, it seems, which sometimes got the better of him. But the
more serious side of his personal life between 1687 and 1692
shows itself chiefly in his writings. From "Military Duties"—a
sermon preached in September, 1686, but not published till the
next year—to the "Midnight Cry,"—the last of his publications
during the period covered by this chapter,—Sibley mentions
twenty-nine titles. Of these, one appeared in 1687, seven in 1689,
ten in 1690, nine in 1691, and two in the beginning of 1692.
Twenty of the twenty-nine were sermons, including some political sermons, and three funeral discourses,—two of which were
enlarged into the biographies of Nathaniel Mather and of the
Apostle Eliot, which appeared again in the Magnalia; two dealt
with the Quakers; five concerned devotional matters in general;
and two—"Memorable Providences," first published in 1689, and
"Late Memorable Providences," published in 1691—concerned
witchcraft.[25] From the moment that his glorious assurances were
justified by the news that King Charles was dead and Kirk's com-

[22] Sewall's Diary, I. 322.   [23] 27 years, 4 months.   [24] Sewall's Diary, I. 339.
[25] Increase Mather's "Remarkable Providences" had appeared in 1684.

ing averted in 1685, this matter seems to have been much on his mind. He was bound by covenant to do special work for the Lord, and here was special work to be done.

So we come to that portion of his diary for 1692 which belongs in this chapter. Like the other volumes I have noted, this one is not the original, but an abridged copy in his own hand of what portions he deemed worth preserving. And it is certainly true that the notes he has copied for this year are less specific and fewer than usual. To those who hate his memory, and they are not few, this fact should count against him; for my part, as I have said, the better I grow to know him, the more honest I believe his intentions. I shall note very briefly all that I have found in the earlier part of this manuscript volume.

"This year finds me," it begins, "in my public Ministry handling the Miracles of our Lord Jesus Christ. . . . Who can tell, what miraculous Things, I may see, before this year bee out?"

The next thing he notes is, that he has induced a meeting of ministers at Cambridge to vote that the churches shall make catalogues of "such things as can indisputably bee found amiss among them," and then shall relentlessly put them down. Most of the churches paid little attention to this vote. But Mather himself drew up an instrument denouncing sixteen distinct common evils and transgressions of the covenant. He preached about this; he wove it into his prayers; and on the 2d of April it was adopted by a vote of the North Church. He had it printed, and conveyed the little book to every communicant. On the 29th of April, he held a day of secret humiliation and prayer. His prayers for the Holy Spirit were answered with assurances. He went on to recount the abasing circumstances of the land, to pray for the awakening of the churches, particularly by himself; therefore he prayed above all for the smiles of God on his "Midnight Cry," "which was just then coming out of the press." He obtained of God an assurance that

"Hee will make use of me, as of a John, to bee an Herald of the Lord's Kingdom now approaching. . . . But my prayers," he goes on, "did especially insist upon the horrible Enchantments and possessions broke forth upon Salem Village,—things of a most prodigious Aspect. A good issue to these things and my own Direction and protection thereabout I did especially petition for."

His next note, undated, tells that his health is "lamentably broken, . . . partly by my Excessive Toyle in the public and private Exercises of my Calling, but chiefly, I fear, by my Sins against the God of my Health." In spite of this, and of preaching when he "had been fitter to have been in my bed," he has had great assistances in the pulpit; "and come easier out of the pulpit than I went into it." Whoever has had crazy nerves knows what that means.

"But now," he goes on, "Illnesse and Vapours, with an Aguish Indisposition, grows upon me at such a rate that indeed I Live in Exceeding Misery: and I can see nothing but a *Speedy Death* approaching. *Blessed be God, that I can Dy!*"

"But the time for Favour was now come!" runs the next note I have copied, "the Sett Time was Come! I am now to Receive the answer of so many prayers as had been employed for my absent parent; and for the Deliverance and settlement of my poor Countrey, for which hee had been Employed in so long an Agencie. We have not the former Charter, but wee have a Better in the Room of it: one which much better suits our Circumstances. And instead of my being made a Sacrifice to Wicked Rulers, all the councellours of the province are of my own Father's Nomination."

Among them were his father-in-law and several brethren of his church. And the Governor was Sir William Phipps, one whom he himself had baptized, in March, 1690.[26]

In fact, the four years' work of Increase Mather had reached a successful issue in October, 1691. Convinced that nothing could revive the old Charter, he had done all he could to make the new one as good as possible. The appointment of the Governor, and the final power of veto, were left with the King; the franchise was made a matter no longer of church-membership, but of freeholds: but the people were to elect the Governor's Council; and above all, the power of taxation was vested in the bodies they elected. Mather's colleagues refused to accept the inevitable: they came back to New England, ready to stir up feeling against him. And Sewall notes that as early as February 8, 1691-2, when the first copy of the new Charter reached Boston, there was much discourse. But Mather's diplomatic tact had actually enabled him to name the chief officers who were to put the government into

[26] See Magnalia, Life of Sir William Phipps.

operation; and the good man came home to his good son with the full conviction that now at last good people were to have their way in New England.

"May 14th, 1692," writes Sewall, "Sir William arrives in the Nonsuch Frigat: Candles are lighted before he gets into Town-house. Eight companies wait on Him to his house, and then on Mr. [Increase] Mather to his. Made no volleys because 't was Satterday night."

Next day, though ill and unprepared, Cotton Mather preached on "the Lord's passing over the water," with much assistance from Heaven.

"Monday, May 16," writes Sewall, 'Eight Companies and two from Charlestown guard Sir William and his Councillours to the Townhouse, where the Comissions were read and Oaths taken. I waited on the Dept. Governour to Town, and there was met by Brother Short . . . who informed me of the dangerous illness of my father, so . . . I was not present at the Solemnity: found my father much better. At Ipswich,[27] as we were going, saw a Rainbow just about Sunset."

"Thus," writes Cotton Mather the same day, "have I seen the wonderful effects of prayer and Faith; and now I will call upon the Lord as Long as I Live."

[27] The elder Sewall lived at Newbury.

VI. *Witchcraft.*

1692-1693 What happened in the next two years was of less consequence to New England than the matters we have been considering. To Cotton Mather, however, and to the cause which throughout his life he had most at heart,—the preservation, the restoration, of the pure polity of the fathers,—these two years were fatal. It was the great tragedy of witchcraft, I think, that finally broke the power of theocracy: it was almost surely the part Cotton Mather played in it that made his life, for the five and thirty years that were left him, a life—at least publicly—of constant, crescent failure. Tragic even if we join with those who read in the records left us no more worthy story than that of frustrated ambition, his career takes an aspect of rare tragic dignity if in his endless, undiscouraged efforts to do God's work we can honestly see what he tells us was there,—an all-mastering faith that the fathers were divinely right, that all which tended away from their teaching was eternally wrong, and that his own failure meant nothing less than the failure of the kingdom of Christ in a land whither Christ's servants had come with high hopes that here, as nowhere else on earth, Christ's kingdom should prevail.

Sir William Phipps, the new Governor, is in certain aspects a most romantic figure. The obscure son of a settler in the wilds of Maine, he was first an apprentice to a ship-carpenter: coming to Boston early in manhood, he learned there to read and write, and soon married a widow of position and fortune decidedly above his own. Prospering for a while as a shipbuilder, he soon took to the sea; and by the year 1684 he had so distinguished himself that he was put in command of a frigate, in which he

sailed to the West Indies in search of a wrecked Spanish treas-
ure-ship. After various adventures and mutinies, he actually discovered the wreck. He brought back to England treasure to the
amount of three hundred thousand pounds, in return for which
feat he was knighted by James II. And in Sir Edmund Andros's
time he came home to Boston with a comfortable fortune of his
own and the office of High Sheriff of New England. By no means
in sympathy with the Governor, he soon went back to England
for a while, where he had more or less to do with Increase
Mather. In 1690 he was again in Boston, where, as we have seen
before, he took command of the successful expedition against
Port Royal. The first real rebuff in the career of this archetype of
self-made Yankees was the failure of the expedition which, too
late in the same year, he led against Quebec. Undiscouraged, he
went back to England with plans for a fresh expedition against
the French. This came to nothing; but Increase Mather, who
saw much of him in London, pitched on him, and obtained the
approval of King William for him, as the man of men to be
the first Governor of the royal Province of Massachusetts.

It would have been hard to find a governor who should
promise more for the polity to which the Mathers gave every
energy of their lives. A man of the people, conspicuous above
any one else of his time for just that kind of material success
which most touches the popular imagination, Sir William, though
hotheaded and full of the pompous tyranny of the quarter-deck,
seems to have had one of those big, hearty, human natures which
command liking even where one cannot approve. He might be
expected at once to command the sympathy of the people, who
would see in him an example of what any one of them might become, and to be very firm in his determination to have his own
way. If such a man be on the right course, he will carry things
farther than any other kind. And, like most self-made Yankees,
Sir William was on exactly the right course, from the point of
view of the clergy. As a class, self-made men to this day grow
up with a rather blind faith in the superiority to other men of
ministers of the Gospel: in worldly moments they may smile at
their spiritual advisers as impractical; but they go to church,
and when it comes to spending their money they are very apt to
spend it as the minister tells them to. And more than most self-

made men Sir William looked up to the clergy, and most of all the clergy to the Mathers. It was Increase Mather's sermon on "The day of trouble is near," in 1674,[1] that first made him sensible of his sins; it was by Cotton Mather, just before the expedition to Port Royal, in 1690, that he was baptized and received into the communion of the faithful; it was to Increase Mather that he owed the office which crowned his worldly ambition. Clearly such a man as this might be trusted, if anybody might, to do the will of God as the Mathers expounded it. And the Mathers meant to expound it in the good old orthodox way; and the new Charter gave the Governor more power than he had ever had under the old; so there was never a moment when the hopes of Christ's kingdom looked brighter.

To understand what followed, we may well recall some things at which we have glanced already. In the view of the Puritans, the continent of America, whither they came to live in accordance with no laws but those of Scripture, had been until their coming the special territory of the Devil. Here he had ruled for centuries, unmolested by the opposing power of the Gospel: whoever doubted this had only to look at the degradation of his miserable subjects, the native Indians, to be pretty well convinced. The landing of the Puritans was a direct invasion of his territories. He fought it in all manner of ways,—material and spiritual. The physical hardship of the earlier years of the settlement was largely his work; so were the disturbances raised within the Colonies by heretics and malcontents; so, more palpably still, were the Indian wars in which his subjects rose in arms against the servants of Christ; so, too, were certain phenomena that every one at the present day would instantly recognize as natural: more than once Cotton Mather remarks as clearly diabolical the fact that the steeples of churches are oftener struck by lightning than any other structures. And from the very earliest days of the settlement the Devil had waged his unholy war in a more subtle way still: appearing in person, or in the person of direct emissaries from the invisible world, to more than a few hapless Christians, he had constantly striven with bribes and threats to seduce them to his service. Whoever yielded to him was rewarded by the possession of supernatural power, which

[1] Cf. page 20.

was secretly exerted for all manner of malicious purposes; these were the witches: whoever withstood him was tortured in mind and body almost beyond the power of men to bear; these were the bewitched. There was no phase of the Devil's warfare so insidious, so impalpable, so dangerous, as this: in the very heart of the churches, in the pulpits themselves, witches might lurk. Their crime was the darkest of all,—deliberate treason to the Lord; but it was the hardest of all to detect and to prove,—the most horrible, both in its nature and in its possibility of evil-doing. Mysterious, horrible, inevitable, it demanded every effort of Christians to withstand its subtle power.

To the Mathers, I believe, all this was very real. In 1684 Increase Mather had written a book against witchcraft. Two years later, as we have seen, Cotton Mather had had what he might well have believed a special message from Heaven that his chief mission for the moment was to fight the witches. The sins of the Colonists had brought on them the most terrible of their misfortunes: the Charter was gone, and Kirk was coming with his red-coats; and, in the deep agony of secret prayer, Cotton Mather was beseeching God to show mercy to New England, and promising, when such mercy came, what special services the Lord might see fit to demand. The good news came, at a moment when the Lord was rewarding his prayers by visions of a white-robed angel from whose lips he heard assurances of Divine favour. King Charles was dead, Kirk was coming no longer. His prayers had availed to save New England from the worst of her dangers. What should he do for the Lord? At that very moment, as we have seen, witchcraft was abroad. It was his duty to collect testimony against it, to denounce it, to fight it with all his might. From that moment, apparently, he began. And the more he studied it, the more real and terrible he found it. In 1688 there was a sad outbreak of it in Boston: Cotton Mather took into his own house one of the afflicted children, whose behaviour as he relates it was in all respects such as to increase his belief both in the reality of the Devil's work, and in the divine sanction of his own efforts against it. And now, in 1692, when the prayers of New England for a righteous charter had been granted, when the best of governors was come, ready to put into execution the best of policies, when at last the material prospects of Christ's kingdom were fairer than for years before, the Devil began such a spiritual assault on New England as had never before been approached.

The story of Salem Witchcraft has been told by Upham with a fulness and a fairness that leave nothing to be added. But he fails, I think, sympathetically to understand a fact which he emphasizes with characteristic honesty,—the tremendous influence on human beings of that profound realizing sense of the mysteries that surround us, to which those who do not share it give the name superstition.

At various periods of history epidemics of superstition have appeared, sometimes in madly tragic forms, sometimes, as in modern spiritualism, in grotesquely comic ones. These are generally classed as pure delusions, based on no external facts. But for my part, though I may claim none of the authority which would come from special study of the subject, I am strongly inclined to believe that from the earliest recorded times a certain pretty definite group of mysterious phenomena has, under various names, really shown itself throughout human society. Oracles, magic, witchcraft, animal magnetism, spiritualism,—call the phenomena what you will,—seem to me a fact. Certain phases of it are beginning to be understood under the name of hypnotism. Other phases, after the best study that has been given them, seem to be little else than deliberate fraud and falsehood; but they are fraud and falsehood, if this be all they are, of a specific kind, unchanged for centuries. The evidence at the trial of the Maréchal de Rais, a soldier of Joan of Arc and the original of the tale of Blue-Beard, relates phenomena that anybody can see to-day by paying a dollar to a "materializing medium." And some of them are very like what are related in the trials of the Salem witches. So specific is the fraud, if only fraud it be, that it may well be regarded, I think, as a distinct mental, or perhaps rather moral disorder.

With no sort of pretension to scientific knowledge, I have found that a guess I made in talk some years ago throws what may be a little light on many of the mysterious phenomena that in Cotton Mather's time were deemed indisputably diabolical. I shall venture, then, to state it here, to be taken for no more than a layman's guess may be worth. If, as modern science tends to show, human beings are the result of a process of evolution from lower forms of life, there must have been in our ancestral history a period when the intelligence of our progenitors was as different from the modern human mind—the only form of intelligence familiar to our experience or preserved in the records of our race —as were their remote aquatic bodies from the human form we know to-day. To-day we can perceive with any approach to distinctness only what reveals itself to us through the medium of our five senses; but we have only to look at the intricate wheelings of a flock of birds, at the flight of a carrier pigeon, at the course of a dog who runs straight home over a hundred miles of strange country, to see more than a probability that animals not remote from us physically have perceptions to which we are strangers. It seems wholly conceivable, then, that in the remote psychologic past of our race there may have been in our ancestors certain powers of perception which countless centuries of disuse have made so rudimentary that in our normal condition we are not conscious of them. But if such there were, it would not be strange that, in abnormal states, the rudimentary vestiges of these disused powers of perception might sometimes be revived. If this were the case, we might naturally expect two phenomena to accompany such a revival: in the first place, as such powers of perception, from my very hypothesis, belong normally to a period in the development of our race when human society and what we call moral law have not yet appeared, we should expect them to be intimately connected with a state of emotion that ignores what we call the moral sense, and so to be accompanied by various forms of misconduct; in the second place, as our chief modern means of communication—articulate language—belongs to a period when human intelligence has assumed its present form, we should expect to find it inadequate for the expression of facts which it never professed to cover, and so we should expect such phenomena as we are considering to be accompanied by an erratic, impotent inaccuracy of statement, which would soon shade into something indistinguishable from deliberate falsehood. In other words, such phenomena would naturally involve in whoever abandons himself to them a mental and moral degeneracy which any one who believes in a personal devil would not hesitate to ascribe to the direct intervention of Satan.

Now what disposes me, scientifically a layman I must repeat, to think that my guess may have something in it is that mental and moral degeneracy—credulity and fraud—seem almost invariably so to entangle themselves with occult phenomena that many cool-headed people are disposed to assert the whole thing a lie. To me, as I have shown, it does not seem so simple. I am much disposed to think that necromancers, witches, mediums,—what not,—actually do perceive in the infinite realities about us things that are imperceptible to normal human beings; but that they perceive them only at a sacrifice of their higher faculties—mental and moral—not inaptly symbolized in the old tales of those who sell their souls.

If this be true, witchcraft is not a delusion: it is a thing more subtly dangerous still. Such an epidemic of it as came to New England in 1692 is as diabolical a fact as human beings can know: unchecked, it can really work mischief unspeakable. I have said enough, I think, to show why I heartily sympathize with those who in 1692 did their utmost to suppress it; to show, too, why the fatally tragic phase of the witch trials seems to me, not the fact that there was no crime to condemn, but the fact that the evidence on which certain wretched people were executed proves, on scrutiny, utterly insufficient. It was little better than to-day would be the ravings of a clairvoyant against one accused of theft. And yet, if there be anything in my guess, this too is just what we might expect. Not knowing what they did, the judges would strain every nerve—just as in their rapt ecstasies the Mathers strained every nerve, along with their Puritan fellows, and the saints of every faith—to awaken from the lethargy of countless ages those rudimentary powers which can be awakened only at the expense of what we think the higher ones that have supplanted them. The motive may make a difference: he who strives to serve God may end as he begun, a better man than he who consents to serve the Devil. But, for all that, bewitched and judges alike, the startled ministers to whom the judges turned for counsel, and perhaps not a few of the witches too, who may well have believed in themselves, vie with one another in a devil's

race, harking back to mental and moral depths from which
humanity has taken countless centuries to rise.

Whoever cares to know in detail the story of 1692 may read it
in Upham, or in Palfrey. In brief, the children of Mr. Parris, minister of Salem Village, were seized early in the year with disorders which seemed of no earthly origin. They accused certain
neighbours of bewitching them; the neighbours were arrested.
The troubles and the accusations spread with the speed of any
panic. By the time Sir William assumed the government, the
whole region was in an agony of superstitious terror; and whoever raised his voice against the matter fell under suspicion of
league with the Devil. At that moment, as the old judicial system had fallen with the Charter, there were no regular courts.
Within a few weeks, Sir William, full of the gravity of the situation, and probably under the direct advice of the Mathers, appointed a special Court of Oyer and Terminer to try the witches.
William Stoughton, the Deputy Governor, was made Chief Justice: his six associates were gentlemen of the highest station and
character in the Province: among them was Samuel Sewall,
whose Diary I have so often quoted. On the 2d of June this
court condemned one Bridget Bishop: on the 10th she was executed for witchcraft. Before proceeding further, the court consulted the ministers of Boston and the neighbourhood. The answer of the ministers is said to have been drawn up by Cotton
Mather: in general terms it urged "the importance of caution and
circumspection in the methods of examination," but "earnestly
recommended that the proceedings should be vigorously carried
on." [2]

It is largely on this document that the charge against Cotton
Mather rests: he is believed by many deliberately to have urged
the judicial murder of innocent people for the simple purpose of
establishing and maintaining his own ascendency in the state.
To me, and what I have written already should show why, the
paper seems the only possible thing for an honest, superstitious
man—himself in direct communication with the blessed part of
the invisible world—to have written. Witchcraft was to him the
most terrible of realities; not to proceed against it would have
been to betray the cause of Christ; but the Devil stood ready to

[2] Upham, II. 268.

beguile the courts themselves; the evidence must be carefully scrutinized, or who could tell what mischief might come? Thus encouraged, the Court proceeded. How many wretched people were committed can never be quite known: Upham thinks several hundreds.[3] Nineteen were hanged; one was pressed to death for refusing to plead to his indictment; at least two died in jail. By the end of September, a revulsion of popular feeling had come. The accusations had spread too far: the evidence on which the witches were executed was beginning to seem too flimsy. On the 22d of September came the last executions. In January, 1693,[4] the special Court of Oyer and Terminer was supplanted by a regular Superior Court, consisting of much the same men. It threw out "spectral evidence,"—that is, it declined to consider the ravings of the bewitched: only three out of fifty indicted for witchcraft were condemned, and none of these was executed. In May, 1693, the panic was over. By proclamation, Sir William Phipps discharged all the accused. "Such a jail delivery," says Hutchinson, "has never been known in New England."[3]

In all this matter Increase Mather seems to have played no conspicuous part. Four years of diplomacy in the capital of the British empire had perhaps taught him practical lessons of prudence not to be learned in any less arduous school. But while these were learning, his son, not yet thirty years old, had been surrounded by influences diametrically different. In the provincial Boston, which was at once the greatest city in America and the only home he ever knew, Cotton Mather had found himself, at an age when most men are still passed by as young, among the chiefs of the leaders. And then, as later, it had been his lot to meet hardly anybody whom he could honestly deem by his own standards superior to himself. As we shall see by and by, his later career was marked by what has often seemed, particularly when we remember his constant failure to achieve the public ends he strove for, a ridiculous and overweening vanity. But I think that few can rise from a careful study of his diary without feeling that this vanity was no blind self-approval; but at most a conviction, in his happier moments, that, far as he was from the attainment of his ideals, there were none about him who were any nearer the attainment of theirs, and that there were many—

[3] Upham, II. 351. [4] Ibid., II. 349.

and year by year more—who were falling away from the ancestral traditions that he never gave up. In 1692 he was still in the flush of youth and of success. No one was more active in fighting the Devil's works as revealed in witchcraft. No one, for well on to two centuries, has borne so much of the odium of what was done as he.

We have seen how his books and his conduct in 1688 tended to stir up public feeling against the witches; we have seen how the letter of the ministers which he drew up encouraged the puzzled Court of Oyer and Terminer to proceed with its deadly work. On the 19th of August, 1692, the most eminent of the victims of the proceedings was hanged; this was the Rev. George Burroughs, a graduate of Harvard College, and for something like twenty years a minister of the Gospel. Four others died with him. One of Sewall's very few notes of this period describes this day.

"A very great number of Spectators . . . present. Mr. Cotton Mather was there. . . . All of them said they were iñocent. . . . Mr. Mather says they all died by a Righteous sentence. Mr. Burroughs, by his Speech, Prayer, protestation of his Innocence, did much move unthinking persons, which occasions their speaking hardly concerning his being executed." In the margin Sewall has written "Dolefull Witchcraft!" [5]

Calef, of whom we shall hear more by and by, gives a fuller account of the scene:—

When [Mr. Burroughs] was upon the ladder, he made a speech for the clearing of his innocency, with such solemn and serious expressions, as were to the admiration of all present: his prayer (which he concluded by repeating the Lord's prayer)[6] was so well worded, and uttered with such composedness, and such (at least seeming) fervency of spirit, as was very affecting, and drew tears from many, so that it seemed to some that the spectators would hinder the execution. The accusers[7] said the black man stood and dictated to him. As soon as he was turned off, Mr. Cotton Mather, being mounted upon a horse, addressed himself to the people, partly to declare that . . . [Burroughs] was no ordained minister, and partly to possess the peo-

---

[5] Diary, I. 363.
[6] It was believed that no witch could repeat the Lord's prayer without error.
[7] The bewitched: a capital example of spectral evidence.

ple of his guilt, saying that the devil has often been transformed into an angel of light; and this somewhat appeased the people, and the executions went on. When he was cut down, he was dragged by the halter to a hole . . . between the rocks, about two feet deep, his shirt and breeches being pulled off, and an old pair of trowsers of one executed put on his lower parts; he was so put in . . . that one of his hands and his chin . . . were left uncovered.[8]

Just a month later, Giles Corey was pressed to death for refusing to plead to his indictment,—the solitary instance in America of this terrible barbarity of the old English criminal law.

"Sept. 20," writes Sewall, "Now I hear from Salem that about 18 years agoe he was suspected to have stamped and press'd a man to death, but was cleared. Twas not remembered till Añe Putnam was told of it by said Corey's Spectre the Sabbath-day night before the Execution." [9]

On this very day, the 20th of September, two days before the last of the executions, Cotton Mather wrote to Stephen Sewall, clerk of the court at Salem, a letter which Upham deems conclusive of his artful dishonesty.[10]

"That I may bee the more capable to assist, in lifting up a standard against the Infernal Enemy," it runs, "I must Renew my most IMPORTUNATE REQUEST, that you would please quickly to perform, what you kindly promised, of giving me a Narrative of the Evidences given in at the Trials of half a dozen, or if you please a dozen, of the principal Witches, that have been condemned. . . . I am willing that when you write, you should imagine me as obstinate a Sadducee and Witch-advocate as any among us: address mee as one that Believ'd Nothing Reasonable; and when you have so knocked mee down, in a spectre so unlike mee, you will enable mee, to box it about, among my Neighbs, till it come, I know not where, at last."

Two days later, on that very 22d of September when the last witches were hanging, Sewall notes that "William Stoughton, Esqr., John Hathorne, Esqr., Mr. Cotton Mather, and Capt. John

---

[8] Page 213.
[9] Diary, I. 364. Upham, II. 341, seq., shows the charge against Corey to have been groundless. There is no more notable example of the popular infatuation.
[10] Upham, II. 487, seq. Cf. Sibley, III. 11.

Higginson, with my brother St., were at our house, speaking
about publishing some Trials of Witches." [11] The result of this
letter and conference seems to have been Cotton Mather's well
known "Wonders of the Invisible World," published the next
year both in Boston and in London.

A few of Sewall's notes show the course of popular feeling
meanwhile. On the 15th of October he went to Cambridge to discourse with Mr. Danforth about witchcraft: Mr. Danforth

"thinks there cañot be a procedure in the Court except there be some
better consent of Ministers and People." On the 26th, "A Bill is sent
in about calling a Fast, and Convocation of Ministers, that may be
led in the right way as to the Witchcrafts. The reason and mañer of
doing it, is such, that the Court of Oyer and Terminer count themselves thereby dismissed. 92 Nos and 33 yeas to the Bill." On the
28th, Sewall, "as had done several times before, desired to have the
advice of the Governour and Council as to the sitting of the Court of
Oyer and Terminer next week: said should move it no more; great
silence, as if should say, do not go." Next day, "Mr. Russell asked
whether the Court of Oyer and Terminer should sit, expressing some
fear of Inconvenience by its fall. Governour said it must fall. Lieut.-
Governour[12] not in Town."

It was nearly a year later, in September, 1693, that Cotton
Mather, in Upham's phrase,[13] "succeeded in getting up" the case
of witchcraft that cost him dearest. One Margaret Rule, a young
woman of Boston whose character seems to have been none of
the best, was seized with all the symptoms of possession. One
symptom, mentioned I think only in her case, throws considerable light on her disorder: the devils prevented her from eating,
but permitted her occasionally to swallow a little rum. Both of
the Mathers visited her, surrounded by her startled and credulous friends; they listened with full faith to her tales of black
spirits and white who haunted her; they examined her person
with what in less holy men might have savoured of indiscretion;
they prayed with her and for her. And finally, the discouraged
devils fled away; and she, returning perfectly to herself, though
extremely weak and faint and overwhelmed with vapours, most

---

[11] Diary, I. 365. Stoughton, Hathorne, and Sewall were judges of the Court
of Oyer and Terminer; Stephen Sewall, clerk of the Court, was the man to
whom Cotton Mather had written on September 20.
[12] Stoughton.   [13] Upham, II. 489.

affectionately gave thanks to God for her deliverance.[14] This case, portending such a diabolical descent on Boston as had passed over Salem, attracted the attention among others, of one Robert Calef, a merchant of the town. He visited Margaret Rule when the Mathers were with her. A perfect matter-of-fact man, thoroughly honest and equally devoid of imagination, he saw in her sufferings only a vulgar cheat, and in the conduct of the Mathers something which seems to have impressed him as deliberate and not wholly decent connivance in her imposture. He made notes of what he had seen, and submitted them to Cotton Mather. The controversy that followed, which has been admirably summarized by Sibley,[15] lasted in one form or another for six years. In 1700, Calef's book on the subject was published in London, and soon found its way to Boston.[16]

Calef's temper was that of the rational Eighteenth Century: the Mathers belonged rather to the Sixteenth,—the age of passionate religious enthusiasm. To me, both sides seem equally honest; and the difference between them seems chiefly due to the fact that, as in a thousand other cases in human history, a man of the future can rarely so rise above himself as to understand men of the past. In such a controversy, it is the man of the future that the future holds right. In the time that has passed since the Mathers and Calef have lain in their graves, the world has seen an age of reason, and not of imaginative emotion. And most of those who have concerned themselves about these dead men have deemed Calef all in the right, and the Mathers foolish, if not worse. But did Calef see all? Is there, after all, in a great epidemic of superstition nothing beyond what those who escape the contagion perceive? Are we not to-day beginning to guess that there may be in heaven and earth more things than are yet dreamt of in your philosophy? If there be, it may in the end prove the verdict of men that neither honest Calef nor the honest Mathers saw all that passed before their eyes; but that each in his own way caught a glimpse of truth, and that each believed that all the truth was comprised in the bit he saw.

But we are come now to a point where we must turn to Cotton Mather himself; where we must look to the diaries he has left us, and to the works he wrote later, for an account of what these

[14] Calef, p. 34.   [15] Harvard Graduates, III. 12-18.   [16] Cf. pages 109, 136.

critical years meant to him. The substance of his later writings seems to me adequately represented by the passages about witchcraft in the "Magnalia" and the "Parentator." A few words of these, and we will pass to his diaries for 1692[17] and 1693.[18]

The substance of his final view of the case, as shown in his published works, seems to have been this: The witchcraft was a real attack of the Devil, permitted perhaps as a punishment for dabblings in sorcery and magical tricks which people had begun to allow themselves.[19] The afflictions of the possessed, which he details in all their petty absurdities, that seem nowadays as monstrously trivial, were really diabolical.

Flashy people may burlesque these things, but when hundreds of the most sober people in a country where they have as much *mother-wit* certainly as the rest of mankind, know them to be *true,* nothing but the absurd and froward Spirit of Sadducism can question them.[20]

The only doubtful question was whether the Devil had the power of assuming before the eyes of his victims the shape of innocent persons. The assumption on the part of the judges that he had no such power led to the conviction on spectral evidence of not a few victims of the court. The abandonment of this assumption led to the cessation of the prosecutions, and to the jail delivery of 1693. Mather asserts in substance that he always opposed spectral evidence; and it is certain that Increase Mather's "Cases of Conscience," published in 1694, clearly condemns it. It is certain, too, that Cotton Mather's letter to John Richards, dated May 31, 1692,[21] warns the judge in the most specific terms against the dangers of spectral evidence. Cotton Mather's own position, as he finally states it, then, seems to have been a persistent belief in witchcraft, a persistent determination to keep the public alive to all the horrors of the crime, and to oppose it by every means in his power, but a growing doubt as to how far so mysterious and terrible an evil can be dealt with by so material an engine as the criminal law. On the whole he inclines more and more to reliance on fasting and prayer. This was undoubtedly the view taken, when the panic was once over, by

[17] In possession of the American Antiquarian Society.
[18] In possession of the Massachusetts Historical Society.
[19] Parentator, XXVIII.   [20] Magnalia, II. App. § 16.
[21] Mather Papers, 392, *seq*. See page 80.

even the most strenuous advocates of the reality of witchcraft, and Cotton Mather undeniably takes to himself the credit of having held and urged it all along.

The part of the "Magnalia" in which these facts appear is the Life of Sir William Phipps, first published separately and anonymously in 1697. On the fact that this book was anonymous, Calef bases much of his charge that Mather wrote it dishonestly to praise himself, and to delude people into believing him free from the responsibility of having urged on the prosecutions. On this fact, on the feebleness of the caution addressed by the ministers to the Court of Oyer and Terminer, and on the letter to Stephen Sewall, rests most of the charge of dishonesty from which Mather's name has never been cleared to the satisfaction of his opponents. It seems to me that the anonymous publication—by no means the only example of it in Mather's voluminous works[22] —may well have been due to no worse motive than a wish for a fair hearing, which might not have been accorded to a name which was held up to public execration. It seems to me, too, that the letter of the ministers may be taken for just what it purports to be,—an honest warning of a danger, in spite of which the Court has no moral right to hesitate in the performance of its official duty. And in the letter to Stephen Sewall I can see nothing inconsistent with the conclusion that what Cotton Mather wished to maintain unshaken was not the fatal penalty of the law, but that belief in the reality of witchcraft which he certainly never abandoned. Calef and posterity seem to me to have confused two distinct things,—this belief in the reality of witchcraft, and insistence on the validity of spectral evidence. But, when all is said, I think two facts against Mather remain: his conduct and his words had as much as any one man's could have to do with the raising of the panic; and in his final presentation of the matter, both in his diaries and in his published works, he never grants or meets the full strength of the case against him.

But before we agree with those who believe him to have been deliberately dishonest, it will be only fair to read what his diaries tell us of these troubled years; and to read it, too, with certain facts in mind that seem to me too little considered. In the first

[22] What is more, he acknowledged the book in 1702, when the "Magnalia" was published.

place, as we have seen, Cotton Mather had for years been a religious enthusiast whose constant ecstasies brought him into such direct communication with Heaven as he believed the witches to maintain with Hell; in other words, he had for years been, what he remained all his life, a constant victim of a mental or moral disorder whose normal tendency is towards the growth of unwitting credulity and fraud. In the second place, I grow to believe more and more that the ceaseless activity of mind and body, of thought, of emotion, of action, into which he never ceased to lash himself,—the activity which produced in actual words and deeds a life-work whose bulk to-day seems almost incredible,—never permitted him, in any act or word, to be really deliberate at all. Striving with all his might to do the Lord's work, believing that the Lord's will forbade him for a moment to relax a particle of his energy, he went through this world from beginning to end in a state of emotional exaltation, of passionate afflation and reaction, which left him in all the sixty years of his conscious life hardly an hour of that cool thoughtfulness without which any deliberation is impossible. It has been his fate—a man whose whole career was a storm of passion—to be judged, in the seclusion of libraries, by unimaginative, unimpassioned posterity. So cool sympathizers with old Calvinism who have sought to defend him, and cooler Protestants who have constantly condemned him, have alike failed to understand.

They have failed, too, adequately to emphasize what seems to me the most notable piece of contemporary evidence. On May 31st, 1692, we have seen,—three days before Bridget Bishop, the first victim of the Court, was sentenced,—Cotton Mather wrote to John Richards, one of the judges, a letter in which he takes, with the utmost decision, exactly the ground he occupied to the end of his life.

"Do not lay more stress upon pure Spectre evidence than it will bear," he writes. . . . "It is very certain that the divells have sometimes represented the shapes of persons not only innocent, but also very vertuous."

There should be confession, or unmistakable signs: he believes in witch-marks, to be sure, and in the water-ordeal. But at the very end he adds this caution:—

It is worth considering whether there be a necessity alwayes by Extirpačons by Halter or fagott [to punish] every wretched creature that shall be hooked into some degrees of Witchcraft. What if some of the lesser Criminalls, be only scourged with lesser punishments, and also put upon some solemn, . . . Publike . . . renunciation of the Divel? I am apt to thinke that the Divels would then cease afflicting the Neighbourhood.

So we come back to the diary for 1692.[23] As I have said already, this is far more abridged and less specific than most of his diaries. But I do not believe it untrue. The last entry I quoted was made in May, when his father had just returned, and the new Charter was just passing into operation. "And now," he wrote, "I will call upon the Lord as long as I live."

The rest of his entries for the year bear no date. He notes briefly that he has preached against temporal persecution of heresy; "And I hope the Lord will own me with a more Singular Success in the suppression of Haeresy by Endeavours more Spiritual and Evangelical." He notes that in his public ministry he has been largely handling the Day of Judgment, from texts in the 25th chapter of Matthew. Then comes a long note beginning, "The Rest of the Summer was a very doleful Time unto the whole Countrey." He tells how devils possessed many people, how witches were accused in the visions of the afflicted, how he himself testified both publicly and privately against the dangers of spectral evidence, and how it was he who drew up the letter from the ministers to the Court of Oyer and Terminer.

"Nevertheless," he goes on,[24] "I saw in most of the Judges a most charming Instance of prudence and patience, and I knew their exemplary pietie, and the Anguish of Soul with which they sought the Direction of Heaven: above most other people, whom I generally saw enchanted into a Raging, Railing, Scandalous and unreasonable disposition as the distress increased upon us. For this cause, though I would not allow the Principles, that some of the Judges had espoused, yet I could not but speak honourably of their Persons, on all occasions: and my Compassion upon the Sight of their Difficulties Raised

[23] In possession of the American Antiquarian Society.
[24] This passage, and indeed the diaries concerning this matter in general, have been studied and cited by Peabody: Sparks's American Biographies, Vol. VI.

by my Journeys to Salem, the Chief Seat of these Diabolical Vexa-
tions, caused me yett more to do so. And merely, as far as I can Learn,
for this Reason, the mad people thro' the Countrey under a fascination on their Spirits equal to what the Energumens had on their
Bodies, Reviled *mee*, as if I had been the Doer of all the Hard Things
that were done in the prosecution of the Witchcraft."

He goes on to note how he offered to provide in his own family
for six of the possessed, that he might try whether prayer and
fasting "would not putt an End to their Heavy Trials"; how
throughout the summer he prayed and fasted weekly for this
heavy affliction to the country; how he visited witches in prison
and preached to them; and how he wrote his "Wonders of the
Invisible World." And at the end of this passage is a note in
brackets, apparently made at some later time:—

[Upon the severest Examination, and the Solemnest Supplication, I
still think, that for the main, I have *Written Right*.]

Later come less coherent notes. One remarks that the spectres
brought books in which they urged the possessed to sign away
their souls. Now, as Cotton Mather worked for God largely by
writing books, this looked as if "this Assault of the Evil Angels
upon the Countrey was intended by Hell as a particular Defiance
unto *my* poor Endeavours to bring the Souls of men unto
Heaven." Whereupon, he wrote "Awakenings for the Unregenerate," which he resolved, if he lived, to give away at the rate of
two a week for two years. In the margin he notes that the evil
angels, through a possessed young woman, reproached him for
never having preached on Rev. 13. 8.[25] "I to oppose them," he
goes on, "and yett not follow them, chose to preach on Rev. 20.
15."[26] Later he makes a memorandum: as the devils bid Energumens sign books, he will sign the best of books. On the fly-
leaves of his favourite Bibles he wrote professions and confes-
sions of his faith: for example, "Received as the Book of God and
of Life by Cotton Mather."

[25] "And all that dwell upon the earth shall worship him [the beast], whose
names are not written in the book of life of the Lamb slain from the foundation of the world."
[26] "And whosoever was not found written in the book of life was cast into
the lake of fire."

"The Hearty Wishes of Cotton Mather," come next. "I have ever now and then gone to the good God with the most Solemn Addresses *That I may be altogether delivered from* Enchantments: *that no* Enchantment on my *mind may hinder mee from seeing or doing any thing for the glory of God, or dispose mee to anything whereat God may be displeased.* The Reason of this Wish is Because I beleeve, that a Real and proper *Enchantment* of the Divels do's blind and move the minds of the most of men: even in Instances of every sort. But I remember, That much Fasting as well as prayer is necessary to obtain a Rescue from Enchantments."

The last entry I have noted for the year, when I remember all the circumstances of the man's life, has for me real pathos: he would carefully avoid personal quarrels,

Because no man can manage a personal Quarrel against another without Losing abundance of precious Time. . . . And one Likely to Live, so little a *Time*, as I, had need throw away, as Little of his Time, as ever he can.

The diary for 1693[27] is a little more full than that for 1692; but, like that, is an abridgement of the original, and omits most of the dates. On his birthday, he preached from the text, "O my God, take me not away in the midst of my days." Then he set to preaching over the whole Epistle of Jude,[28] "intermingled with occasional texts." A little later he notes that a young woman possessed of devils has been delivered after he has held three fasts for her. He holds a thanksgiving accordingly; but, her possession being renewed, falls again to fasting and prayer:—

And unto my amazement, when I had kept my *Third Day* for her, shee was finally and forever delivered from the hands of the *Evil Angels:* and I had afterwards the satisfaction of seeing, not only *Her* so brought home unto the Lord that she was admitted into the *Church,* but also many others, even some scores, of young people Awakened by the picture of *Hell* exhibited in *her* Sufferings, *to flee from the wrath to come.*

The next note I have copied tells more than any other I have found of Cotton Mather's pastoral methods:—

[27] In possession of the Massachusetts Historical Society.
[28] A most minatory scripture.

"The church having hitherto extended a *Church Watch* unto none but Communicants, and confined *Baptism* unto *Them* and *Their Children*, I was desirous to bring the church into a posture more Agreeable unto the Advice of the *Synod*, in the year, 1662." So he preached on the subject, and allowing no disputation, proceeded to circulate among the brethren of the church "an instrument containing my Sentiments and purposes." The brethren "generally signed a Desire and Address unto myself thereto annexed that I would act accordingly. As for the few . . . who were Disaffected unto my proceedings, I carried it so peaceably, and obligingly, and yett resolutely, towards them, that they patiently Lett me take my way: and some of them told mee, they thought I did well to *do* as I did: tho' they could not yett come to *see* as I did. . . . Thus was the church quietly brought unto a point, which heretofore cost no Little Difficulty. But my Charge of such as now submitt themselves to my *Ecclesiastical Watch* was exceedingly increased.—Lord, LETT THY GRACE BEE SUFFICIENT FOR ME."

He notes that during the spring his days of fast and humiliation were so frequent that he lost record of them; that he kept, too, one or two days of Thanksgiving in his study. On one of these days, he goes on,—

My Special Errand unto the Lord was this: That whereas His Good *Angels,* did by *His Order,* many good offices for His people, Hee would please to grant unto mee the Enjoyment of all those *Angelical Kindnesses,* which are to bee done by *His Order,* for His *Chosen Servants* . . . in a manner and measure more *Transcendent,* than what the great *Corruptions* of the generalty of *Good Men,* permitted them to be made partakers of. Now that I might bee *Qualify'd* for this Favour, I . . . Entreated that I *may* not, and Engaged that I *will* not, on the Score of any *Angelical Communications,* forsake the Conduct of the Lord's *Written Word.*

He goes on to state certain lines of conduct which he proposes to follow, with the hope of making his behaviour as agreeable to that of angels as he can. And his closing purpose is this:—

"To *Conceal* with all prudent Secrecy whatever *Extraordinary Things* I may perceive done for mee, by the *Angels,* who love *Secrecy* in their Administrations. ☞ I do now believe," he adds, "That some Great Things are to be done for mee by the *Angels* of God."

On the 28th of March his first son was born. The child had a malformation beyond the reach of contemporary surgery. On the 1st of April it died unbaptized. It was buried beneath the epitaph, "Reserved for a glorious Resurrection."

"I had great reason," writes the bereaved father, "to suspect a *Witchcraft*, in this præternatural Accident; because my Wife, a few weeks before her Deliverance, was affrighted with an horrible *Spectre*, in the porch, which fright caused her Bowels to Turn within her; and the *Spectres* which both before and after, Tormented a young woman in the Neighbourhood, brag'd of their giving my Wife that Fright, in hopes, they said, of doing mischief unto her *Infant*, at Least, if not unto the *Mother*: and besides all this the child was no sooner Born but a suspected Woman sent unto my Father a Letter full of Railing against myself, wherein shee told him *Hee little knew what might quickly befall some of his posterity*. However, I made little *Use* of, and laid little *Stress* on, this Conjecture: desiring to submitt unto the will of my Heavenly Father without which, *Not a sparrow falls unto the Ground*."

He notes how during the summer he testified against the sin of uncleanness, on the occasion of the execution of two young women for child murder. "I accompanied the wretches to their execution," he writes, "but extremely fear all the Labours were lost upon them: however sanctify'd unto many others." He notes how his preaching at Reading started a revival there; how he conceived the idea of writing the Church History which, under the name of "Magnalia Christi Americana," remains by far the most notable of his publications; how in July a fleet arrived, and he started down the harbour to preach to it, but fell so ill that he had to go home; and how he recovered in the afternoon to find that there was yellow-fever aboard the ships, and to be convinced that an Angel of the Lord had upset his stomach for the purpose of preserving him from infection. He notes how he has prayed and preached against vices which are bringing judgments on the community, "and such of these vices as called for the Correction of the Magistrates, I hope, I did effectually stir up some of the Justices to prosecute." Then, very ecstatically, he notes how in these dying times he feels himself quite ready for death: yellow-fever was abroad now. He notes a resolution to visit widows and the fatherless: he tells how he wrote a "True and Brief Representation of the Country," which was transmitted "with all the Secrecy desirable, unto the KING's own hand: who Read it with much Satisfaction, and I hope, formed from thence, in His own Royal Mind, those Characters of the Countrey whereof we shall reap the good Effects for many a day." He notes how he wrote a book called "Winter Meditations," which when winter came on was published; and how towards the end of the summer he began his great commentary on the Bible,—a collection of every scrap of learning he can discover which has any bearing on Scripture. He worked at this for twenty years: it still remains in manuscript, under the name of "Biblia Americana." [29]

Early in September, he went to preach at Salem, where he sought "Furniture" for his Church History, and endeavoured "that the complete *History* of the Late *Witchcrafts and Possessions* might not be Lost." The notes from which he intended to preach were stolen "with such Circumstances, that I am . . . satisfy'd, the Spectres, or Agents in the *Invisible World,* were the Robbers." But he preached from memory, "so the Divel gott nothing." He had an interview with a pious woman, lately visited by shining spirits. Along with some things "to be kept secret," she prophesied a new "Storm of Witchcraft . . . to chastise the Iniquity that was used in the wilful Smothering . . . of the Last." On his return home, he found Margaret Rule down.

To avoid gratifying of the *Evil Angels,* . . . I did . . . concern myself to *use,* and *gett* as much *prayer* as I could for the afflicted Young Woman; and at the same time, to forbid, either her from *Accusing* any of the Neighbours, or others from *Enquiring* anything of her.[30] Nevertheless, a Wicked Man wrote a most Lying Libel to revile my Conduct in these Matters, which drove me to the Blessed God with my supplications. . . . I did at first, it may bee, too much Resent the Injuries of that Libel; but God brought *good* out of it: it occasioned the multiplication of my *prayers* before Him; it very much promoted the works of *Humiliation* and *Mortification* in my Soul.

He resisted the temptation to desert, in consequence of the libel, the lecture at the Old Meeting-House. As for his missing

---

[29] In possession of the Massachusetts Historical Society.
[30] In Calef himself I find nothing to contradict this.

notes, he adds, the spectres bragged to the possessed girl that they had stolen them, but confessed that they could not keep them. Sure enough,

> On the fifth of October following Every Leaf of my Notes, . . . tho' they were in eighteen separate . . . sheets, . . . were found drop't here and there about the Streets of Lyn; but how they came to bee so Dropt I cannot Imagine, and I as much wonder at the Exactness of their preservation.

On the 3d of October, his little daughter Mary[31] was ill. He prayed for her

> With such Rapturous Assurances of the Divine Love unto *mee* and *mine*, as would richly have *made Amends for the Death of more Children, if God had then called for them.* I was Unaccountably Assured, not only that *this child* shall be Happy forever, but that I never should have *any Child*, except what should bee an everlasting Temple to the Spirit of God: Yea, *That I and Mine should bee together in the Kingdome of God, World without End.*

On the 6th, the child died: next day she was buried: her epitaph was "Gone but not Lost." On the 8th, in spite of his bereavement, he administered the sacrament;

> And, I hope, that I now so exemplify'd such a Behaviour as not only to embolden my Approaches to the Supper of the Lord, but also to direct and instruct my Neighbourhood, with what frame to encounter their Afflictions.

On the 10th, a military training day, he prayed and fasted, particularly for a possessed girl,—doubtless Margaret Rule. A white spirit appeared to her, with word that God had made Cotton Mather her father, and thereupon she was delivered.

He notes in detail how he drew up a plan for a Negro meeting, in which he carefully attended both to the spiritual welfare of the Africans and to their temporal duties in the station of slavery to which it had pleased God to call them; and how he prayed and preached at the almshouse. He tells then how he was himself accused of witchcraft: the tormentors of a possessed young woman made

> my Image to appear before her, and they made themselves Masters of her tongue so far, that she began in her Fits to complain that I

[31] Born in 1691.

Threatened her, . . . tho' when shee came out of them, shee owned that They could not so much as make my *Dead Shape* do her any Harm. . . . Her greatest outcries when shee was *herself,* were for my poor prayers.

Aware of the terrible danger to his influence, if these rumours should gain credence,

"I was putt," he writes, "upon . . . Agonies, and Singular . . . Efforts of Soul, in the *Resignation* of my *Name* unto the Lord; content that if Hee had no further Service for my *Name,* it should bee torn to pieces. . . . But I cried unto the Lord as for the Deliverance of my *Name* from the Malice of Hell, so for the Deliverance of the Young Woman whom the powers of Hell had seized upon. And behold! . . . the possessed person . . . was Delivered . . . on the *very same day;* and the whole *plott of the Divel* to Reproach a poor Servant of the Lord Jesus Christ was Defeated."

In January, his only surviving child, Katharine, was very ill; praying for her, he was assured that she should recover, and presently she did. His last note for the year tells how he offered to give up a part of his salary to some members of his church who lived at a distance, and were for starting a new meeting nearer home: but nothing came of it.

Meanwhile he had published nine works: two,—a volume of sermons, and some meditations on the last judgment,—in 1692; and seven,—a preface to Mosten's "Spirit of Man," two volumes of sermons, his warnings against uncleanness, his "Winter Meditations," a letter on Witchcraft, and his "Wonders of the Invisible World," which was printed both at home and abroad,—in 1693.

I have cited with perhaps tedious detail his account of himself during these years that proved the most critical of his life, because I have not found it much noticed elsewhere, and without it he cannot, I think, be fairly judged. I have told enough, I hope, to enable whoever cares, to pass honest judgment on him. There remain two or three facts, without which our notion of the great tragedy of witchcraft would be incomplete.

Sewall, it will be remembered, was one of the judges who accepted spectral evidence. In the years that followed, he suffered many afflictions. In his diary for January, 1696-7, is this note:—

Copy of the Bill I put up on the Fast day; giving it to Mr. Willard as he pass'd by, and standing up at the reading of it, and bowing when finished; in the Afternoon.

Samuel Sewall, sensible of the reiterated strokes of God upon himself and family; and being sensible, that as to the Guilt contracted upon the opening of the late Comission of Oyer and Terminer at Salem (to which the order for this Day relates) he is, upon many accounts, more concerned than any that he knows of, Desires to take the Blame and shame of it, Asking pardon of men, And especially desiring prayers that God, who has an Unlimited Authority, would pardon that sin and all other his sins; personal and Relative: And according to his infinite Benignity, and Sovereignty, Not Visit the sin of him, or of any other, upon himself or any of his, nor upon the Land: But that He would powerfully defend him against all Temptations to Sin, for the future; and vouchsafe him the efficacious, saving Conduct of his Word and Spirit.

It is said that when Stoughton, the Chief Justice of the Court of Oyer and Terminer, heard what Sewall had done, he declared that he had no such confession to make, having acted according to the best light God had given him.[32]

In Cotton Mather's diaries for later years[33] are two entries that belong here. The first was made at this very time, January 15th, 1696-7.

"Being afflicted last Night," it runs, "with Discouraging Thoughts as if unavoidable *marks* of the *Divine Displeasure* must overtake my Family, for my not appearing with *vigour* enough to stop the proceedings of the Judges, when the Inextricable Storm from the *Invisible World* assaulted the Countrey, I did this morning in prayer with my Family, putt my Family into the merciful Hands of the Lord. And with Tears I Received Assurance of the Lord that *marks* of His Indignation should not follow my Family, but that having the *Righteousness* of the Lord Jesus Christ pleading for us, *Goodness and Mercy* should follow us and Signal Salvation of the Lord."

The other entry comes years later. On the night between the 15th and 16th of April, 1713, he held a vigil: in it he prayed that many books which he had published might do the good in the

[32] Sewall's Diary, I. 446, note.
[33] Both diaries are in possession of the American Antiquarian Society.

hope of which he had written them; and finally, in the troubled perplexity of spirit that had been growing during these long years, when his public influence and the public power of the church had been constantly waning, he wrote these words:—

I also entreated of the Lord, that I might understand the meaning of the Descent from the Invisible World, which nineteen years ago produced in a Sermon from me, a good part of what is now published.

VII. *The End of Sir William Phipps.*

1692-1695 The importance to the Mathers of
the tragedy of witchcraft has warranted me, I think, in treating
the matter by itself. Before we proceed, however, we must glance
at certain other matters that were in progress at the same time.
It was not witchcraft alone, perhaps hardly witchcraft at all,
which in 1694 brought to a close the administration of Sir William
Phipps, and with it the control of the Mathers in affairs of state.

Witchcraft was by no means the only thing that bothered poor
Sir William. There were French and Indian wars, Canada way,
which he managed rather clumsily. And there was a great deal
of political trouble at home. The new Charter was not popular.
The people had been used to electing their own governors: what
privileges Increase Mather had secured for them failed, in the
popular imagination, to balance the fact that their chief executive
officer was a nominee of the King, and that he proved, after all, by
no means the sort of man they would have chosen. Honest
enough, everybody knew, this hot-headed, uneducated, self-made,
self-willed Sir William was in nobody's opinion a man of much
administrative ability. The democratic spirit declared itself more
and more vigorously against him: not a few ministers took that
side. And the old theocracy, represented by the Mathers, found
itself at last quite divorced from the popular party; and at most
a power behind the throne of the royal Governor. From this time
on, in fact, the politics of Massachusetts was not a question of
theocracy and democracy, but was rather a struggle, which
culminated in the American Revolution, between the royal power
and the rights of the people.

The chief figure in the opposition was Elisha Cooke, a gentleman who had been associated with Increase Mather in the mission to England, and who had bitterly opposed the acceptance of the new Charter. A few of Sewall's notes show how matters ran in Boston. In November, 1692, Cooke came home; and on the 15th he kept a day of thanksgiving for his safe arrival. Most of the Boston worthies joined him in the festival; but Sewall notes: "Mr. Mather not there, nor Mr. Cotton Mather. The good Lord unite us in his Fear, and Remove our Animosities." The next May, in the teeth of an election sermon preached by Increase Mather on the great benefit of primitive counsellors,[1] Cooke was elected a member of the Governor's Council, along with certain other opponents of the government. On the 1st of June, Sir William used his privilege to veto the election of Cooke. "June 8," notes Sewall, "Mr. Danforth labours to bring Mr. Mather and Mr. Cook together, but I think in vain. Is great wrath about Mr. Cook's being refused, and 'tis supposed Mr. Mather is the cause." We begin to see more of what poor Cotton Mather meant by resolving not to waste precious time in personal quarrels towards the end of 1692. On the 11th of July, Sewall notes, Cotton Mather prayed at the opening of the Council; he prayed there again on the 15th; and in the afternoon of that day the Governor dissolved the assembly, being "much disgusted . . . about the not passing of the Bill to regulat the house of Representatives."

The bill in question was passed on the 25th of November. To all appearances a mere political device for strengthening the power of the government at a given moment, it has proved perhaps the most mischievous measure in the whole madcap history of American legislation. So far as the Mathers were responsible for it, they did their utmost to weaken the character of legislative bodies throughout this continent. As a matter of fact, in 1693, the opposition to the government was far stronger in Boston than in the country: chiefly, if not wholly, to weaken the opposition in the legislature, this bill provided that a representative must reside in the place he represented. It has been followed in practice throughout America: as a consequence no American constituency is able today to elect a competent representative unless, by the blessing of providence, a competent person happens to reside among them. And as, in the nature of things, the most able men

[1] See Quincy, I. 73.

generally congregate in large cities, the greater part of every
American legislature is composed of men personally insignificant.

But even this device proved of little use. In addition to his
other troubles, Sir William was always getting into hot water on
his own account. Early in his administration, he had a difficulty
with the collector of the port of Boston, which culminated in a
hand-to-hand fight. In January, 1693, another difficulty with the
captain of a royal frigate brought upon the captain a caning at
the hands of Sir William in the streets of Boston. It was chiefly
for this, apparently, that he was summoned to England to explain his conduct. After all, the godly, self-made adventurer had
not proved the Governor the Mathers hoped for: he was not one
to make friends for the new Charter.

A few of Sewall's notes for November, 1694, give the most vivid
pictures of his last days in New England.

"Nov. 1. . . . Capt. Dobbins refusing to give Bail, the Sheriff was
taking him to Prison, and Sir William Phips rescued him, and told
the Sheriff He would send him, the Sheriff, to prison, if he touch'd
him, which occasioned very warm discourse between Him and the
Lieut. Governour."—"Nov. 3. . . . Governour adjourns the General
Court. . . . Several of the Council desired a dissolution, lest some
Emergency should require the Calling of an Assembly, and this adjournment bind our hands: but the Governour would not hearken to
it. . . . Said, This Court is dissolved to such a time; being put in
mind of his mistake, said I mean Adjourn'd."—"Nov. 9. . . . Lieut.
Governour and Council dine at James Meers's: The Treat was in-
tended for the Governour; but is so offended at Capt. Dobbins Im-
prisonment, that He comes not, nor Mr. Mather the Father, nor Son
. . . ; so chair at the uper end of the Table stands empty. Note. Mr.
Cotton Mather was sick of a grievous pain in his face, else He had
been there, as he told me afterward."—"Seventh-day, Nov. 17th.
. . . Just about Sunset or a little after, the Governour goes from his
House to the Salutation Stairs, and there goes on board his Yatcht;
Lieut. Governour, many of the Council, Mr. Cotton Mather, Capts.
of Frigatts, Justices, and many other Gentlemen accompanying him.
'Twas six oclock by that time I got home, and I only staid to see them
come to sail. Guns at the Castle were fired about seven: Governour
had his Flagg in main top. Note. Twas of a seventh day in the even
when the Governour came to Town, and so tis at his going off, both in
darkness: and uncomfortable, because of the Sabbath."

Stoughton, the Lieutenant Governor, was left at the head of affairs for several years. In March, Cooke was elected to the Council, where he served annually till Joseph Dudley's time.

Two or three more notes of Sewall's tell a little of Cotton Mather, and all the rest there is to tell of poor blundering Sir William.

Monday, April 29, 1695. . . . About 2 P.M. a very extraordinary Storm of Hail, so that the ground was made white with it, as with the blossoms when fallen. . . . Mr. Cotton Mather dined with us, and was with me in the new Kitchen when this was; He had just been mentioning that more Ministers Houses than others proportionably had been smitten with Lightening; enquiring what the meaning of God should be in it. Many Hail Stones broke throw the Glass and flew to the middle of the Room. . . . I got Mr. Mather to pray with us after this awfull Providence; He told God He had broken the brittle part of our house, and pray'd that we might be ready for the time when our Clay-Tabernacles should be broken. . . . I mentioned to Mr. Mather that Monmouth made his descent into England about the time of the Hail in '85, . . . that much cracked our South-west windows.

Whether Sewall thought this storm equally portentous does not appear. But on

"May 5, 1695. About 3 hours News comes to Town of the death of Sir William Phipps, Feb. 18th, at which people are generally sad. Lay sick about a week of the new Fever as 'tis called."—"May 6th. . . . Mourning Guns are fired at the Castle and Town for the Death of our Governour."—"May 8, 1695. I visit my Lady, who takes on heavily for the death of Sir William. Thinks the Lieutenant and Council were not so kind to him as they should have been."

VIII. *Harvard College.*

1636-1701 From this time on, the history of Massachusetts takes a course of less interest to us. Stoughton, the Lieutenant Governor, remained at the head of affairs until 1699, when Lord Bellomont, who had been appointed Governor some time before, came to Boston. Two years later Bellomont died. In 1702 Joseph Dudley, who had been virtually an exile from Massachusetts since he was shipped to England with Andros, was appointed Governor. There is reason to believe that his appointment was much advanced by a letter from Cotton Mather, which Dudley showed the King, stating that "there was not one minister nor one of the Assembly but were impatient for his coming." [1]

The chief public affairs in Stoughton's time were connected with the French and Indian wars in Maine. In Bellomont's time, the legislature established a judiciary in a form which ultimately led to trouble with England, and began the series of squabbles with the Governor about his salary which lasted well through Cotton Mather's day. Bellomont's most notable act was perhaps the suppression of piracy: it was he who brought Captain Kidd to justice. In brief, the political history of Massachusetts up to the time of Joseph Dudley may be said to have been a slowly strengthening opposition in the legislature—and so among the people—to the power of the Governor and the Crown.

With all this the Mathers had far less to do than with the politics of earlier times. It is very typical of their history, and of the history of the theocratic party in Massachusetts, that, from this time on, their most notable public activity concerns not the

[1] Palfrey, III. 183.

Province, but Harvard College. It will be worth our while, then, hastily to glance at the history of this institution.

This has been very thoroughly written by President Quincy. In 1636, only seven years after the arrival of Governor Winthrop with the first Charter of the Colony, the General Court voted four hundred pounds "towards a School or College." Two years later, the Rev. John Harvard, a young graduate of Cambridge who had emigrated to Charlestown, died, leaving half of his estate and his whole library to the new College. With this encouragement, the College was immediately opened, and, in honour of its first benefactor, received the name of Harvard. In 1642 a Board of Overseers was established, consisting of the Governor and Deputy Governor, all the magistrates, and the teaching elders of the six adjoining towns. In 1650, a charter was granted by the General Court, placing the government of the College in the hands of a Corporation, consisting of the President, the Treasurer, and five Fellows named in the act, and empowered, with the counsel and consent of the Overseers, to perpetuate themselves. Under this charter, after various vicissitudes and some very radical changes in the nature of the Board of Overseers,—who are now elected by the alumni,—the College is governed at the present day.

Amid the utmost poverty and privation the College began its work, which was chiefly to educate the more promising youth of the Colony to a point which should render them efficient ministers of the Gospel in the inevitable days when the emigrant ministers should be no more. What manner of men it turned out we should know by this time: both Increase and Cotton Mather were graduates of Harvard; and Sibley's[2] amazingly careful biographies of those who graduated before 1689 prove the Mathers to have been typical men. It is curiously characteristic of Harvard, however, that the first two Presidents—if we except, as the records do, a rather disreputable person who was for a little while made master of the school—were decidedly inclined to heresy in the matter of baptism. Earnest, devoted, learned, ill paid, half starved, they gave every energy to the College; and before Chauncy, the second President, died, he began to see the gifts to the College come in, which have continued to the present

[2] Harvard Graduates, 3 vols.

time. The third President, Leonard Hoar, came from England to take office. For some obscure reason he was unpopular: there were intrigues against him, which encouraged the students—in the words of Cotton Mather[3]—to turn "cud-weeds, and, with great violations of the fifth Commandment, set themselves to *travestie* whatever he *did* and *said*." He resigned, and is believed to have died of a broken heart. His successor, Urian Oakes, seems to have been the leader of the intrigues against him: he seems to have been orthodox, however, if we may credit the words in which, as we have seen, he addressed young Cotton Mather in 1678.[4] When he died, in 1681, Increase Mather was chosen his successor. He declined, and so did another reverend gentleman; but John Rogers, who became the fifth President of the College, survived his inauguration less than a year; and in 1685 Increase Mather finally accepted the office. He took it on condition that he should not reside at Cambridge, but should be permitted to continue, at the same time, his pastoral work at the Second Church in Boston. He held it throughout his mission to England: he retained it throughout the administrations of Phipps, Stoughton, and Bellomont, under circumstances which we shall have to consider in some detail.

For what reason no man knows, the acts of the General Court which founded and moulded the College contained no phrases which could fairly bind it to any sectarian policy. In 1642, *piety* is the only term used that connects the College with any distinct religious principle; in 1650, there appears no more stringent term than *godliness;* and the first seal of the College, adopted on the 27th of December, 1643, bears only the word "Veritas." [5] It was not until Increase Mather's time, in all probability, that affairs led to the adoption of the other, and far less characteristic, motto still in use,—"Christo et Ecclesiæ." [6] Whether, as President Quincy inclined to think, this apparently studied religious liberality was real, may perhaps be doubted: there is, I think, about as much reason for supposing that, at the time the charter was granted and the seal adopted, piety, godliness, and truth meant to the men who used these terms nothing more or less than orthodox Calvinism; that to have defined this further would

[3] Magnalia, IV. I. § 5.   [4] Cf. page 28.   [5] Truth.
[6] For Christ and the Church.

have seemed to them a waste of words. But, whatever the reason, as the political power of the clergy began to weaken, it became evident that there was a dangerous flaw in the construction of their innermost stronghold. To the defence of this, then, the Mathers devoted their utmost energy.

In 1686—the year after Increase Mather had accepted the presidency—came, as we have seen, the final news of the vacating of the Charter of the Colony. With this, of course, fell all the minor rights that the Colonial authorities had granted under it, and among others the charter of Harvard College. For twenty-one years, until, in December, 1707, the old charter of 1650 was not too regularly revived, the College had no settled government. Throughout this period the Mathers, with whomever they could get to follow them, fought, and worked, and prayed for a charter which should permanently commit the College to the care of men whose chief thought should be to preserve uncontaminated the traditions of the fathers. They hopelessly failed; the College they longed to see the perpetual breeder of a priesthood has grown to be perhaps the most potent nurse of every shade of liberal protestantism and toleration in the English-speaking world. So those there who remember the Mathers at all nowadays either scoff at their memory or abuse it. But I think we shall grow to feel, as we read their story, that, whatever their errors, they fought their earnest fight with all their hearts, with all their souls, with all their might.

During Increase Mather's stay in England, he was constantly endeavouring to get a royal charter for the College. In an interview with James II., on the 2d of July, 1688, he asked the King directly to grant a charter for the non-conformist institution.

" 'Certainly, Syr,' " he said; " 'they may think it hard that the College built by Non-Conformists, should be taken from them and put into the Hands of Conformists.' The King replied, 'It is Unreasonable, and it shall not be.' "—"What?" notes Cotton Mather in the margin, "King James himself declare so!" [7]

But before long poor King James was where he could grant no more charters, and Increase Mather paying court to William and Mary. He had his last interview with the king on the 3d of January, 1691-2.

[7] Parentator, XXV.

" 'We have in *New England,'* " he said, as he took his leave, " 'a
COLLEGE where many an Excellent Protestant Divine has had his
Education.' The KING said, 'I know it.' He thereupon added, 'If Your
Majesty will cast a favourable Aspect on that Society, it will yet Flour-
ish more than ever.' The KING returned, 'I shall willingly do it.'—And
so *Ended* the *Final Conference.*" [8]

Home again, he busied himself at once to obtain a new charter
for the College. On the 27th of June, 1692, the very month when
the first of the Salem witches was hanged, Sir William Phipps
signed one. This charter vested absolute power in a Corporation
of ten persons, every one of whom was selected by Increase
Mather; and it made no provision for any kind of visiting board.
It was immediately sent to England for royal approval. Meantime the new Corporation assembled as if the new charter had
been thoroughly sanctioned, and among their first acts conferred
the first honorary degrees. They made Increase Mather Doctor of
Divinity: Leverett and Brattle, who had managed the College in
his absence, were at the same time made Bachelors of Divinity.
There is something significant in this very fact: Leverett and
Brattle were men of far more liberal sentiment than Mather;
Brattle is believed to have given Calef much assistance in the
preparation of his book against witchcraft;[9] and the two Bachelors
of Divinity proved leaders in the movement that finally drove
the Reverend Doctor from power.

In 1693, Increase Mather published his Election Sermon on
the benefit of primitive counsellors.[10] "Bene agere et male audire
regium est,"[11] was its motto; and in his preface he tells how he
had been warned in England that he should find New England
ungrateful for his public services; and how he had replied, that
he would go to New England and see, and that if he found their
prognostications true he should see his call clear to return to
England again. In spite of this warning, the General Court, far
from sending him to England again, passed a vote that the
President of Harvard College ought to reside at Cambridge.
Mather, who had no notion of resigning his church, offered his
resignation of the presidency to the Corporation; they refused it,

[8] Parentator, XXVIII.   [9] Sibley, III. 17, 18.   [10] Cf. page 92.
[11] "It is the lot of kings to do good and to hear evil."

and requested him to go on in the old way. Here matters stood in July, 1696, when word came from England that the King had vetoed the Charter of 1692, for the reason that it provided no visiting board. The effect of this news on Increase Mather was the renewal of a special assurance, which persisted for years, that he should once more be permitted to do work for the Lord in England.[12]

A note in Sewall relates what next happened.

> Oct. 12. [1696.] Lt. Governour goes to Cambridge. . . . Complemented the Pressedent etc., for all the respect to him, acknowledg'd his obligation and promis'd his Interposition for them as become such an Alumnus to such an Alma Mater: directed and desired the Presdt and fellows to go on: directed and enjoined the students to obedience. Had a good diñer. . . . Mr. Cotton Mather took off Mr. Chauncy and Oakes's Epitaphs as I read them to him.

A vivid little note I find this: Mather the father succeeding for the time in somehow continuing his power over the nursery of the old faith; Mather the son busy meantime in gathering material for the great Church History which remains its most notable literary monument.

It is Sewall, too, who gives the most vivid account of what came next. On the 17th of December, 1696, the Council passed a new charter.

> "Dec. 18," writes Sewall, "Mr. Mather, Allen, Willard, C. Mather give in a paper subscribed by them, shewing their dislike of our draught for the Colledge charter, and desiring that their names might not be entered therein. One chief reason was their apointing the Govr. and Council for Visitor.[13] . . . I doe not know that I ever saw the Council run upon with such a height of Rage before. The Lord prepare for the Issue. . . . The Ministers will go to England for a Charter, except we exclude the Council from the Visitation."

In 1697 Increase Mather drew up a new charter, which was somehow fought through the legislature. And the first public indications of the troubles that were brewing within the College appeared in the dropping of Leverett's name from the Corpora-

[12] Quincy, I. App. IX.
[13] I. e. Lay overseers threatened the predominance of the clergy.

tion. "How the Deputies will resent it," writes Sewall,[14] "I know not." And there was a petition of some ministers that Increase Mather be sent to England to push the charter; and the General Court refused it; and Mather threatened to resign. Late in the same year, Sewall gives another glimpse of the poor man's troubles:—

> Nov. 20. Mr. Willard [15] told me of the falling out between the President and him about Chusing Fellows last Monday. Mr. Mather has sent him word, He will never come to his House more till he give him satisfaction.

Next January came another petition that Mather be sent to England, likewise rejected. And at the end of 1698, the General Court renewed the vote that President Mather "remove to the College, and take up his residence there."

Two accounts are extant of the interview that followed, on the 8th of December, between Mather and the representatives of the General Court who brought him this order.

"I told them," writes Increase Mather himself,[16] "that I was discouraged. . . . Col. Byfield said . . . every one in the House desired that I should be the President, etc. I objected that I was not willing to leave my preaching work. Mr. Sewall's reply was, I might preach to the scholars by expositions every day. I told them, I could not go till the church spared me."—"Oh," he writes two days later, "that God would accept of service for me in England according to my faith!"

Sewall's account of the interview runs thus:—

> Twas near 7 in the even before we got thither. I began, and ask'd excuse for our being so late. The reason was, most of us were come from a Wedding: However, I hop'd it was a good omen, that we were all coming to a Wedding. . . . We urged his going all we could; I told him of his Birth and education here; that he look'd at work rather than Wages,[17] all met in desiring him, and should hardly agree so

---

[14] Diary, I. 450.
[15] Minister of the Old South. The year before, Willard and Mather had joined in protesting against the charter of 1696.
[16] Quincy, I. 480, 481.
[17] Among other troubles was a dispute about salary.

well in any other. Mr. Speaker, in behalf of the House, earnestly desired him. Objected want of a House, Bill for Corporation not pass'd;
Church; [his attachment to it] Must needs preach once every week,
which he prefered before the Gold and Silver of the West Indies. I
told him would preach twice a day to the students. He said that . . .
was nothing like preaching.

All of which Mather repeated formally in a letter to Stoughton
on December 18.[18] And putting the question of leave of absence
to his church a few weeks later, he had the satisfaction of being
refused. In April, 1699, came news that the King would not approve the charter of 1697.

The next month Lord Bellomont, the new Governor, arrived.
In his message to the General Court, on the 2d of June, he expressed a wish to promote a charter for the College. A few days
later, Cotton Mather had a spiritual experience perhaps worth
recording here. On the 7th of June, 1699,[19] one of his children
was very ill. He had had a particular faith that she should recover; but as she grew worse, "being in distress lest my particular Faith should prove but a Fancy, and a Folly, and end
in Confusion," he held a special fast; and the child mended
forthwith.

"God has ordered this Matter," he goes on, "for my Encouragement
about several greater points of my particular Faith not yett accomplished. . . This day as I was, (may I not say?) in *the Spirit*, it
was in a powerful manner assured me from Heaven, That my Father
shall one Day be carried into England: and that he shall there glorify
the Lord Jesus Christ: And that the *particular Faith* which has Introduced it, shall be at last made a matter of wonderful glory and
Service unto the Lord. And thou, O Mather the Younger, shalt Live
to see this Accomplished. And thy Son[20] too shall glorify the Lord
Jesus Christ, after thou also hast followed thy Father into the Kingdom of God."

On the 7th of July,[21] the Mathers and six other ministers addressed to the General Court a request that in the new charter
our holy religion may be secured to us and unto our posterity, by a
provision, that no person shall be chosen President, or Fellow, of the
College, but such as declare their adherence unto the principles of

---

[18] Sewall's Diary, I. 493, 494.
[19] The diary for 1699 is in possession of the American Antiquarian Society.
[20] Cf. pages 128-29.   [21] Quincy, I. 99.

reformation, which were espoused and intended by those who first settled the country and founded the College, and have hitherto been the general profession of New England.

Such a provision was inserted in the charter passed on the 13th of July; none of the previous charters had contained anything of the kind. On the 16th, Cotton Mather had another ecstatic assurance that all should be well. On the 18th, Lord Bellomont objected to the religious proviso in the new charter, which he probably deemed a direct attack on the Church of England. This charter, then, and the fervent particular faiths of the Mathers came to nothing.

Meantime another matter had been growing that sorely troubled the Mathers. Quincy tells the story clearly. We have seen already that Leverett and Brattle had begun to show a tendency to heterodoxy. In 1697, Cotton Mather published a Life of Jonathan Mitchel, Minister of Cambridge.[22] To this Increase Mather prefixed a dedicatory letter to the church in Cambridge and the students in the College there. The substance of this long assertion of the pristine principles of New England is, that "to admit persons to partake of the Lord's Supper, without any examination of the work of grace in the heart, would be a real apostacy and degeneracy from the churches of New England"; and he warns the tutors of the College not to become "degenerate plants or prove themselves apostate." This was a direct attack on Leverett, Brattle, and their friends. They were not slow in retorting. At the beginning of 1698, they organized a new church in Boston on new principles, expressly rejecting "the imposition of any public relation of experiences" as the condition of admission to the Lord's Supper.[23] In November, 1699, the Rev. Benjamin Colman arrived to take charge of the new church; an accomplished young man, graduated at Harvard College seven years before, and since that time resident in England, where under William of Orange clever Dissenters had been having a very comfortable time. A few notes from Cotton Mather's diary and from Sewall's[24] will tell the rest of the story.

[22] Reprinted in the Magnalia, IV. IV.
[23] Quincy, I. 130, 131. For a somewhat fuller account of their principles, see Palfrey, III. 170, seq.
[24] All these are cited in the Appendix to the first volume of Quincy.

"7th, 10th m. [1699]," writes Cotton Mather, "A company of head-strong men in the town, the chief of whom are full of malignity to the holy ways of our churches, have built in the town another meet-ing-house. . . . And without the advice or knowledge of the minis-ters in the vicinity, they have published, under the title of a *manifesto*, certain articles that utterly subvert our churches. . . . This drives the ministers that would be faithful unto the Lord Jesus Christ, and his interest in the churches, unto a necessity of appearing for their de-fence. No little part of these actions most unavoidably fall to my share."

Two days later Colman called on Sewall, who talked at some length about the startling manifesto.

"At his going away," writes Sewall, "I told him, If God should please by them to hold forth any Light that had not been seen or entertained before; I should be so far from envying it, that I should rejoice in it: which he was much affected with."

On the 5th of January, 1699-1700, poor Cotton Mather's mood was far from placid.

"I see Satan," he writes, "beginning a terrible Shake unto the Churches of New England, and the *Innovators* that have sett up a New Church in Boston, (a *New* one indeed!) have made a Day of Temptation among us. The men are Ignorant, Arrogant, Obstinate, and full of malice and slander, and they fill the Land with Lyes, in the misrepresentations whereof I am a very singular sufferer. Where-fore I set apart this day again for prayer in my study, to cry mightily unto God."

But by the 21st of January, he had so far controlled himself as to be able to draw up a proposal of terms on which the old party and the new might agree. Sewall tells the rest of the story for the moment.

Jany. 24th. The Lt. Govr. calls me with him to Mr. Willards, where out of two papers[25] Mr. Wm. Brattle drew up a third for an Accomo-dation to bring on an Agreement between the New-Church and our Ministers; Mr. Coleman got his Brethren to subscribe to it.—Jany. 25th. Mr. I. Mather, Mr. C. Mather [and others] wait on the Lt. Govr.

[25] This phrase seems to me to dispose of Quincy's charge that Cotton Mather falsely claimed the authorship of the agreement. One of the "two papers" was doubtless his. See Quincy, I. 237.

. . . to confer about the writing drawn up the evening before. Was some heat; but grew calmer, and after Lecture agreed to be present at the Fast which is to be observed Jany. 31.—Jany. 31. Fast at the New Church. Mr. Coleman reads the Writing agreed on. . . . Mr. I. Mather preaches, Mr. Cotton Mather prays. . . . Mr. Mather gives the Blessing. His text was, Follow peace with all men and Holiness. Doct. must follow peace as far as it consists with Holiness. . . . C. Mather pray'd excellently and pathetically for Mr. Colman and his Flock. Twas a close dark day.

The next May, Lord Bellomont in his address to the General Court advised that "the settlement of the College will best be obtained . . . by addressing the King for his royal charter of privileges." Accordingly the General Court prepared an address to his Majesty, humbly soliciting his approval of a charter they prepared in form. The influence of the Mathers appears in the fact that neither Leverett, nor either of the Brattles, the Rev. William, and Thomas, the Treasurer, was named in this charter. How matters now appeared to Cotton Mather, his diary tells.[26] On the 16th of June, 1700, he writes in much detail of his particular faiths about the College: he was holding a day of fasting and special prayer.

"I beg'd of the Lord," he goes on, "that if my *particular Faith* about my Father's voyage to *England,* were not a Delusion, He would please to Renew it upon mee. All the while my Heart had the Coldness of a Stone upon it, and the Straitness that is to be expected from the bare Exercise of Reason. But now all on the sudden, I felt an inexpressible Force to fall on my Mind, an *Afflatus* that cannot be described in words; *None knows it, but he that has it;* If an *Angel* from Heaven had spoken it Articulately, the communication would not have been more powerful. It was told me that the Lord Jesus Christ Loved my Father, and Loved mee, and that Hee took Delight in us as in Two of His Faithful Servants: and that Hee had not permitted us to be Deceived in our *particular Faiths,* but that my Father should be carried into *England,* and there glorify the Lord Jesus Christ before his passing into Glory: . . . and that I shall also live to see it; and that a Sentence of *Death* shall be written on . . . our *particular Faith,* but the Lord Jesus Christ, who *Raises the Dead,* and

[26] The whole passage from which I make selections is printed in Quincy, I. 484-86. The diary for 1700 is in possession of the Massachusetts Historical Society.

is *the Resurrection and the Life* shall give a New Life unto it! Hee
will do it! Hee will do it!—Having Left a Flood of Tears fetched from
me by these Rayes[27] from the *Invisible World* on my study-floor, I
Rose and went unto my chair. There I took up my Bible, and the
First place that I opened was at Act 27. 23. 24. 25,[28] 'There stood by
me an angel of God, whose I am, and whom I serve, saying, Fear not,
thou must be brought before Cæsar.' . . . A New Flood of Tears immediately gush'd from my flowing Eyes, and I broke out into these
Expressions: 'What! Shall my Father yett appear before *Cæsar?* Has
an *Angel* from Heaven told me so? And must I believe what has been
told me? Well then, It shall be so! It shall be so!' "—"And now," runs
the next entry, "what shall I say? When the affair of my Father's
agency . . . came to a turning point . . . some of the Tories so
wrought upon the Governour that he deserted [29] it. The Lieutenant
Governour . . . appeared with all the Little Tricks imaginable to
confound it. It had, for all this, been carried, had not some of the
Council been inconveniently called off. . . . The whole affair of the
College, was left unto the management of the Earl of Bellomont. So
that all expectation of a Voyage for my Father unto *England* on any
such occasion, is utterly at an end. What shall I make of this Wonderful matter. Wait! Wait!"

Before he had waited a month, his particular faith had a worse
buffet still. On the 10th of July, the General Court, far from
bidding Increase Mather go stand before Cæsar, voted more decidedly than ever that the President of Harvard College ought
to reside there; and that Increase Mather should "repair to
Cambridge as soon as may be." Sewall visited him the same day,

at three in the afternoon. I told him the Honor of Athanasius, *Maluit
sedem quam Fidei syllabam mutare:*[30] Worthies of N. E. left their
Houses in England, and came hither where there were none to preserve[31] Religion in its Purity. Put him in mind how often God has
renewed his Call to the work which was to be consider'd. That were
19 in the Council: and had every vote.

[27] Not *rages,* as Quincy read.
[28] Like most of Cotton Mather's quotations, this is not quite accurate in detail. It is characteristic of his eternal hurry, that, while he rarely misses the
spirit of a quotation, he is apt, even when citing Scripture, to make verbal
slips.
[29] Not *deferred,* as Quincy read.
[30] "He would rather change his home than a jot of his faith."
[31] May not this be a misprint for *persecute?*

But poor Increase Mather, who had stood before three Cæsars, had no mind to "leave preaching to 1500 souls . . . only to expound to 40 or 50 Children, few of them capable of Edification by such Exercises." [32] At least he must get the consent of his church, the official representative of the 1500 souls. To his grief, they gave their consent. A note of Cotton Mather's early in July tells the story.

"There was a coincidence of many things," he writes, "to incline the Church unto such a Vote; but the chief was, The Ferment and the Tumult of the Countrey, about the State of the too-corrupted College, and the Danger of its falling into Ill Hands, if my Father should not have answered the Cry of the publick about it. And it was the apprehension of his best Friends, that if my Father had now declined going to Cambridge, the Clamour and Reproach of all the Land against him, would have been insupportable; he must have Died with Infamy. My Father upon the vote of the Church immediately (the next week) hastens away to Reside at Cambridge. But I am now plunged into Distresses of two sorts. First, The Strangely melancholy and Disconsolate Condition of Mind which my Father has carried with him to *Cambridge*, (the place, which of all under Heaven, was most Abominable to him) fills me with Fear, what may be the Event. If he would be cheerful, all would be easy; but his Spirit is prodigiously unframed, unhing'd and broken; and if the Lord be not very merciful to Him, the Name of the Lord Jesus Christ will suffer more Dishonour from his Uneasiness than I am willing to see. Lord, Rate off, and Chain up, the Tempter, that falls upon my poor Father with such molestation. Secondly, I am now Left alone in the care of a Vast congregation, the largest in all these parts of the world. I am afraid, lest now they grow foolish and froward, and lest the Devices of Satan may some way or other prevail to scatter them, or Lest some Distemper arise among them. And, I am feeble; and in this Town I have many Enemies: indeed, all the Enemies of the Evangelical Interests are mine. I need a more than ordinary prudence and patience, and the Defence of Heaven."

For all this time there were other troubles entangled with those directly concerning the College. The dissensions with the Brattle Street people had broken out afresh. Before the reconciliation of January, 1700, the two Mathers had, "with many prayers and studies, and with humble resignation of our names unto the

---

[32] I. Mather to Stoughton, 16 December, 1698. Sewall's Diary, I. 493.

Lord, prepared a faithful antidote for our churches against the infection of the example, which we feared this company had given them." [33] The reconciliation stopped the publication of this antidote: but in March, the Mathers published it,—a book entitled the "Order of the Gospel." It was a direct, violent attack, in general terms, on the innovations that were creeping into the churches of New England. Some notes from Cotton Mather's diary for 1700 tell how this matter showed itself to him. On the 1st of March, the day the book came out, he writes,

The Venome of that malignant Company who have lately built a New Church in Boston disposes them to add unto the Storm of my present persecution; for it may bee never had any men more of that Character of *Grievous Revolters*, To bee *walking with Slanders*, than too many of that poor people have.

On the 14th of April, he comforted himself with the reflection that as Christ was persecuted on earth, so would naturally be His faithful servants: he ought, then, to be thankful for his sufferings.

"It was powerfully sett home upon my heart," he adds, "that I have in this Disposition an *Infallible Symptome*, That my Lord Jesus Christ will ere Long fetch me away to *Heavenly Glory*, and that he will *glorify* me with Himself world without End." On the 11th of May, he had an assurance "That something shall befall the Disorderly Society of Innovators (now causing much Temptation and Iniquity in the place) that shall confirm these Churches in the Right Ways of the Lord."

In spite of this assurance, "sundry ministers of New England" published the "Gospel Order Revived," [34]—a vigorous reply to the Mathers' "Order of the Gospel." On the 4th of July, less than a week before his ecstatic assurance, so dreadfully disappointed, that his father should be carried into England, Cotton Mather writes that there are hardly any but his father and himself

to appear with any strength of Argument or Fortitude in Defence of the invaded *Churches*. Wherefore I thought I must cry mightily unto the Lord that He would mercifully Direct me . . . in all my feeble,

[33] Cotton Mather's Diary, 21 January, 1700, quoted from Quincy, I. 487. For all this matter of the Brattle Street Church, see Quincy, Chap. VII.
[34] For a curious contemporary comment on this controversy, see Sewall's Letter-Book, I. 255.

but faithful Endeavours to serve Him . . . and preserve me from
all the Devices of Satan . . . to blast me with Reproaches that may
. . . Incapacitate me for Eminent Serviceableness. I also thought,
that if it be the purpose of Heaven that the Apostasy should go on,
they that will vigorously . . . stand in the way of that *Apostasy* may
be in danger of a Stroke from the *Angel of Death,* that so a *way may
be made for the Anger of God.* But then I resolved . . . I will oppose
it, tho' it cost me my *Life.* Hereupon the Lord sent into my Spirit a
Sweet Meditation, That my Life which I am thus willing to venture,
shall the rather be prolonged; and my Name, which I thus cast overboard, shall be the more precious in the Churches of the Lord.

On the 2d of September, when poor Increase Mather was at
work expounding to his "40 or 50 children" at Cambridge, Cotton Mather writes,

Observing how powerfully the *Devices of Satan* are operating to
bring on *Apostasies* and *Innovations* upon the Churches, and particularly, a Minister of some Note in the Churches for his piety[35] having
published a Book of Wretched Novelties, which, tho' it be offensive
to the generalty of Good Men, yett is Entertained with Gladness by
a carnal, Giddy Rising generation, I thought it my duty to defend
the Churches.

So he wrote a "Defence of the Evangelical Churches," "whereto
my Father joined with me, in setting his Name." This was apparently the pamphlet full of passionate vituperation which is
described by President Quincy.

At the same time, another attack, and a more direct one, was
making on the Mathers. We have already seen[36] how profoundly
unimaginative Robert Calef was stirred by what seemed to him
the deliberately monstrous conduct of the Mathers in the matter
of witchcraft. In the intervening years he had put together his
book on the subject, for which, Sibley says,[37] "he was furnished
with materials . . . by Mr. [Wm.] Brattle of Cambridge and his
brother of Boston, gentlemen who were opposed to the Salem
proceedings." Likewise gentlemen, I may add, who started the
Brattle Street Church, and in College matters were leaders of
the opposition to the Mathers.[38] An honest book, I have said, it
seems to me; a sensible one, if it be good sense to have no glim-

---

[35] Colman, I believe.   [36] See page 77.   [37] Harvard Graduates, III. 17, 18.
[38] See page 105.

mer of imagination; but about as appreciative of what the
Mathers really were as a good, practical Yankee of to-day might
be of Cardinal Newman. It was printed in England: it arrived
in Boston in November, 1700. Increase Mather had it publicly
burned in Harvard Yard, thereby doubtless increasing its vogue.
Just at this moment no blow could have hit the Mathers harder.

"First Calef's book," writes Cotton Mather on the 28th of December,
"and then Coleman's do sett the people in a mighty Ferment. All the
Adversaries of the Churches Lay their Hands together as if by Blasting
of us they hoped utterly to blow up all."

So this day he prayed and fasted. His devotions consisted
largely of the singing of psalms. His psalm-book, he remarked
with some surprise, opened of itself at places

the most agreeable perhaps of any that I could have chosen. This
observation may easily be abused unto superstition: but yett sometimes there is an Angelical Agency in these occurrences.

But the losing fight was almost over. On the 17th of October,
1700, Increase Mather, professing ill-health, had returned from
Cambridge, desiring in a letter to Stoughton that another President be thought of. In February, 1701, Samuel Willard, Minister
of the Old South, was made Vice President. On the 5th of March,
Lord Bellomont died in New York, leaving the administration
once more in the hands of Lieutenant Governor Stoughton. On
the 4th of July, Sewall visited him, confined to his bed, with a
committee of the General Court, who wished to arrange an
adjournment.

"He agreed to it," writes Sewall, "very freely. I said the Court was
afflicted with the sense of his Honors indisposition; at which he rais'd
himself up on his Couch. When coming away, he reach'd out his hand;
I gave him mine, and kiss'd his. He said before, Pray for me! This was
the last time I ever saw his Honor."

Three days later the grim old Puritan was dead: he had been
one of the crew of Andros; with the favour of the Mathers he
had retained office in the time of Phipps; with the best light God
had given him, he had done to death the Salem witches; and all

that is left of him now is the forbidding portrait in Memorial
Hall, with the stiff open hand that tells how he was the first
native benefactor who built a hall for Harvard College.

The executive authority now vested in the Council. On the
6th of September, 1701, the General Court voted that Increase
Mather, who had meanwhile gone back to Cambridge and again
returned to Boston, be replaced by Mr. Samuel Willard, who
promised to reside at the College one or two days and nights in
a week. And so the "good President" who had stood before
Cæsar, who had won for Massachusetts the Charter under which
she flourished for more than eighty years, who had given every
energy of his life to the defence of the old theocracy of the
fathers, was left at sixty-two just what he had been at twenty-
five, and what he remained all the rest of his life,—nothing but
the Minister of the Second Church in Boston.

Twenty-three years later, when Cotton Mather wrote his
father's life, he could speak thus:—

His abdication was after all brought about, I will but *Softly* say,
Not so fairly as it should have been. I think, there are Thanks due to
me, for my forbearing to *Tell the Story.*[39]

At the time he was not so calm. It is probable that, almost at
this moment, he had the sagacity to make his last forlorn attempt
to master the government, by writing to Joseph Dudley the letter
which clinched his appointment to the governorship.[40] Dudley
might be grateful; things might still go better. But how he took
it at the moment appears most vividly in a note of Sewall's.

Oct. 20 [1701]. Mr. Cotton Mather came to Mr. Wilkins's shop,
and there talked very sharply against me[41] as if I had used his father
worse than a Neger; spake so loud that the people in the street might
hear him.

Later notes of Sewall's show that some kind of reconciliation
soon followed. So does a letter in Sewall's Letter-Book.[42] But to
one who has learned from Sewall's artless record how close the

[39] Parentator, XXIX. See pages 134-35.   [40] Cf. page 95.
[41] Sewall was of the Council that finally dismissed President Mather.
[42] Cf. pages 134-35.

good old man's fists were, the most startling of all his notes—a note that shows how, after all, his conscience smote him—is this:—

> Octr. 9. I sent Mr. Increase Mather a Hanch of very good Venison: I hope in that I did not treat him as a Negro.[43]

[43] Diary, II. 44.

IX. *Cotton Mather's Private Life*
until the Death of His Wife.

1696-1702 It is during the years we have just
been considering, and the two that immediately follow, that Cotton Mather's diaries give us the most continuous view of his private life. The revised copies of his diaries from 1696 to 1705 are preserved. The story of Increase Mather's presidency seemed important enough to be considered by itself. In this chapter I purpose telling what I have found concerning Cotton Mather's personal career until the death of his wife in 1702.

In 1694, Sibley tells us, he published two books: a treatise of Early Religion, and a lecture on the History of New England. In this year, too, his fifth child, Abigail, was born. In 1695, he published seven distinct books: four volumes of sermons, a book against the Devil, a volume of biographies of eminent emigrant ministers, and a Life of Queen Mary, who was just dead. In this year, I take it, was born his sixth child, Mehitabel. These were the years, we shall remember, when Sir William Phipps came to grief and died, and when Increase Mather's first charter for Harvard College was still in the hands of the King.

The next year, 1696, was that in which news came of the royal disapproval of the College charter; in which, as we have seen, Stoughton authorized Increase Mather to continue his presidency on the day when Cotton Mather was copying the epitaphs of Chauncy and Oakes; the year in which the objections of the Mathers killed the first College charter drawn by the Council; the year whose close brought the fast at which Sewall put up his confession of penitence for his share in the witch trials, and Cotton Mather put his family into the hands of God.

His diary[1] shows that he began the year in a state of depression, and closed it with more or less satisfactory assurances that his work was grateful to the Lord. The entries, which occur about once a week, are mostly in general terms: perhaps the most notable thing they show is an increasing interest in foreign affairs, concerning which he had occasional prophetic assurances. Early in the year he wrote his Life of Phipps, which Lady Phipps sent abroad for publication. I have found only two or three entries which seem worth noting in detail.[2]

The first is for the 22d of February, a day on which he fasted, with abasement and depression, and was rewarded by assurances that something should come of his prayers for England, Ireland, and Scotland.

"After this Day," he goes on, "I continued full of such Dejected and Abasing Thoughts of my own extraordinary Vileness as did fill mee in the Day itself. Oh! the Lord is laying of me Low! . . . So I wrote: and so it must Come to pass. For 28. 12.[3] Early this morning my daughter Mehitabel dyed suddenly in its Nurse's Arms: not known to bee dying till it was dead of some sudden stoppage by wind: *The wind passed over the Flower, and it was presently gone.*" Next day the child was buried: its epitaph was, "In Faith of the Resurrection your Bones shall flourish like an Herb." In the margin he notes that he "Forgot to pray for M. that morning": reproaching himself, he found that the child was dead at the time. "Alas," he adds, "the child was overlaid by the Nurse."

The only other notes I have copied for this year come in the following January. One I have already quoted,[4] in which, on the occasion of the fast, he commends his family to God. The other, for the 23d of January, 1696-7, gives a little glimpse of fact:—

"So extremely cold was the weather that in a Warm Room on a great Fire the Juices forced out at the end of short billets of wood by the Heat of the Flame on which they were laid, yett froze into Ice on their coming out." So he gave up a projected fast, "because I saw it impossible to serve the Lord without such Distraction as was Inconvenient."

[1] In possession of the American Antiquarian Society.
[2] For another, see Sparks's American Biographies, VI. 261.
[3] 12 = February. Mather begins his years with March.
[4] See page 89.

On the 29th, the weather seems to have moderated: at all events, he had an assurance that his consort should have easy travail. The next day she was out of order; his servant was ill; and little Nibby[5] fell into the fire, happily without much hurt.

This year he published five books: four volumes of sermons, and an account of memorable experiences of those captured by Indians.

The next year, 1697, was that in which Increase Mather drew up his second charter for the College, in which the first application for his agency to England was refused, in which he threatened to resign, and fell out with Mr. Willard about the choosing of Fellows.

Cotton Mather's diary for this year[6] is more interesting than the last. One of its mottoes is characteristic: "Tully, in his Second Book, De Natura Deorum, says, 'Nemo Vir Magnus sine aliquo Afflatu Divino unquam fuit.'"[7] He began the year by an ecstatic birthday. A week later, he was writing to Connecticut for relief for famine-stricken Massachusetts. A few days later, prayer and fasting were rewarded by an assurance that he should "ere long bee with the Innumerable company of Holy Angels," and that his offspring should want for no good thing. And on the 27th of February another fast, ending with assurances of a speedy revolution in England and France, led him to resolve on daily prayers, like Daniel's, for the emancipation of the Church from captivity, and later to start a prayer-meeting for the coming revolution and reformation. The close of this note is a good example of his manner of recording his afflations in general:—

In the close of the Day, when I lay prostrate on my Floor, in the Dust, before the Lord, I obtained Fresh and Sweet Assurances from Him, That altho' I have been the most Loathsome Creature in the World, yett His *Holy Spirit*, would with Sovereign and Glorious Grace, Take possession of me, and Accept mee, and employ mee, to glorify His Name exceedingly. And I successfully Renewed my Cries unto the Lord, that Hee would visit *France*, and *Great Britain*, speedily, with a mighty *Revolution*.

A little later, his seventh child, Hannah, was born.

[5] Abigail.
[6] In possession of the Massachusetts Historical Society.
[7] "No man was ever great without some afflation from God."

A note of Sewall's for the 8th of April gives a characteristic glimpse of Mather:—

> Mr. Cotton Mather gives notice that the Lecture hereafter is to begin at Eleven, . . . an hour sooner than formerly. Reprov'd the Towns people that attended no better; fear'd twould be an omen of our not enjoying the Lecture long, if did not amend.

But it is not till August that I find in Mather's own diary anything else noteworthy. On the 20th, he held a private thanksgiving for his life, his health, his speech freed from impediment, his library, his dwelling-house, his consort, his children, his unblemished reputation, "and such deliverances granted unto the Countrey that my opportunities to be serviceable have not been overwhelmed in the Ruines of it." That evening he went into his empty church, where he had much ecstasy. In the midst of a thousand other works he had finished his "Magnalia," his great Church History of New England.

Though several years passed before this most notable of his works was published, we may perhaps best consider it here, at the moment of its completion. Its scope and purpose are well expressed, I think, in a few words from the General Introduction:—

> It may be, 't is not possible for me to do a greater service unto the Churches on the *best Island* of the universe, than to give a distinct relation of these great examples which have been occurring among Churches of *exiles*, that were driven out of that Island, into an horrible wilderness, merely for their being well-wishers unto the Reformation. . . . 'Tis possible that our Lord Jesus Christ carried some thousands of Reformers into the retirements of an American desart, on purpose that, with an opportunity granted unto many of his faithful servants, to enjoy the precious *liberty* of their Ministry, though in the midst of many temptations all their days, He might there, *to* them first, and then *by* them, give a *specimen* of many good things, which He would have His Churches elsewhere aspire and arise unto; and *this* being done, he knows not[8] whether there be not *all done* that New England was planted for; and whether the Plantation may not, soon after this, *come to nothing*.

He has written nothing but truth, he says:—

[8] Should not this rather be "I know not"?

I have not commended any person, but when I have really judged, not only that he *deserved* it, but also that it would be a benefit unto posterity to know wherein he deserved it; . . . yett I have left unmentioned some censurable occurrences in the story of our Colonies, as things no less unuseful than improper to be raised out of the grave, wherein Oblivion hath now buried them.

That defines the whole book, I think; it seems to me an honest effort, at a moment when the old order was changing, to preserve and emphasize all the best things that in the olden time had been thought, and said, and done. If the sons could but be brought to emulate the virtues of the fathers, all might still go well. And those old days were glorious days that filled Cotton Mather with enthusiasm; and their sins and errors might best be tenderly forgotten. He had conceived the book, we have seen,[9] in 1693. Meanwhile he had been incredibly busy with all sorts of other matters: his pastoral duties, politics, the College, his incessant private devotions, his many other writings, including the great "Biblia Americana," on which he worked for twenty years.

"All the time I have had for my Church History," he writes, "hath been . . . chiefly that which I might have taken else for less profitable recreations; and it hath all been done by *snatches*. . . . I wish I could have enjoyed, entirely for this work, one quarter of the little more than two years[10] which have rolled away since I began it."

The "Magnalia" bears throughout traces of the crowded haste with which it was written. It is flung together, not composed at all. There are seven chief divisions, or books: the first recounts the history of the Colonies; the second contains the lives of governors and magistrates, closing with that of Sir William Phipps; the third contains the lives of some sixty emigrant ministers; the fourth tells the history of Harvard College, and contains the lives of ten eminent ministers graduated there; the fifth gives an account of the orthodox creed and discipline of the New England churches; the sixth contains a record of many remarkable providences, judgments, and the like, that have been experienced in

[9] See page 85.
[10] According to his own diaries, the book was begun at the end of 1693, and finished in the middle of 1697. This inaccuracy is characteristic,—palpable, unimportant. Anyway, before the "Magnalia" was published, he revised it and inserted new matter.

New England; the seventh tells of the "Wars of the Lord," or the various disturbances that have attacked the churches and the people there. Along with much new matter, these books contain reprints of at least fifteen volumes published separately: ten before the end of 1697, five after. Just as these volumes were naturally independent, so are all the chapters in the whole work. And there is no question that it is full of superstitions now incredible, and of hasty errors of date and the like.

For all this, the "Magnalia" has merits which dispose me to rate it among the great works of English literature in the Seventeenth Century. The style, in the first place, seems to me remarkably good. Any one can detect its faults at a glance: it is prolix, often overloaded with pedantic quotation, now and then fantastic in its conceits. But these were faults of Mather's time. And he has two merits peculiarly his own: in the whole book I have not found a line that is not perfectly lucid, nor many paragraphs that, considering the frequent dulness of his subject, I could honestly call tiresome. In the second place, admitting once for all every charge of inaccurate detail, I am inclined to think the veracity of spirit that pervades the book of very high order. Somehow, as no one else can, Cotton Mather makes you by and by feel what the Puritan ideal was: if he does not tell just what men were, he does tell just what they wanted to be, and what loyal posterity longed to believe them. In the third place, not even the sustained monotony of his style and temper can prevent one who reads with care from recognizing the marked individuality of his separate portraits. It was my conviction of this that made me, in my account of his grandfathers, tell their story as nearly as might be in his own words. A glance back at what I have said about John Cotton and Richard Mather[11] will show as clearly as need be the strength and the weakness of the "Magnalia." I have known the book for eleven years; and the better I know it, the more I value it. Whatever else Cotton Mather may have been, the "Magnalia" alone, I think, proves him to have been a notable man of letters.

But to return to the diary for 1697. A few days after his ecstasy in the empty church, he notes, as a serious matter, a week's

---

[11] See pages 7-14. For an admirable example of Mather's best work, see his account of the last days of Theophilus Eaton, Magnalia, II. IX. §§ 9, 10.

journey to Salem and Ipswich. I believe he never went much
farther from home. On the 18th of September, he held a fast,
rewarded by assurances from Heaven, "in a manner which I may
not utter." This probably means that a visible angel appeared;
for the next day he writes:—

"The Spirit of the Lord came near unto mee; Doubtless, the angel
of the Lord made mee sensible of his Approaches. I was wondrously
Irradiated. My Lord Jesus Christ shall yett be more known in the
vast Regions of *America;* and by the means of poor, vile, sinful mee
he shall be so." And Great Britain shall undergo a reformation, and
France shall feel a mighty impression from the hand of Christ, and
Cotton Mather shall be concerned in these matters. "Nor was this all,
that was then told mee from Heaven; but I forbear the rest."

His next note shows a phase of him rarely seen in his diary.
He was reputed, they say, good company: here, for once, he
gives us a bit of his conversation. On the 24th of September,

Discoursing with a worthy minister who lay . . . sick, I said unto
him, to *praise Christ,* in the midst of Myriads of *Angels* in *Heaven,*
may in some respects bee as good as to *preach Christ,* in the midst of
Hundreds of *Mortals* on Earth. Hee replied, *It's true.* I added (for
our Discourse was managed with a certain serious and sacred Hilar-
itie), But, Syr, have you . . . thought what to say when you arrive
among the Blessed *Angels?* Hee replied: *Why, pray what do you
intend to say?* I answered, I 'l say, *Behold, o ye Holy Spirits, the most
. . . Loathsome Sinner that ever arrived among you; but it is the
Glorious Christ that hath brought me hither. . . . I have as good a
Righteousness as any of you.* I 'l say, *Oh! you Illustrious Angels, if you
don't wonderfully glorifie the Grace of the Lord Jesus Christ in fetching so vile a Sinner into these mansions, you 'l never do it.*

Just how vile the man really felt himself is hard to tell. One
thing is certain, however: the fate that six days later befell his
uncle, John Cotton, minister of Plymouth, affected him very
profoundly. Sewall tells the story[12]: A Council of ministers "advised the Church to dismiss [Mr. Cotton] with as much Charity
as the Rule would admit of. . . . This was for his Notorious
Breaches of the Seventh Commandmt." A few days later, Sewall
notes that Increase Mather "declar'd among the Ministers . . .
that they had dealt too favourably with Mr. Cotton." On the 9th

[12] Diary, I. 460. 30 Sept., 1697.

of October, and again on the 16th, Cotton Mather, full of agony for his "fallen uncle," and full of self-abhorrence and of fear lest his own sins should likewise be condemned, prostrated himself before the Lord, and enjoyed assurances from Heaven.

The next notable entry shows him in a character as yet new to us. His daughter Katharine was getting old enough to take life seriously: she was past her fifth birthday. On November 7th, a Lord's Day, he writes:—

I took my little daughter, *Katy*, into my Study, and there I told my child That I am to *Dy* Shortly and Shee must, when I am *Dead*, Remember every Thing, that I now said unto her. I sett before her, the sinful . . . condition of her Nature, and I charged her to *pray in secret places* every day, . . . That God for the sake of Jesus Christ, would give her a *New Heart*. . . . I gave her to understand that when I am taken from her, shee must look to meet with more Humbling *Afflictions*, than she does, now she has a . . . Tender *Father* to provide for her. . . . I signified unto her, That the people of God would much observe how shee carried herself, and that I had written a Book, about *Ungodly Children*, in the conclusion whereof I say, that this Book will bee a forcible Witness against my own children, if any of them should not bee *godly*. At Length, with many Tears, both on my part and hers, I told my child, that God had from Heaven satisfied me, . . . *That shee shall be brought Home unto the Lord Jesus Christ.* . . . I . . . made the child kneel down by me; and I poured out my cries unto the Lord, That Hee would . . . Bless her, and Save her, and make her a *Temple* of His Glory. It will bee so! It will bee so! I write this, the more particularly, that the child may hereafter have the Benefit of Reading it.

This curious note shows but one side of his domestic discipline, however. And perhaps here, as well as anywhere, I may mention his son Samuel's account of how Cotton Mather treated his children.[13] He would constantly tell them delightful stories, especially at table; "and he would ever conclude with some lessons of piety." He would constantly "put them upon doing . . . Kindnesses . . . for other Children," and "would applaud them when he saw them delight in it." As soon as possible, he made them learn to write and copy "profitable Things."

[13] S. Mather, Life, I. 4. 7.

He incessantly endeavoured, that his Children might betimes be acted by Principles of *Reason* and *Honour*. . . . The *first Chastisement* he would inflict for any ordinary Fault, was *to let the Child see and hear him in an Astonishment* . . . that the Child could do so *base* a Thing. . . . To be *chased for a while out of his Presence*, he would make to be look'd upon as the sorest Punishment in his Family. . . . The *Slavish* way of *Education*, carried on with *Raving, and Kicking, and Scourging*, . . . he looked upon as a dreadful Judgment of GOD on the World; . . . and express'd a mortal Aversion to it. . . . He would often tell them of the *good Angels*, who love them; . . . who likewise take a very diligent Notice of them, and ought not in any measure to be disobliged. He would not say so much to them of the *evil Angels*, because he would not have them entertain any frightful Fancies about the Apparitions of *Devils*: But yet, he would briefly let them know, that there are *Devils*, who tempt them to Wickedness, who are glad when they do wickedly, and who may get leave of GOD to kill them for it.

And there is every reason to think that all his children loved him dearly.

But in 1697, only Katy was old enough for much discipline. We must go back to the diary, in which there is little more to concern us. The rest of the notes refer chiefly to his devotions: he had fasts, and thanksgivings, and ecstasies. A case of adultery in his church caused him special humiliation. He preached on peace, and forthwith ships arrived with news of peace. A note of Sewall's on December 10th gives another glimpse of him:—

Mr. Cotton Mather was at the Townhouse Chamber pretty merry and pleasant: but was made sad by Col. Hutchinsons telling him of the death of his Unkle Mr. N. Mather. . . . Visited the President in the evening. He is sorrowful.

That very day Cotton Mather's Life of Phipps had come from England. In January he was laid up with an epidemic influenza. On his first Sunday out he enjoyed angelic help to such a degree that he was seized next day with a "cholic"; but angels interfered again, and by Thursday he was well enough to preach the lecture. The volume closes with two closely written pages of texts he preached from during the year.

In this year (1697) he published nine books: his Lives of

Mitchell, Phipps, and Moodey; three devotional works; another book about captivity among the Indians; a volume of sermons; and a volume of hymns.

The next year, 1698, was that in which the second application for Increase Mather's agency was refused; and at the close of which the General Court renewed its request that the President remove to Cambridge, and the church refused consent. It was the year, too, when the Brattle Street Church was founded.

The mottoes in the diary for 1698 [14] are the queerest of all.

"Ego Sic semper et ubique Vixi," runs the first, "tanquam ultimam Diem, numquam redituram, Consumerem.[15] EUMORP. C. M. Can't say so!" Then come three other Latin phrases, with the notes, "C. M. would say so!" Lett C. M. . . . take the Caution!" and "C. M. heartily subscribes to This!"

The first month of the year shows him extremely ecstatic. On the 4th of March, in a secret fast, he put his Church History and another book into the hands of Christ; and it was told him from Heaven

"that they shall bee carried safe to *England,* and there employed for the Service of my glorious Lord."—"The . . . Beginning of this month," he goes on, "brought with it little that was Remarkable, besides multiplied Experiences of Strange *Dejections* and sad *Buffetings* upon my mind, just when I have been going to do some *special service* for the Lord Jesus Christ in my public ministry, and then a more than *Assistance* and *Enlargement* in the service itself."

Later he notes that a gentleman has remarked that good men speak well of Cotton Mather, and bad men ill. On the 7th of April, a lecture day,

The Lord having Helped me beyond my expectation in preparing a Discourse for the Lecture,[16] Hee yett more gloriously *Helped* mee, in uttering of it, unto a vast Assembly of His people. I first Laid my Sinful mouth, in the Dust on my Study-floor before the Lord, where I cast myself, in my supplications for His Assistance and Acceptance, as utterly unworthy thereof. But the Lord made my sinful mouth to

[14] In possession of the Massachusetts Historical Society.
[15] "I have always and everywhere lived as if each day were my very last."
[16] This was the "Bostonian Ebenezer," reprinted as an appendix to the first book of the "Magnalia."

become this Day, the Trumpet of His glory; and the Hearts of the Inhabitants of the Town were strangely moved by what was Delivered among them.

Immediately afterwards he fell ill of a fever, from which he recovered in a duly thankful mood.

He eagerly renewed his prayers and fasts. On the 13th of May two of his special subjects were the College and the scandals in his church; on the 20th his particular subject was one of his flock, to be censured for adultery,—"and one whom I had formerly, with many Cries to Heaven, rescued from the Hands of Evil Angels, which had a Bodily possession of her." On this occasion he humbled himself as a very vile sinner; and when the time came for pronouncing the censure, he enjoyed an extraordinary presence of the Lord. On the 29th comes a long note, in which he recapitulates the astonishing verifications of some of his particular faiths about public affairs, and goes on to assert his faith that certain prophesies point to a speedy completion at the end of one hundred and eighty years, of the "Half Reformation" of 1517: "Make mee a very Holy, prayerful, watchful, and prudent man," he writes, "that I may bee fitt for my master's use." The next note, written on the 10th of June, is in Latin: he confesses to the Lord "peccatorum meorum aggravationem";[17] he prays that the blood of Christ may wash him clean, and he enjoys an assurance that he shall actually see angels once more. The close of the note is worth quoting:—

Latiné haec scribo, ne chara mea Conjux, has chartas aliquando inspiciens, intelligat.[18]

The next note is a very long one about Calef, a man "who makes little conscience of Lying," and who is attacking Mather for "public Asserting of such Truths as the Scripture has taught us about the existence and Influence of the *Invisible World*." This man's book was about to be sent to England for publication. Cotton Mather prays that the Lord

"Forgive him, and do him Good even as to my own Soul."—"But then," he goes on, "I could not but cry unto the Lord that Hee would

[17] "A heavy addition to my sins."
[18] "I write this in Latin, lest my dear wife, sometime looking over these papers, should understand it."

Rescue my *opportunities* of serving my Lord Jesus Christ from the Attempts of this man to damnify them. . . . So I putt over my Calumnious Adversary into the Hands of the *Righteous God*. . . . And I now Beleeve, That the *Holy Angels* of my Lord Jesus Christ, whose operation this Impious man denies (which is one great cause of his enmity against mee!) will do a *wonderful Thing* on this occasion."

Immediately afterwards, he remarks that pressure of work has caused him to give up the practice of taking notes as he listens to sermons: his attention is consequently flagging; he must take notes again.

A month of ecstatic afflations and reactions followed. Towards the end of July,

"my Mind Being . . . Easy, and Ready to Dy, I . . . besought of the Lord, nevertheless, that Hee would yett spare my life, to work for Him, a Little more, among His people." And one Lord's Day in August, he writes thus: "Whereas one of the Last Times I was at the *Lords-Table*, I made my particular Application unto the Lord Jesus Christ in the way of *Sacramental Communion*, to obtain from Him, the Cure of that One Distemper, *An Heart Wandering with Impertinent Thoughts in Religious Exercises*, I must now Record that I have seen an Extraordinary Success of my Faiths making those Applications. On the *Lords-day* particularly I know not that one sentence passed mee, in all the Five prayers made by Father, or One Head or Text of all the Long Sermon preached by him, in the Forenoon, but what my Heart accompanied with some Agreeable *Ejaculation*. And my own Services in the Afternoon were under the Special Operation of Heaven."

On the 5th of September, he went to Salem for five days. Two of his notes during this considerable journey are worth recording. The first is this:—

Finding, That whenever I go abroad, the *curiosity* and *vanity* of the people discovers itself in their *great Flocking* to hear me . . . causes me . . . exceedingly to *Humble* myself before the Lord, and cry from the *Dust* unto Him that the *fond expression* of the people, may not be chastised upon myself, in His Leaving of *mee* to any Inconvenience. By this Method, I not only am in a Comfortable Measure kept from the Foolish Taste of *popular Applause* in my own Heart, but also from the Humbling Dispensations from Heaven, whereto the Fondness of the people might otherwise Expose mee.

The other is this:—

One Day, while I was at Salem, I Retired into the Burying place, and att the Grave of my dear Younger Brother[19] there, I could not but fall down on my knees before the Lord; with praises to His Name, for granting the *Life* of my dead Brother to be writt, and spread, and Read among His people, and bee very serviceable; and for sparing me, a barren wretch, to survive these many years upon the Earth, to Serve His people, in Several parts of the World. I then considered, What if I were speedily to bee called away by *Death,* after my *younger Brother?* I found my Spirit, Gloriously Triumphing in the Thought of going by Death, to bee with the Lord Jesus Christ, and among his *Angels.* But when I further Thought of *Staying* to Glorify Him, in the midst of *many Temptations,* among his people here, I did, at present, because of my *Age,* prefer *This;* and Request it of the Lord.

Some three weeks later, he went to Reading. On the way,

riding over a Bridge, one of *the Rotten poles* upon it Broke: and my Horse broke thro' and broke in, and *sank down* his very *Breast.* I chose rather to keep the *Saddle,* than go off into the *River;* and the *Horse,* to the Astonishment of my Company *Rose* again (tearing off a *Shooe* in his Rising) and Leap'd over, with mee safe upon him. How happily do the *creatures* all serve us, while wee are serving their and our Lord, the Blessed Jesus.

In the middle of October came inspiring news from Medfield. A deaf old woman there had been greatly stirred by reading a book of Cotton Mather's, and had presently recovered her hearing; she remained piously afraid "that shee is not thankful enough unto the Lord Jesus Christ for so great a mercy." The same month Cotton Mather preached at the execution of a young woman for child-murder.[20]

In this October, too, Cotton Mather took his final leave of his fallen uncle, John Cotton. Some months before Sewall had seen the disgraced man at Plymouth.

"March 10," . . . he writes, "Had large discourse in the even with Mrs. Cotton, Mr. Cotton, Mr. Rowland.[21] I told Mr. Cotton, a free

[19] Nathaniel, ob. 1688. Cf. page 60.
[20] Sarah Threeneedles. Sewall's account of her is vivid: Diary, I. 486.
[21] Their son.

confession was the best way; spake of Davids roaring all the day long
and bones waxing old whilest he kept silence. . . . When ready to
come away, March 11. I said his danger was lest catching at shadows,
he should neglect the cords thrown out to him by Christ and so be
drown'd. Some of my last words to him was Kisse the Son, lest he be
angry! This was in the house between him and me alone. Just as was
mounting, He desired me to pray for him till I heard he was dead."

John Cotton was now called to take charge of a church in
South Carolina. He came to take leave of his nephew. They
prayed together with heartfelt pathos. And the broken man's
last words were a solemn denial of "the most and worst of the
charges against him."

The remaining months of the year passed amid Cotton Mather's
habitual ecstasies and activity. In November he preached at the
execution of some murderers, where the assembly was so vast
that he had to climb into the pulpit over the heads of the people.
In January, little Nancy[22] fell into the fire, without permanent
injury. But her father took the matter very seriously.

"The fire that hath wounded the child," he writes, "hath added a
strong fire to the zeal of my prayer for her; and God has now raised
my prayer for her to this degree of a particular Faith in her behalf.
If this Writing of her poor Father ever come to bee Readd by her,
Lett her give Thanks to God, that ever Hee cast her into a *Fire* which
thus enflamed the supplications of her Father for her." He resolved
that he would be more attentive to his family duties, and finally determined to "see whether there be nothing further that I may do, to
save the *Children* of my flock from falling into the unquenchable *Fire*
of the Wrath of God."

About this time, too, "a few Leisure minutes in the evening
of Every Day, in about a Fortnight or Three weeks Time, so accomplished me I could write very good Spanish." So he composed
a body of Protestant religion for the conversion of Spanish
America. Later in the year he fell ill again, and was much depressed with fear of premature old age. The record closes with
four pages of texts from which he has preached in his public
ministry during the year.

In 1698 he published six works: two discourses, and a preface

[22] His daughter Hannah, born early in 1697.

to a third; a history of the Non-Conformists; a devotional volume; and a pastoral letter to English Captives in Barbary.

The next year, 1699, was that in which news came that the College charter of 1697 was disapproved, and in which, under Bellomont's advice, the new charter was drawn that contained the religious proviso which made Bellomont disapprove it. It was the year, too, in which Coleman arrived and published his manifesto, and the Brattle Street Church was finally opened, and the Mathers prayed and preached there. We have already seen what Cotton Mather wrote in his diary about these public matters.[23]

His diary for 1699[24] shows his personal and pastoral experiences going on just as before. Two or three notes are perhaps worth remembering. He sent his Spanish book to a Jew who turned up in Boston; he translated some of the Psalms into French verse; he heard of bears on the Ipswich road; he was much disturbed by an impostor named May, who pretended to be a minister and made trouble, but ultimately ran away, having been detected in very unministerial overtures to the ewes of his flock;[25] and when in Cotton Mather's opinion the Church of England was conspiring against him, he sent the conspirators a message,

That tho' I am every way Little, yett I hope, thro' the Help of Christ, I may Live to do for them the same kindness that Sampson did for their philistine Brethren, and pull down their Temple about their Ears.

But what makes this year notable, besides its public history, is what happened in his family. His relations with his father were growing more and more intimate and tender; at every turn he sustained and comforted the worried old President; he shared and encouraged his particular faith that he should by and by do great works for Christ in England. The other family matters he tells of I shall mention in detail.

Towards the end of February, little Katy's head-dress caught fire, and the child was severely burned. As she lay in a fever, her father was assured that this

[23] See pages 102, 104-05.
[24] In possession of the American Antiquarian Society.
[25] The curious may find a pretty full account of May in the Magnalia, VII. VI. § 9.

Blessed Affliction . . . shall prove the salvation of my child. It shall
bee so! It shall bee so! Lord, How much ought I to *Love* Thee, when
Thou dost *Rebuke and Chasten me.*

The same day Mrs. Mather's mother died.

"I count it a Singular Favour of God unto mee," writes Cotton
Mather, "(and it might bee so unto *her!*) that tho' shee was Delirious
the First Night of her Illness, yett shee had the Free Use of *Reason*
all the Rest of the Little Time: and hereby I enjoyed an opportunity
for Two Dayes together, to *Talk* with her, and *pray* with her, and Do
all that it was possible for mee to Do, in assisting her, about the *Great
Acts* of Resigning her Spirit unto the Lord. She was a pious Woman,
and one full of *prayers* and *Alms;* and tho' shee were of a very *Fearful Temper,* and was particularly in her Life-Time under some
Slavish Fear of *Death,* yett as her Death approached, shee com-
fortably gott over it."

In June, little Nancy fell ill. Reading in the Book of Job, her
father broke off to pray that, like Job, he might retain three
daughters.

"I purposed," he writes, "that I would grow yett more Fruitful in
my Conversation with my Little Birds, and Feed them with more
frequent and charming Lessons of Religion." And he resolved to start
schools, to make more pastoral visits, to give away more copies of
his book about a "Family Well-Ordered," to write a book for the
Indians. "Lord, Pitty mee," he begs, "Assist mee, Accept mee!"

The child did not mend; but his Bible, opening by chance at
Mark 10. 13-16,[26] assured him that she should live. Then he
prayed for her again, and had fresh assurances, and she grew
better; and, as we have seen,[27] he took this for an omen of good
concerning his particular faith about the College.

This particular faith, we may remember, was accompanied by
an assurance that his son should glorify the Lord Jesus Christ
after he himself had followed his father into the kingdom of God.
At the moment he had no son; he had had none but the mal-
formed child whose fate he attributed to witchcraft.[28] But his
wife was again near her time, and on the 8th of July showed

[26] "Suffer the little children to come unto me," etc.
[27] See page 102.   [28] See page 85.

symptoms of travail; so he made a fast to obtain mercy for his family and his ministry.

"In the Evening of this Day," he goes on, "near eleven o'clock my Consort fell into her Travail. Just before this, the Text with a meditation whereon I chose to entertain my Family at our evening-prayers was that in Joh. 16. 21. A woman when shee is in Travail hath sorrow, because her Hour is Come; but as soon as shee is delivered of the Child, shee Remembreth no more the Anguish, for Joy that a Man is born into the World. After I had commended my Consort unto the Lord, I Laid mee down to sleep, after midnight, that I might be fit for the Services of the Day Ensuing. But after one a clock in the morning I awoke, with a concern upon my Spirit, which oblig'd mee to Rise, and Retire into my Study. There I cast myself on my knees before the Lord, confessing my Sins that rendered mee unworthy of His Mercy, but imploring His Mercy to my Consort, in the Distress now upon her. While my Faith was pleading that the Saviour who was Born of woman would send His good Angel to Releeve my Consort, the people ran to my Study-Door, with Tidings *That a Son was Born unto mee*. I continued then on my knees, praising the Lord; and I received a wonderful Advice from Heaven, That this my Son, shall bee a Servant of my Lord Jesus Christ throughout eternal Ages. Hee was Born about three Quarters of an Hour past One, in the morning of the (Lords-Day) 9d. 5m.[29]—an Hearty, and Lusty, and comely Infant. . . . In the Afternoon, I Baptised my Son, and in Honour to my Parent, I called him, INCREASE. After which, Retiring to my Study, it was again assured mee from Heaven, That this Child shall glorify my Lord Jesus Christ, and bee with Him, to Behold His Glory."

In October came sad news from Carolina. The plague had broken out in Charleston, and poor Uncle John Cotton had been stricken down at the beginning of his pastoral work there. In the diary is a brief note about him. But the letter which Cotton Mather wrote the same day to his uncle's faithful widow, who had been waiting at Plymouth for a chance to rejoin her husband, is more touching. I will quote a little from that, then.

In their confusion, they tell us not the precise Time of his Death; nor do they relate any Circumstances of it, only that hee lay sick Two Days, and hee Dy'd the Third, which is the period, wherein the sick of that pestilential Distemper use to dy. That circumstance will make

[29] July 9, 1699.

you think of *Lazarus,* and you'l join with mee in hopes That my
uncle was *one whom the Lord loved.* I need not say unto you, how
near the Death of so beloved a Friend goes to the Hearts of his Relatives, . . . and in a special manner to mine. I had not many Friends
on Earth like him. But in the midst of our sorrowes, . . . wee have a
peculiar satisfaction in the Lord's accepting my uncle to Dy with
Honour in the service of the Gospel and kingdom.—As it was no great
mercy (I beleeve) unto Plymouth, for their Laborious, and good-
spirited, and well-tempered Pastor to be driven from them, so it was a
great Mercy unto my uncle to bee employed in gathering a church
for the Lord Jesus Christ in a Countrey that had never seen such a
Thing, from the Beginning of the world.[30]

In this year, 1699, Cotton Mather published nine separate
works: a history of the Indian wars; a statement of the orthodox
faith of New England; the "Family Well-Ordered"; his Spanish
book, of which part was reprinted separately; an account of religious impostors; a book for sailors; and a book called the
"Serious Christian." He also edited a collection of Cases of Conscience, made at a meeting of ministers at Cambridge.

The next year, 1700, as we have seen, was very troublous. Increase Mather, disappointed of his agency, deceived in his particular faith, was finally forced to Cambridge; the Brattle Street
controversy broke out again, and waxed fierce; and Calef's book
arrived. What Cotton Mather wrote about these matters we have
read already.[31]

The other notes in the diary for 1700[32] show few new traits.
His children were ill: little Increase had a terrible time with
convulsions; Nibby's head-dress caught fire, as Katy's had the
year before; and Nancy had a serious disorder. In the course of
the year his ninth child, and third son, Samuel, was born.

A few of his notes, however, are worth remembering. In April,

A Gentleman came to mee with a Desire that I would write a Sheet
upon the horrid Evils of Debauching the Indians by Selling Drink unto
them: a crime committed by too many in the country; a crime fruitful
in wickedness and confusion.

[30] Mather Papers, 403. To Mrs. Joanna Cotton, 23 October, 1699.
[31] See pages 106-10.
[32] In possession of the Massachusetts Historical Society.

So he wrote the book: it would do good, he thought. A little later, on a lecture day, he writes of

"Torturing pains in my Head, which have diverse days molested mee; (such as I have so often found præludious unto my doing some special service for my Lord Jesus Christ, that I cannot but have particular Thoughts about the Original of them.)" In spite of them he prepared his lecture. "And now, When I came to my public Services, I felt a Wonderful Force from Heaven, Strengthening, and Assisting, and Enlarging of mee. . . . The Vast Assembly, which was come together, saw That the Lord was with mee of a Truth—Now, o my Soul, Feed, Feed upon these Experiences."

In June he held a special fast.

"I this day putt up my Church History," he writes, "and pen down directions about the publishing of it. It . . . has lain by me, diverse years, for want of a fit opportunity to send it. A Gentleman, just now sailing for England, undertakes the Care of it; . . . and by his Hand I send it for London. O my Lord Jesus Christ, lett thy good Angels accompany it."

In October, he had doubts whether his habit of giving away good books was not too expensive; and indeed his son Samuel says[33] that he sometimes gave away a thousand volumes a year. But he rebuked his doubts, and looking for a sign soon found one: calling, for "pure religion," on a widowed gentlewoman, he was offered as many books as he chose to take from the late President Chauncy's library; he took about forty, which raised his own library to something near three thousand volumes. It was a sore trial to him a little later, though, when Calef's book arrived, and his own Church History had not even gone to press. A number of pious friends joined him in more than one day of prayer about this.

Another note of this year has a charm of its own.

"There was an old man," it runs, "(called Ferdinando Turyl) scarce known to me. . . . On a Saturday night [28d. 7m.] I was very strongly accosted in my sleep, with a Dream, of this importance. That this old man was brought into my Sight and that it was (I know not how) said unto me, *Take Notice of this Old Man. . . . Speak to him.*

[33] Life, II. 1. 116.

Do for him. On the Day following, I saw the Old Man, at our public sermons, very attentive: (where I suppose he had rarely attended.) On the Day after this, I mett the Old Man in the Street, and I Lett fall some such words as these unto him: *How d' ye do, Old Man. I am glad to see you still in this World: I pray God, prepare you for another; I suppose it won't be long before you are called away: Can I do you no service?* And so I turned from him. On the Day after that the old man came to me at my House: and I then Instructed him, how to prepare for Death: and I gave him a Little Book (of Grace Triumphant) further to assist him in it: Adding a peece of money to Encourage him. Afterwards he came to me several times: but in about seven weeks, after our first Interview, he Dyed suddenly. Going to his Funeral, I was told (from some who did not understand how much I had been concerned for him) and afterwards . . . from people of the House where the old man Lived, That he had been a poor Carnal Sorry old man until near seven weeks, before he dyed: but in his Last Six or Seven Weeks, they had observed a Wonderful Change upon him: he spent his whole Time in praying and Reading, and the Little Book (of *Grace Triumphant*) was his continual companion Day and Night. They never saw a man so altered; and they are verily persuaded he dyed a *Regenerate Man.*—Truly I have several Times observed That God hath strangely stirred up my Heart sometimes to visit persons, that were Strangers to me, and employ my particular methods, to excite and assist their giving themselves to Him. . . . And they have presently after dyed with great symptoms of Regeneration upon them."

On the 18th of January, Cotton Mather mentioned to his wife and his father a matter that troubled him deeply. In spite of many prayers, he could not feel a faith that his baby Samuel would serve the Lord in his churches. So, though the child was "lusty and heavy," he feared it would die in infancy. On the 7th of February comes this note:—

The Evil that I feared is come upon me. On Tuesday night this week, my little son Samuel, was taken with very sad Convulsions. They continued all Wednesday incurable, and we were all that day in continual expectation of his expiration. But he lived all *Thursday,* too, and outlived more than a hundred very terrible Fitts. The Convulsions of my own mind, were all the while, happily composed and quieted; and with much Composure of Mind, I often and often in prayer Resigned the Child unto the Lord. Preaching the lecture, on *Thursday,* while we were every minute Looking for the Death of the Child, I chose to insist on that Joh. 19. 25., *I know, that my Redeemer Lives;* as a matter of satisfaction to us, at the Sight of our Dying Friends. On Thursday, about midnight, an odd thing fell out. The child, coming out of One of its worst Fitts most unaccountably fell a Laughing, and this held for diverse minutes; unto the amazement of the Spectators, who indeed were so amazed, that they could hardly keep from Swooning. After This, it had no more such Fitts as before; but Lingered along, till about ten a'clock this morning, when one of its fitts carried it off.

Cotton Mather preached as usual on Sunday, the 9th. On Monday, the child was buried. Its epitaph was, "Not as they that have no Hope."

The last note in the volume tells how friends have insisted on publishing a vindication of the Mathers from the attack of Calef, —a "laudable example of a people appearing to vindicate their injured pastors when a storm of persecution is raised against them." There are six pages, too, of an address to an assembly of ministers concerning an "offensive book about Churches"; and four pages of notes of texts preached from. On the back cover is a memorandum through which a pen has been very lightly drawn:—

Ab Amico Satis Adulatore[34]

ON COTTON MATHER.

For *Grace* and *Art* and an Illustrious *Fame*
Who would not look from such an Ominous Name?
Where *Two Great Names* their Sanctuary take,
And in a *Third* combined, a *Greater* make.

Too Gross flattery for me to transcribe; (tho' the poetry be good.)

In 1700, Cotton Mather published eighteen distinct works: five devotional books; three sermons; four monitory letters, including that about selling drink to Indians and one to Indians themselves in their own tongue; a pamphlet against balls and dances; an exposure of religious impostors; two books for young people and children; a Defence of Evangelical Churches; and another statement of the old Principles of New England.

[34] "By a sufficiently flattering friend."—This verse is a palpable imitation of Dryden's lines on Milton:

"Three poets in three distant ages born," etc.

The next year, 1701, was that in which Bellomont died, and Stoughton; in which Willard was made Vice President of the College, and in which, amid all the heat of the Brattle Street controversy and Calef's attack, Increase Mather was excluded from the presidency.

It is notable that Cotton Mather's diary contains very little about these terribly grave matters. In fact, as I have read his diaries, nothing has impressed me more than his resolute abstinence from evil speaking. He had a hot temper and a quick tongue. But he did his best not to leave behind him written records that should defame any man. It would be hard, I think, to find another diary so long and so free from scandal. To get a clear notion of how he really felt at this moment, then, we must turn to Sewall again.

In the last chapter, I cited two of Sewall's notes.[35] Here are a few more:—

Oct. 20. Mr. Cotton Mather . . . went and told Sam,[36] That one pleaded much for Negroes,[37] and he had used his father worse than a Negro, and told him that was his Father. I had read in the morn Mr. Dod's saying; Sanctified Afflictions are good Promotions. I found it now a cordial. And this caus'd me the rather to set under my Father and Mother's Epitaph,—Psal. 27. 10.[38] It may be it would be arrogance for me to think that I, as one of Christ's Witnesses, am slain, or ly dead in the street.—October 22. 1701. I . . . speak with Mr. Cotton Mather at Mr. Wilkins's. I expostulated with him from I Tim. 5. 1. Rebuke not an elder. He said he had considered that: I told him of his book of the Law of Kindness for the Tongue, whether this were correspondent with that. Whether correspondent with Christ's Rule: He said, having spoken to me before there was no need to speak to me again; and so justified his reviling me behind my back. Charg'd the Council with Lying, Hypocrisy, Tricks, and I know not what all. I ask'd him if it were done with that Meekness as it should: answer'd, yes. Charg'd the Council in general, and then shew'd my share, which was my speech in Council: viz. If Mr. Mather should goe to Cambridge again to reside there with a Resolution not to read the Scriptures, and expound in the Hall: I fear the example of it will do more

---

[35] See page 111.   [36] Sewall's son.
[37] Sewall had published a tract against slavery.
[38] "When my father and my mother forsake me, then the Lord will take me up."

hurt than his going thither will doe good. This speech I owned. Said
Mr. Corwin at Reading, upbraided him, saying, This is the man you
dedicat your books to! I ask'd him if I should suppose he had done
something amiss in his Church as an Officer; whether it would be well
for me to exclaim against him in the street for it. (Mr. Wilkin would
fain have had him gon into the iñer room, but he would not.) I told
him I conceiv'd he had done much unbecoming a Minister of the
Gospel, and being call'd . . . to the Council, . . . I went thither.
. . . 2 Tim. 2. 24. 25.[39]—Sign'd Mr. Mather's order for £25.
Hañer'd out an Order for a Day of Thanksgiving.—Oct. 23. Mr.
Increase Mather said at Mr. Wilkins's, If I am a Servant of Jesus Christ,
some great Judgment will fall on Capt. Sewall, or his family.—Oct.
24. Rainy day. . . . I got Mr. Moody to copy out my Speech, and
gave it to Mr. Wilkins that all might see what was the ground of
Mr. Mather's Anger. . . . Mr. Wilkins carried [it] to Mr. Mathers;
They seem to grow calm.

On the 30th of November, Sewall writes:—

I spent this Sabbath at Mr. Coleman's [church], partly out of dis-
like to Mr. Josiah Willard's cutting off his Hair, and wearing a Wigg:
. . . Partly to give an example of my holding Comunion with that
Church who renounce the Cross in Baptisme, Humane Holy days etc.
as other New-english Churches doe. And I had spent a Sabbath at the
Old Church, and at Mr. Mathers.[40]

In Sewall's Letter-Book we find how the quarrel ended. On
December 31, 1701, he wrote to Cotton Mather thus:—

Sir,—I once intended an Answer to yours of the 30th of Octobr.
last, principally as to some matters of fact therein recited. But since
you were pleased to sit with me last Tuesday was fortnight, and to
honour my Pue, with publishing there the very acceptable News of
Liberty again granted to our dear Brethren of the Palatinat, I do now
Remise, Release and forever quit claim, as to any personal Contro-

---

[39] "And the servant of the Lord must not strive; but be gentle unto all men,
apt to teach, patient; in meekness instructing those that oppose themselves;
if God peradventure will give them repentance to the acknowledging of the
truth."

[40] The Old Church was the First; Mr. Mather's, the Second; Mr. Willard's,
the Old South, the Third; Mr. Colman's, the Brattle Street, the Fourth.
There were as yet no other Congregational churches in Boston; and Sewall
was doing his best to make the brethren dwell together in unity.—And concerning Willard's wig, cf. pages 26, 59.

versy we were lately managing at Mr. Wilkins's. It has been my thought ever since, and the consideration of this being the last day of the year, suffers me to delay it no longer. And at the same time I assure you that I am your truly loving friend and humble Servant S. S.

In Sewall's Letter-Book for this year is one other document worth remembering. On October 6th, he and Isaac Addington wrote a long letter of advice to the gentlemen who were about to start a new college in Connecticut. They enclosed hints for an act of incorporation; and went on,

> We should be very glad to hear of flourishing Schools and College at Conecticut, and it would be some relief to us against the Sorrow we have conceived for the decay of them in this Province.

Sewall and the Mathers agreed in feeling that Harvard was lost to orthodoxy; and no three men hailed with more prayerful enthusiasm the rising star of Yale.

Cotton Mather's diary for 1701[41] shows the general condition of his activity, his enthusiasm, and his affections unchanged. In the beginning of the year, he was much excited by Calef's book.

"One Vile Tool," he writes on the 5th of April, "namely R. Calef,[42] . . . employed by [the Enemies of the Churches] to go on with his Filthy Scribbles to hurt my precious opportunities of glorifying my Lord Jesus Christ,"—disposes him to special fast and prayer. And on the 11th, "because I would *bespeak the Lord thrice*," he summoned six friends, for the third time, to pray with him that "the Lord would send his Angel to stop the Adversary in the Course of his Wickedness [Which the Lord will do!]"

The other matter which seems most on his mind is his Church History, concerning which his prayers and assurances were frequent throughout the year. On the 13th of June came a letter from Mr. Broomfield, in London: Mr. Robert Hackshaw had agreed to print the book at his own expense.

"I told him," wrote Mr. Broomfield, "*Syr, God has answered* Mr. Mather's *prayers.*—He declared he did it not with any expectation of Gain to himself, but for the Glory of God, and that he might be a

[41] In possession of the Massachusetts Historical Society.
[42] This opprobrious mention of a name, a very rare thing in Cotton Mather's diary, indicates his overwrought condition. Cf. pages 77, 109.

means to midwife so good a work into the World. And did you know him so well as I do you would believe him."

But in September came news of some complications about the printing: on the 27th, Cotton Mather held a special fast for the History, being also moved to supplications by the fact that his father-in-law, after the orthodox manner of New England, was already "upon a second marriage." Among his other memoranda for the year, the most notable seems to be that he had started thirteen or fourteen "private meetings." He believed in organizing the work of the Lord: throughout his life he was getting together prayer-meetings, and societies for the suppression of disorders; working with the commissioners to convert and civilize the Indians; and so on.

I find but four notes in 1701 which are worth remembering in detail. In September came news that a friend had been killed in the wars. Cotton Mather immediately went to pray with the widow; and found with her another widow, her sister.

"Now in my prayer," he goes on, "I found myself strangely diverted from the Condition of the person to whom only I intended my Visit. I was as it were compelled so to word my prayer as take in all along the condition of her Sister; even as if my prayer had been cheefly, if not only, for her. I wondered a little at my frame in this matter. But the Spirit of the Lord knew what I did not know. Within Two Days there arrived Intelligence that the young man, the husband of the supposed widow to whom I gave my visit, was yett living."

On the 3d of October, he held a thanksgiving for his health, for the defeats of the "subtil and raging malice" of his enemies, for the safety and prospects of his Church History, and for his opportunities to do good by preaching and printing.

"But there was another signal article," he goes on, "cf my praises to the Lord on this day. And this was the Confluence of Blessings, which I enjoy in my dearest Consort, who bore me company in some of the duties of the day. Her piety, the agreeable charms of her person, her obliging Deportment unto me, her discretion in ordering my and her Affairs and avoiding everything that might be dishonourable to either of us, and the lovely offspring that I have received by her, and her being spared unto me for more than fifteen years: These are things that I should thankfully acknowledge before the Lord."

At the end of the year come two notes without date. The first concerns the Church History, which he had prayed for time and again.

"All that I have to add," he writes, "is That when I am committing my Church History (which great work runs great hazard of miscarrying) into the hands of the Lord Jesus Christ, I receive wonderful Assurances (I think, I know) from Heaven That the Lord will accept it, and preserve it, and publish it, and that it shall not be lost. An Heavenly Afflatus causes me sometimes to fall into Tears of Joy, assured that the Lord has heard my supplications about the matter. And now, its having been thus long delayed, and obstructed and Clogg'd, proves but an opportunity for that prayer and Faith, which if I had gone without, the publication of that book would not have proved near so sweet a mercy to me. But if it should miscarry after all, O my God, what confusion would ensue upon me!"

The second of the undated entries is a copy of part of a printed letter, expounding from personal experience a passage of Baxter, to the effect that whoever has a special virtue will probably be defamed for the contrary vice.

"It has in some former years commonly happened unto me," he writes, "That when I visited, in the way of my *pastoral Duty*, persons possessed with Evil Spirits, the persons, tho' they knew every one else in the room, yett, thro' the unaccountable operation of the *Evil Spirits* upon their Eyes, I must appear so Dirty, so ugly, so *Disguised* unto them, that they could have no knowledge of me. I have a thousand times thought, That the Lord ordered This for some Intimation unto me, That when *Times of Temptation* come, wherein *Evil Spirits* have so much operation on the *Minds* of my people, as they have on the eyes of Energumens, a Minister of the Lord Jesus Christ that will be faithful unto his Interests, must Look to be all over *Disguised* by Misrepresentation unto the *Minds* of them that are under the power of *Temptation*."

On the cover of the volume are these lines:—

A Good Note in a Little Book entituled A Spiritual Legacy. Pray for those you Love, And assure yourselves you shall never have comfort of his Friendship for whom you pray not.

It is a very curious fact, that the diary for this most troublous of years shows, on the whole, more spiritual calm than any of the preceding. Mather seems to have realized this himself. On the 6th of December, he was afraid lest he "fall into Security."

In 1701 he published nine works: four volumes of sermons; a poem addressed to an old gentlewoman afflicted with blindness; a preface to his friends' answer to Calef; a book on the Greek Churches; a book on the Wonders of Christianity; and a book concerning which he writes as follows:—

> Many (it may be, more than seven) years ago, a Bookseller going from hence to *London*, carried certain Manuscripts of mine with him, declaring his Intentions to publish them. He carelessly left them in the Hands of . . . a Bookseller there; who sometime after dyed; and I could never hear what became of my Manuscripts. . . . A friend of mine going the last Summer for *London*, did . . . Enquire after my Manuscripts; and strangely recovering of them, he carried them to another Bookseller, who published them. . . . The Book, which has had such a *Resurrection* from the *Dead*, has this Title, DEATH MADE EASY AND HAPPY.[43]

The year 1702 brought to Boston Joseph Dudley, the new Governor. As we have seen, it is believed that a letter of Cotton Mather's urging his popularity in Massachusetts—a popularity which there is reason to fear that Mather either invented or imagined—had much to do with his appointment.[44] Son of the old Puritan Governor, Thomas Dudley, Joseph Dudley had from the first appearance of Randolph in Massachusetts been a pronounced Royalist. He had been President of the provisional government which held power until Andros arrived. Under Andros he had held high office; and with him he had been overthrown and sent to England for trial by the Revolution of 1689. Since that time he had been virtually an exile, but had enjoyed several honors. As Chief Justice of New York he had hanged Leisler, the leader there of such a revolution as had driven Dudley from Massachusetts. As Lieutenant Governor of the Isle of Wight, and later as a member of Parliament, he had been high in royal favour. And now, as the official representative of Queen Anne, —for William of Orange died in March, 1702,—he returned triumphantly to Massachusetts. This final triumph he perhaps owed to the influence of the Mathers, whose crushing defeats

[43] Sibley, Harvard Graduates, III. 6. [44] See page 95.

were probably not appreciated in England. They believed that he would be grateful, that with his help something might still be done to preserve the system of the fathers. On June 11th, the day he arrived, there was a grand official banquet at the Town-house, and "Mr. Mather crav'd a blessing and Mr. Cotton Mather Returned Thanks." [45]

But Cotton Mather's diary for 1702[46] tells little of all this; and much of matters that came nearer to him. "Prophesia quae dicit aliquid tale futurum impletur per aliquid tale," [47] is its motto. His first entry is this:—

Thursday. On a Thursday just Thirty-Nine years ago, I first appeared in the World. I cannot express either my Amazements at the Goodness and Mercy of God, in sparing me thus far beyond my expectation to enter upon the Fortieth year of My Age: (methinks, *Forty* sounds Old and Big!) or my Distresses in Reflecting upon my Sinful and foolish misspend of my Irrevocable Time. (Alas how little, how nothing have I done in all this Time!) I considered these things a little this Day, in my Supplications before the Lord. But more on the Day following, which was with me a Day of prayer, (albeit I did three Dayes ago keep a Day of Thanksgiving in my Study.)

He notes then how he had started a society for the Suppression of Disorders, and another for the Propagation of the Christian Religion. On the 14th of March he held his first recorded vigil: all the rest of his life he held these night-watches of prayer and fasting, as well as those he kept by day. And the same month he began the practice of reading Scotch commentators to his family at evening prayers. The first he took up was Hutchinson on Job.

"And many times after I had begun," he writes, "I had this Darted into my mind; That I might expect some Trials (perhaps of Long Sick-ness) to come shortly upon my Family; and that the Lessons fetch'd from the Study of Job were to prepare me for those Trials."

The rest of his notes until the 25th of May record only such ecstasies, vigils, activities, as by this time we know well. On that day his consort miscarried, at four or five months. He thought it his duty to humble himself before the Lord; but the dispensation remained mysterious, for

[45] Sewall's Diary, II. 59.

[46] In the possession of the Massachusetts Historical Society.

[47] "A prophecy that some such thing shall be is fulfilled by some such thing."

when I more particularly examined, whether I had ever troubled the Churches of the Lord with any *False Conception,* I could not find myself conscious to any such matter.

For seven months there are few notes in the diary which concern anything but his domestic affairs. What few there are indicate that all the while his busy work went on unchecked. And besides the "Magnalia," which was published this year, he gave no less than eleven books to the press in the course of 1702. But what concerns us now is what went on at his home.

His wife grew worse. On the 3d of June, holding a special fast for her, he had a "sad experiment. . . . I can't Beleeve what I will or when I will." A dulness was on his spirit; impure thoughts assailed him; he feared she was about to die. His distress increased for three days. Then, on the 6th,

in the Forenoon, while I was at prayer with my Dying Wife, in her Chamber, . . . I began to feel the blessed breezes of a *particular Faith,* blowing from Heaven upon my mind. . . . In the Afternoon, when I was alone in my Study, crying unto the Lord, . . . my *particular Faith* was again Renewed, and with a Flood of Tears, I thought I received an assurance from Heaven, That she should Recover. Whereupon I begg'd of the Lord, That He would by His Good Spirit incline me to be exemplarily wise, and chast, and Holy, in my whole Conversation, when I should again *obtain such favour of the Lord,* as to have my *Good Thing* with me, in former Circumstances.

Next day, for all this, she grew worse; her physician was called out of church to attend her; and Mather "was called up, in the middle of the following Night, because they thought her Dying." At one or two in the morning he retired to his study, where the Lord renewed "assurances of His purpose to Recover her." She lingered on. In a special fast for her on the 4th of July, he prayed too for the town, where small-pox had broken out; for the land, where war had been proclaimed;[48] and for "other said circumstances we have in our government."[49] On the 12th, he held his seventh fast for her:—

On which Day I also made Seven several Addresses for her, wherein I resigned her unto the Lord, and submitted unto all the sorrowful Consequences of a Rejected prayer, and a Defeated Faith, and a

[48] "Malbrook s'en va-t-en guerre," etc.   [49] See Chapter X.

desolate broken Family, if He should order them for me. But while I thus *gave up* my dear consort, still I could not *give her over*.

And his particular faith was renewed. On the 21st, as she was still terribly ill,

> I chose . . . to Spread my Distress before the Lord, in the way of a Vigil. I Retired into my Bed-Chamber, and spent good part of the Night, prostrate on the Floor (with so Little of Garment on, as to render my lying there painful to my Tender Bones) crying to God for the Life of my poor Consort. . . . I think, before I went unto my Rest, I obtained some further satisfaction that my God has heard me.

On the 1st of August, she was a little better:—

> And yett, after This, . . . her Feebleness grows again to that extremity, as to render her condition, as dubious perhaps as ever. I am kept up all Night that I may see her Dy, and therewith see the Terrible Death of my prayer and Faith. But in this Extremity, when I renew my Visits unto Heaven, . . . a strange Irradiation comes from Heaven upon my Spirit that her Life shall not as yett come unto an End.— My Heavenly Father will still have me attended with some special Exercise, that shall keep my prayer and Faith employed. And that which His Fatherly Wisdome has ordered for me, in these later weeks, has been the singular Calamity of my poor Consort: and an Illness which none of the ablest physicians know, what to Judge of, or what to do for.

On the 29th, reflecting that his consort had been "strangely upheld, and tho' *chasten'd sore, yett not given over to Death,* for twice seven weeks together," he determined to hold a thanksgiving: it might be, he thought, that "a *Day of praise,* would be followed with salvations, beyond what any *Dayes of prayer* had yett obtained." But though she mended a little hereupon, it was only a little.

So in September he writes:

> I suspect, I have been too unattentive unto the meaning of the Holy Spirit, and His Angel, in the *particular Faith,* which I have had about my Consort's being Restored unto me. . . . When she has been Several Times on or near the Last Agonies of Death, . . . I cry to the Lord, that He will yett spare her. He tells me, That He will do it. Accordingly, to our Astonishment, . . . she stayes yett longer with us. . . . But it may be, after the Lord has given me admirable Demonstra-

tions, of His being Lothe to Deny me anything that I importunately ask of him, and therefore does one Month after another Delay the Thing which I fear; yett I must at Last Encounter the Death which I have so deprecated, when both my wife and myself shall be better prepared for it.

On the 22d of October, matters still unchanged, he held a vigil, at the close of which he writes:—

I took my *psalm-book* into my hand that I might sing something for the Quickening of my uneasy Mind. And unto my Surprize, the very first Verse, that at the opening of the Book, my Eye was carried unto was that: Psal. 105. 37.

> *And there was not among the Tribes*
> *A Feeble person told.*

Lord, I thought!—This won't be fulfilled until the *Resurrection of the Dead*. The *Tribes* of the *Raised* will not have one *Feeble person* among them. And must I resign the condition of my Consort at last unto what shall be done in the future state? Lord, *Thy Will be Done*.

The next night his wife had a vision. A grave person appeared to her,—"she supposes, in her sleep,"—leading a woman in such "meagre and wretched circumstances" that Mrs. Mather was presently stirred to praise God that "her condition was not yett so miserably circumstanced." The grave person proceeded to suggest remedies that had not occurred to the doctors; the doctors approved the suggestions; and Mrs. Mather grew better,

Insomuch that she came twice on Saturday out of her Sick Chamber, unto me in my Study; and there she asked me to give Thanks unto God with her, and for her, on the Account of the Recovery in so surprising a Degree begun unto her.—After this, my dear Consort continued much Refreshed, and yett Feeble. We had Great Hopes of her becoming a Strong person again; and yett great Fears, Lest some further Latent mischief within her, prove after all too hard for her.

On the 30th of October comes this note:—

Yesterday, I first saw my CHURCH HISTORY, since the publication of it. A Gentleman arrived here from *Newcastle,* in *England,* that had bought it there. Wherefore, I sett apart this Day, for solemn THANKS-GIVING unto God, for His Watchful and gracious providence over that Work and for the Harvest of so many prayers, and cares, and Tears, and Resignations, as I had employ'd upon it. My Religious Friend, Mr. *Broomfield*, who had been singularly helpful to me in the publication of that great Book (of Twenty shillings price, at *London*) came to me, at the Close of the Day, to join with me, in some of my praises to God.—On this Day my little daughter Nibby began to fall sick of the small-pox. The dreadful Disease, which is raging in the Neighbourhood, is now gott into my Family. God prepare me, God prepare me, for what is coming upon me. The child is favourably visited, in comparison of what many are.

The pestilence increased through November. So did the fervency of Cotton Mather's prayers. Late in the month, he writes:—

Humiliations are coming thick upon me! My Study, is tho' a Large, yett a Warm Chamber, (the hangings whereof, are Boxes with between two and three thousand Books in them,) and we are so circumstanced, that my House, tho' none of the smallest, cannot afford a safe Hospital now for my Sick Folks, anywhere so well as there. So I Resigned my Study, for an Hospital to my little Folks, that are falling sick of a Loathsome Disease.

The first patient there was his "godly maid"; Nancy came down on the 24th; little Increase on the 29th.

The Little Creatures," he writes, "keep calling for me so often to pray with them that I can scarce do it less than ten or a dozen times in a day; besides what I do with my Neighbours.

Two days later,

At last, the Black Day arrives. . . . I had never yett seen such a Black Day, in all the Time of my Pilgrimage. The *Desire of my Eyes* is this Day to be taken from me. . . . All the Forenoon, . . . she lies in the pangs of Death; sensible until the last minute or two before her final expiration. I Cannot Remember the Discourses that passed between us. Only, her Devout Soul was full of Satisfaction, about her going to a State of Blessedness, with the Lord Jesus Christ, and as far as my Distress would permitt me, I studied how to confirm her satisfaction and consolation. This I Remember, That a little while before she died, I asked her to tell me Faithfully, what Fault she had seen in my Conversation, that she would advise me to rectify. She replied, (which I wondred at,) That she knew of none, but that God had made what she had observed in my Conversation, exceedingly serviceable unto her, to bring her much nearer to Himself. When I saw to what a point of Resignation I was now called of the Lord, I Resolved, with His Help therein to glorify Him. So, Two Hours before my Lovely Consort Expired, I kneeled by her Bed-Side, and I took into my two Hands, a dear Hand, the dearest in the World. With her thus in my Hands, I solemnly and sincerely gave her up unto the Lord: and in token of my Real RESIGNATION, I gently putt her out of my Hands, and Laid away a most Lovely Hand, Resolving That I would never touch it any more. This was the Hardest, and perhaps, the bravest Action, that ever I did. She afterwards told me, *That she sign'd and seal'd my Act of Resignation.* And tho' before that, she call'd for me, continually, she after this never asked for me any more. She continued until near two a clock in the Afternoon, And the last Sensible Word that she Spoke, was to her weeping Father, *Heaven, Heaven, will make amends for all.* When she was expired, I immediately prayed with her Father, and the other weeping people in the chamber, for the grace to carry it well under the present Calamity, and I did Consummate my Resignation, in terms as full of glory to the wisdome and Goodness and Alsufficiency of the Lord, as I could utter. She Lived with me just as many years, as she had Lived in the World, before she came to me, with an Addition of the seven months, wherein her Dying Languishments were preparing me to part with her.

x. Cotton Mather's Private Life.
—His Second Marriage.
—Charter of Harvard College.
—Quarrel with Joseph Dudley.

1702-1707 Before proceeding with Cotton Mather's private life, we may best glance at the history of Massachusetts and of Harvard College for the next five years; and first, perhaps, glance back at Cotton Mather's account of his first interview with Governor Dudley.

On the last page of his diary for 1702 is this memorandum:—

June 16. I received a Visit from Governour *Dudley*. Among other things . . . I said to him, . . . "Syr, you arrive to the Government of a people, that have their various and their Divided Apprehensions, . . . particularly about your own Government over them. I am humbly of opinion, That it will be your Wisdom to carry an Indifferent Hand towards all parties. . . . I would approve it . . . if any one should say to Your Excellency: *By no means lett any people have cause to say, That you take all your measures from the Two Mr. Mathers.* By the same Rule, I may say without offence: *By no means lett any people say, That you go by no measures in your conduct but Mr. Byfield's and Mr. Leverett's.* This I speak not from any personal prejudice against the Gentlemen, but from a due consideration of the Disposition of the people; and as a service to your Excellency." The Wretch went unto those men, and told them, that I had advised him to be no ways advised by them: and inflamed them into an implacable Rage against me.

For some years Mather maintained friendly relations with the "wretch" in question; but they were straining more and more. The verdict of posterity is that from beginning to end Joseph Dudley was a self-seeker. Such verdicts, of course, are to be taken with caution; and in estimating this one it is but fair to remember that Dudley was the first of the native Tories, and that

New England tradition has never done the native Loyalists justice. At the same time, I have found little to show that in this
particular case posterity has erred. At home and abroad Dudley's
whole training had been that of a gentleman,—an aristocrat. In
his eleven years of exile he had been in constant contact with
intriguing, self-seeking courtiers. How foreign his temper was
to that of the compatriots he came to govern appears most vividly
in a misadventure which befell him in December, 1705.[1]

"Dec. 7," writes Sewall, "Went to Brooklin. . . . After Diñer met
with the Govr. upon the Plain; . . . told me of what haꝑened on the
road, being in a great passion: threaten'd to send those that affronted
him to England."

What had happened on the road was this. Driving in his
travelling chariot, Governor Dudley found his way stopped by
two carts loaded with wood. He ordered the carters to move
aside. They declined, one of them saying, "I am as good flesh and
blood as you; . . . you may goe out of the way." The Governor
drew his sword on the man, who snatched it and broke it, declaring that he acted in defence of his life. "You lie, you dog; you
lie, you devill!" cried Dudley.—"Such words don't become a
Christian," said the carter.—"A Christian, you dog!" cried Dudley.
"A Christian, you devill! I was a Christian before you were born."
And snatching the carter's whip he lashed him. Then he had both
carters arrested, and apparently tried to make their conduct
appear treasonable. The case hung on until the following November, when the Superior Court discharged the prisoners. This was
the Governor that the Mathers had fondly hoped to manage.

The temper Dudley thus showed in private appears, more
decorously, in his public conduct. Palfrey[2] tells in detail the
story of his relations with the legislature, and of the wars which
harassed the frontiers. It was during these wars that Deerfield
was sacked, Cotton Mather's cousin Mrs. Williams killed, and her
husband and family carried off by French and Indians. And
before 1707, the people of Massachusetts had generally come to

---

[1] See Sewall's Diary, II. 144, seq., and note. Meantime Sewall's son had
married Dudley's daughter.
[2] Book IV. Chapters VIII.-X.

believe that Dudley's administration was corrupt; and that he was personally interested in illicit trade with the enemy.

Harvard College meanwhile proceeded under the provisional government of Vice-President Willard. From the time of President Mather's dismissal Cotton Mather never attended a meeting of the Corporation. On the 10th of August, 1703, he was reckoned to have abdicated; and Mr. Brattle elected in his place.[3] As a minister of Boston, he remained an Overseer; but apparently attended only one other meeting of the board. Willard and Dudley had married sisters,—a fact which might well have had influence on such a temper as the Governor's. Whatever the reason, no steps were taken for a new charter during Willard's administration beyond two mentions of the subject in the Governor's messages: one in 1703, the other in 1705.[4]

So we come back to Cotton Mather's diary. It was on Tuesday, December 1, 1702, that his wife died. On Saturday she had been buried; and we find him holding a day of prayer and fasting,

That I may obtain the pardon of all the sins for which the Lord is now chastening me; and Grace and Help from Heaven to glorify the Lord with a wise Behaviour, under the Temptations of the Condition which is now come upon me.

Next day he preached on the death of the prophet Ezekiel's wife; and he notes that in many ways the people showed their love to him,—among other tokens of affection subscribing to build Mrs. Mather a costly tomb. A little later, the pestilence began to abate; the children grew better, and escaped scarlet-fever, which was also abroad. Cotton Mather himself remained well. His godly maid recovered, too; but so "distracted" that she had to go.

His next note is very long and curious. The seven months' strain has brought reaction. With a good deal of deliberation, he proceeds to consider the "Dispensations of Heaven, that have been Rolling over" him.

"Has not the Death of my Consort," he asks, "that most astonishing Sting in it: A miscarriage of a particular Faith? Truly, Nothing has ever yet befallen me, that has come so near it. But"—he finds reassuring thoughts. In the first place, it was compassionate in God to remove

[3] Quincy, I. 151.   [4] Quincy, Vol. I. Chapter VIII.

her: she could never have grown strong enough to perform her con-
jugal and maternal duties. "More than all this. She was a Gentlewoman
of a Melancholy Temperament; and there were come dreadful changes
in her Father's Family. He had extremely broken her Spirit by bringing home a mother-in-law. . . . Her youngest Brother, and a considerable Interest of mine with him, (some hundreds of pounds perhaps) was newly fallen into the Hands of the French Enemy. Her
Second Brother, who was her Darling, . . . was dead in *London*.
. . . Her Eldest Brother proves an Idle, profane, Drunken, and sottish
Fellow, and a Disgrace to all his Relatives. . . . The sight of these
Things, would without a miracle, have brought such a Disorder of
Mind upon her, as would have rendered my Condition Insupportable.
And now, who can tell, what way may be made for Blessings unto
me, and mine, by her Translation to the Heavenly World?" In the
second place, she herself had prayed that she might never live to hear
of the death of her favorite brother; and this prayer was granted. In
the third place, within a fortnight after her death he had preached on
John 4. 47,[5] from which he had expounded the doctrine that "Tho'
Faith be no Folly, yett Faith may be mixed with Folly; and particularly
with the Folly of Limiting the Wisdome of God, unto our own way
of *answering it*." And a gentlewoman, who heard the sermon, had been
so moved as to address him thereupon in verses, ending—

> Your whole Discourse is Swol'n with its own praise,
> But this fair Article, does wear the Baies.

"It may be," he writes at last, "The Lord will ere long Enable me,
to penetrate further into the Nature, meaning, and mystery of a *particular Faith*. However, I have mett with enough to awaken in me a
more exquisite Caution, than ever I had in my Life, concerning it."

In January, Nancy was very ill: but when her life was despaired of, his prayers recovered her. The only other note I have
recorded for this month runs thus:—

Before the late Weeks of my Life, I had rarely known Tears, except
those that were for the Joy of the Salvation of God. But now, scarce
a day passes me without a Flood of Tears, and my Eyes even Decay
with weeping. One Day, considering how frequently and foolishly
widowers miscarry, and by their miscarriages dishonour God, I earnestly with Tears besought the Lord, *That he would please to favour*

[5] "When he heard that Jesus was come out of Judea into Galilee, he went
unto him, and besought him that he would come down, and heal his son:
for he was at the point of death."

me, so far as to kill me rather than to leave me unto anything that
might bring any Remarkable Dishonour unto His Holy Name. (Within
a few Minutes, I found myself grow very Ill. . . . I suspected that
the Lord was going to take me at my word. But anon, I perceived that
it was nothing but *Vapours*.)

The next month began a new trial. He received a visit from
a very attractive young gentlewoman, who declared that she had
long admired his public character, and now felt herself at liberty
to confess herself equally pleased with his person. The state of
perplexity into which this address threw him lasted for two
months.

His diary for 1703[6] begins with a birthday fast on this occasion.
His note of it is typical of all on the subject.

"Nature itself," he writes, "causes in me a mighty Tenderness for a
person so very amiable. Breeding requires me to treat her with Honour
and Respect, and very much of Deference to all that she shall at any
time ask of me. But Religion, above all, obliges me instead of a rash
Rejecting her Conversation, to Contrive rather how I may Imitate the
Goodness of the Lord Jesus Christ in his dealing with such as are
upon a Conversion unto him.—On the other side I cannot but fear a
fearful Snare, and that I may soon fall into some error in my Conversation, if the point proposed unto me be found after all unattainable thro'
the violent Storm of Opposition which I cannot but foresee . . . will
be made unto it."

So on the 18th of February he begged her to desist; and, finding her inflexible, devoted himself to the task of converting her.
And on the 20th he held a vigil, partly for himself, whom he
feared "rejected and abhorred of God,"—relatives and friends
being displeased with gossip about the gentlewoman,—but partly
for his church.

"It was a consolation unto me," he writes, "to think That when my
people were all asleep in their Beds their poor pastor should be watch-
ing and praying and weeping for them."

On the 27th, he held another fast, in which he gave up to the
Lord "the Ingenious Child that sollicits my Respects unto her."
On the 6th of March he was in great trouble; the gentlewoman's
reputation turned out to be somewhat damaged; to marry her

[6] In possession of the American Antiquarian Society.

would seriously interfere with his ministry; and her attentions were beginning to cause much tattle.

On the 12th, his state of mind was confused: the Assembly had voted

"the most unworthy man in the world to be Præsident of the Colledge in Cambridge. God knows what further trials are coming upon me." But at the same time, "the Spirit of the Lord sometimes does Visit me with Raptures of Assurances, That He has loved me, and that I shall glorify Him. I am sometimes even ready to faint away with the Rapturous prælibations of the Heavenly World."

On the 15th, he definitely renounced the gentlewoman. "I struck the Knife into the Heart of my Sacrifice by a Letter to her Mother." But next day comes this:—

Was ever man more Tempted than the miserable Mather? Should I tell in how many Forms the Devil has assaulted me, . . . it would strike my Friends with Horrour. Sometimes Temptations to Impurities: and sometimes to Blasphemy and Atheism and the Abandonment of all Religion as a mere Delusion: and sometimes to Self-Destruction itself. These, even These, O miserable Mather, do follow thee with an astonishing Fury. But I fall down into the Dust on my Study-floor, with Tears before the Lord: and then, they quickly vanish: Tis fair weather again. Lord, what wilt thou do with me?

On the 3d of April he held another fast, to guard against the temptations of widowhood. He would like to remain a widower, he thought; but his father and his friends advised otherwise. On the 13th, 14th, and 15th, he kept three successive days of fasting and prayer, in which extraordinary things were done for him.

"The Angels of Heaven are at work for me," he writes, "And I have my *own* Angel, who is a better Friend unto me, than any I have upon Earth."

But the "desirable frame" in which this left him lasted only two days. Still, on the 18th of May he found himself assured that

for the sake of the Lord Jesus Christ, whose I am, a desireable consort should be bestowed upon me; and a glorious Angel of the Lord, should be concerned for me (as for Isaac of old) in this important matter.

His friends, it appears, were trying to make a match for him; but succeeded only in getting him distressingly talked about. A "marvellous providence of God" diverted him from "doing a thing whereto . . . Friends had mightily urged" him. On the 19th, he went to Salem for five days. The gentlewoman and her mother took advantage of his absence to call on Increase Mather, who had been suffering with gout; and to urge their case. But Cotton Mather, though distressed, remained resolute. And a little later he writes,

> While the Lord is otherwise laying me exceedingly low, He yett gratifies me with Strange Favours on that point which is the very Apple of my Eye: and that is, my being employed in Service for His Blessed Name.

In other words, his condition had proved unusually favourable to pulpit eloquence.

In June, when gossip began to accuse him of jilting the gentlewoman, she joined her mother in loyally protesting that his conduct had been thoroughly honourable.

> "Yea," he writes, "they have proceeded so far beyond all bounds in my vindication, as to say, *They verily look on* Mr. M——r *to be as great a Saint of God as any upon earth.*"

The poor gentlewoman had a worse trial coming, though. Sundry fasts of Cotton Mather's early in July directed his attention to Mrs. Elizabeth Hubbard, a godly and comely widow who lived near by. On the 14th, he paid her his first visit. In a few days more they were engaged. The gentlewoman raged, but relented. People in general approved. And Cotton Mather's troubles reduced themselves to groundless fears that he should die before his wedding day. On the 18th of August, after spending the day in Heaven, he became in the evening the husband of "the most agreeable Consort (all things considered) that all America could have afforded me."

Of this lady her son Samuel wrote:—

> She was one, of finished *Piety* and *Probity*, and of an unspotted *Reputation;* one of *good sense*, and bless'd with a compleat *Discretion* in ordering an Household; one of singular *good-Humour* and incomparable Sweetness of Temper; one, with a very handsome and engaging *Countenance;* and one *honourably descended* and related; . . .

the Daughter of Dr. JOHN CLARK. She had been a Widow *four years* when Dr.[7] MATHER married her.[8]

The rest of Cotton Mather's notes for this year show him very busy with pastoral and literary work, and quite relieved of the morbid tension that preceded his marriage.

My summary of his annual literary work in the last chapter should be sufficient. A glance at Sibley's catalogue of his works[9] will show that the years I have summarized are typical. Of this matter I shall say no more, save that his publications in 1703 amounted to twelve; and in 1704 to the same number. And so he kept on all his life.

His diary for 1704 is not preserved. The only facts I have noted for this year are these. A daughter, Elizabeth, was born to him. It was the year when Deerfield was sacked. In June, certain pirates were hanged in Boston; and Cotton Mather preached to them and went with them to execution, where, "when the scaffold was let to sink," Sewall writes, "there was such a Screech of the Women that my wife heard it sitting in our Entry, . . . yet the wind was sou-west. Our house is a full mile from the place." In July, Sewall notes that Cotton Mather was at Commencement; on October 12th, that Cotton Mather prayed for the College. Two days before, Samuel Mather[10] tells us, a dying man had sent for Cotton Mather, to beg his forgiveness for wanton slanders. Mather forgave him: and "the Man . . . kept continually crying for him to be with him the next Day in the Forenoon, and he died in the Afternoon." I incline, also, to attribute to the period of his troubles with the gentlewoman of 1703 the anecdote preserved in a vituperative pamphlet of 1707, and probably a good example of the stories told of him by his enemies. It runs thus:—

A Gentlewoman of *Gayety*, near *Boston*, was frequently visited by the Reverend Mr. *C. M.* which giving offence to some of his Audience, he promised to avoid her Conversation. But *Good* intentions being frustrated by *Vicious* Inclinations, he becomes again her humble Servant: the *Reciprocal* promise being first made, that NEITHER OF THEM SHOULD CONFESS THEIR SEEING EACH OTHER: However it be-

[7] The title is premature. Cotton Mather was not Doctor of Divinity until 1710.
[8] Life, page 13.   [9] Harvard Graduates, III. 42-158.   [10] Life, page 64.

coming again publick, his Father accused him of it, who after two or three HEMS to recover himself, gave this *Aequivocal* Answer, INDEED, FATHER, IF I SHOULD SAY I DID SEE HER, I SHOULD TELL A GREAT LYE.[11]

Which story, having read his diaries, I do not believe.

The diary for 1705[12] records a busy year, more wholesome than usual. I have noted a few entries. On the 16th of March, maligned for falsehood, he held a very earnest day of fasting and prayer.

"And I considered," he writes, "That tho' my whole Time all the Day long, and all the Week long, is employ'd in a continual Contrivance of . . . Zeal to do good, yett few men meet with more clogs in it, from the malignity of Evil people. . . . And if I had jogg'd on in an Indifferent manner as others do, and less thwarted and vexed the Divel in his interests, I might have been as little envied and maligned as they: But I resolved, That I would not at all Abate of my Endeavors to be universally Serviceable."

In May, Nancy had another severe illness.

"I cannot be at rest," he writes, "until I have obtained of the Lord that this Child shall in Spiritual Blessings have an abundant and glorious Compensation for all her Temporal Sufferings."

In May he was specially maligned by a "very wicked fellow," who, with Cotton Mather's approval, had been disciplined by the Church of Woburn. Early in June, then, he examined himself for

"what marks I can find in myself, that might carry me cheerfully thro' the Dark Valley of the Shadow of Death, if I should be (which I have abundance of Reason to look for) immediately called into it." He found eleven, of which the last was compassion for personal enemies. "I am afraid," he writes, "of allowing my Soul a Wish of Evil to the Worst of them All. . . . Q. Whether the man that can find these *marks* upon himself may not conclude himself *mark'd out* for the City of God?"

At this time he was very busy, starting Societies for the Suppression of Disorders.

"I am well content," he writes, "that I have not the Time, to Record a hundredth part of the *methods to bring forth Fruit* wherein I am

[11] Sewall's Diary, II. 81*. See page 163.
[12] In possession of the Massachusetts Historical Society.

endeavoring to *glorify God,* so that they should be utterly buried in oblivion for this world."

In July, hearing in a hymn the words,

With persons merciful that be
Thou merciful thyself wilt show,

he was affected to tears by the thought that the merciful dispositions he could discover in himself were but faint rays of the sun of God's mercy. In November, he examined himself curiously.

"A man Bitten with a *Mad-Dog,*" he writes, "has not only his *Body,* but his very *Soul* also poisoned. The poison . . . pervades the Nervous Fluid. . . . The *Spirit* of such a man, will cause him to say to his Friend, . . . *I would not hurt you.* Notwithstanding this, yett when his Fitt arrives the *Spirit* must knock under and ly fettered. . . . The Soul of every man is *Dog-Bitten,* or, which is as bad, *serpent-bitten,* or *Divel-bitten. Original Sin* has depraved it. . . . A *Regenerate Spirit* . . . chuses above all Things, to Glorify God, . . . and it has gotten an *Empire* over the *Soul,* in doing of it."

By this test, he found himself probably regenerate.

In January, there was a thanksgiving for successes in the war with France.

"For the best part of Two Hours together," he writes, "my soul kept soaring and Flaming towards Heaven in the wondrous praises of God. Such length in this kind of Devotions being somewhat unusual, and unto some folks (I fear'd) uneasy, I took occasion in my Sermon to make this Apology for it."

The apology I will not quote; it is very long.

The volume closes with five elaborate notes: one about the dispositions of his mind relating to a great reputation in the world, concerning which he believes himself to care little; one about the education of his children, which is substantially what his son Samuel reports of his practices;[13] one about several points of conduct, in which he resolves to practise Christian humility; and one about his flock, which he purposes to edify by pastoral visits, and by edifying speeches on all occasions,—giving them many books, too, with the charge that they are to remember that he

[13] See pages 120-21.

speaks to them whenever the books are before them. The fifth
note is similar to that which closes nearly every volume of the
diary,—a memorandum of the texts he has preached from this
year: it covers four closely written pages.

The diary for 1706 [14] opens with a very long memorandum of
how his time is occupied: this is digested under thirty-one heads.
It appears that he rises at seven or eight;[15] sings a hymn of praise;
writes a short paragraph,—"hereby sometimes I have insensibly
prepared whole sermons"; adds illustrations to the "Biblia Americana"; prays in private and then with his family; works; dines,
edifying the family meanwhile; retires to his study for a short
prayer; goes out visiting; about the shutting in of the evening
hears the children say the catechism, and makes an evening
prayer chiefly of thanksgiving; sups at ten, edifying the adult
part of his family; prays and reflects on the day in his study; and
reads himself to sleep with some agreeable book at eleven or so.
Sermons, the children, the sick, calls from all manner of visitors,
the fourteen or fifteen religious societies he belongs to, new books
to be read, frequent days of fasting and prayer, and the discipline
of his church constantly engage his attention. He notes all this in
the hope that by perusing it he may be kept up to work. Four
pages of notes of his correspondents follow: I observe no names
of permanent importance.

His birthday note is worth remembering. He would like to
record thoughts

that carry in them a peculiar Advancement of my Soul towards the
perfection after which I am aspiring. One of them, which has been of
late singularly useful to me in my pressing after the true temper of
Christianity is This. I see all Creatures everywhere full of their Delights. The Birds are singing; the Fish are sporting; the Four-footed
are glad of what they meet withal; the very Insects have their satis-
factions. Tis a marvellous Display of Infinite Goodness. The Good
God has made His Creatures capable of Delights: He accommodates
them with continual Delights. These Delights are the Delicious Enter-
tainments of His Infinite Goodness. His Goodness takes pleasure in
. . . the Delights of His Creatures.—Well: Is there no way for me

[14] In possession of the Massachusetts Historical Society.
[15] Thus habitually sleeping eight or nine hours, which is probably what kept
him alive.

to Resemble and Imitate this Incomparable Goodness of God? Yes: I
see my Neighbours all accommodated with their various Delights. All
have some, and some have many. Now I may honestly make their
Delights my own. . . . I may make their prosperity, not my *Envy*,
but my *pleasure*. . . . Oh, the glorious Joy of this Goodness! Lord,
Imprint this thy Image upon me!

With good resolutions, one against evil-speaking, for example;
with prayers and assurances, among others for the prisoners
among the French and Indians, the year went on. In March, little
Increase having begun school, Cotton Mather wrote a verse daily
for the child to get by heart, that he might "improve in goodness
at the same time that he improv'd in Reading"; these verses ultimately made a popular book. In April, he was pleased to find
that he had "no Fondness at all for Applause and Honour in this
World": for which disposition "in the midst of . . . Humiliations," he gave thanks. Late in May, languishing in health, he
hurried work and finished the first draft of the "Biblia Americana." He kept adding to it, however, for years. As late as 1720
he wrote John Winthrop[16] that he had inserted in the "Biblia
Americana" an account of the discovery in New England of a
water-dove, probably the species employed by Noah. The manuscript of the "Biblia Americana," by far the most voluminous of
Cotton Mather's works, is preserved by the Massachusetts Historical Society. He could never find subscribers enough to publish it; and I have not had the time or the courage to examine
it. At a superficial glance, it seems to be a marvellously industrious, uncritical collection of every scrap of learning he could
find which might by any chance have bearing on Holy Writ. It
includes a great deal of such matter as is most familiarly known
nowadays in Burton's "Anatomy of Melancholy"; and a great
deal, too, of that eager observation of nature[17] which some years
later made Cotton Mather a Fellow of the Royal Society.

His next work, printed in June, was an essay to promote the
Christianizing of Negroes.[18] He determined to give a copy of this

[16] Mather Papers, 436.

[17] For examples of this, see Cotton Mather's letters to John Winthrop, in
the Mather Papers.

[18] See Sibley, III. 93; and in regard to Cotton Mather's relations to negroes
in general, see a paper by Professor Haynes in the Proceedings of the American Antiquarian Society.

to every family in New England who possessed a Negro, and to send copies to the West Indies.

In July, he was much disturbed about illicit trade with hostile Indians. These Indians made a descent this very month on the Andover road, over which he had passed a few days before. On this journey, he writes,

being desirous to do some Good on the Road in the Woods, I called some children to me, which I met there, and bestowed some Instructions with a little Book upon them: which I understood afterwards made no little Impression upon the Family. But it proved a family which in a few Dayes the Indians visited, and murdered the mother, and several of the children.

So the year went on, busier than ever. In October I find two notes worth recording. On the 17th, he writes:—

One of my more special Actions . . . was to make my Children, Four of them,[19] successively to come into my Study, and observe and mention to me the special mercies which they were sensible they had received of God; and then charge them immediately to Retire and give Thanks unto the Lord, and beg to be possessed by the Spirit of the Lord.

On Wednesday, the 30th, he writes:—

With many favourable Circumstances for which the Lord had been sought unto, my Consort fell into Travail; and after a Wondrous Good and Quick Time, was about three-quarters of an hour past nine at Night, happily delivered of a Son; to appearance a hearty and an handsome Infant.—On the Lord's-day following I Baptized this my Son, and called him SAMUEL. Tis my desire to have him devoted unto the Service of the Lord as long as he lives.

That night, accordingly, he held a vigil for his whole family. This Samuel lived to grow up into a very commonplace divine, whose biography of his father is probably the most colourless book in the English language.

In November, Cotton Mather's assurances were rewarded by the return of his cousin, Mr. Williams of Deerfield, from captivity. In December some gentlemen gave Mather a negro, named Onesimus, worth forty or fifty pounds.

[19] Katharine, Abigail, Hannah, and Increase; their ages ranged from fourteen to seven.

"I would use the best endeavours," he writes, "to make him a servant of Christ, and also be more serviceable than ever to a flock which laies me under such obligations."

The same month comes a note that shows his temper up. He has two wicked brothers-in-law, he writes:—

The first of these prodigies, namely J. O.,[20] married my Lovely Sister Hannah, a most Ingenious and sweet-Natured, and good-carriaged Child: one that would have been a Wife, to have made any Gentleman Happy; but married unto a Raving Bruit. The Fellow, whom they called, Her Husband, perfectly murdered her, by his base and abusive way of treating her; and he chose to employ in a special manner, the ebullitions of his venome against me, to weary and worry her, out of her Life, who Loved me dearly. . . . At last on 1d. 10m., . . . the pangs of Death came upon her. Her Death was Long and Hard, and has awakened me more than ever, to pray for an Easy Death. She kept in her dying Distresses much calling on me: her *Brother*, her *Brother!* As I had heretofore used all possible Diligence and Contrivance, to prepare her for her Death, so I now assisted her, as well as I could, in her last Hours. I prayed with her Six Times this Day: and in the Night following she died. The Monster, to whom she owes her Death, now with Anguish, bears a most honourable Testimony for her; as the best Wife in the World; and a great example of piety. And from a convinced conscience, he now also speaks of *me*, with no little pretence of Honour and Acknowledgement. Indeed, she had Cause to Bless God for the Wretch, for he was a great occasion of her growing a serious and gracious Christian, weaned from this World and fitted for a better.

The other wicked brother-in-law was a Phillips, whose offences seem less a matter of opinion. On the 10th of January, Cotton Mather writes:—

My Father-in-Law at Charlestown has of late been in a very froward and Evil Frame. The elder of his Two wicked Sons, has been lately Fined by the General Assembly of the Province for his unlawful Trade with the Enemy. The crime of the Traders, whereof he was one filled the Countrey with a mighty Inflammation. On that occasion, it was necessary for me, to bear my part with the other ministers, in a faithful Testimony. And I did my part as easily and as modestly, tho' as Faithfully as I could. The Humoursome Old Man is so very unhappy, as to be enraged at me, and express himself, as I hear, very Enragedly

[20] John Oliver.

and Abusively. . . . His Two Wicked Sons do also strangely manage him.

So Cotton Mather was afraid that old Mr. Phillips would disinherit his Mather grandchildren and offered up prayers accordingly.

The very next note, however, is of different tenor:—

My little Son waits upon his Grandfather every day, for his Instruction, as well as upon other Tutors and Teachers. This day I sent him on an Errand, where the person imposing on his Flexible Temper, detained him so long that his Grandfather was displeased at him, for coming so late; and his punishment was, that his Grandfather, did Refuse to Instruct him, as he used to do. The child, unable to bear so heavy a punishment, as that his Grandfather should not look favourably upon him, repairs to me, full of weeping Affliction. Hereupon, I applied myself with a Note, unto my *Father*, as an *Advocate* for the Child. I pleaded all that could be said by way of Apology for the Infirmity of the Child. I asked, that I might bear the displeasure due for it, because of what had passed relating to it. I assured my Father, the child should no more in this way displease him. So the Child was presently received into favour with my Father: My Father looked on him with a pleased Aspect, and bestowed agreeable Illumination upon him. I thought, the Lord ordered this little Accident this Day, to raise in my mind, the Thoughts of the Reconciliation, which the Son of God, who is my Advocate with the Father, would obtain for me, with God.

The diary closes with a painful record of how Cotton Mather was persistently vexed with vile thoughts: but he fought them hard, he resolved that they should not tempt him to forbear testimony against sin in others, and he meditated

on the inexpressible evil, which there would be, . . . if one of my . . . many and mighty obligations, to the most unspotted Sanctity, should harbour or indulge in myself any wicked Thing in the World.

Of the diary for 1707 only a fragment remains;[21] in which I have remarked nothing of more note than that Cotton Mather was praying fervently for the expedition against Port Royal that came to nothing. For the notable events of this year, then, we must turn to other authorities.

[21] In possession of the Massachusetts Historical Society.

Palfrey tells with great clearness the story of Joseph Dudley's administration.[22] Frequent notes of Sewall's, a member of the Council, a judge of the highest court in the Province, and closely connected by marriage with the Governor, become very vivid when we keep in mind the state of politics. In brief, with his overbearing temper, so thoroughly foreign to the temper of New England, Dudley had been doing his best to strengthen the power of the Crown. Without much success, he had been carrying on the war against Canada; in 1707 a fruitless expedition was sent against Port Royal, restored to the French by the Peace of 1697. Meantime, like other men in office before and since, he had taken good care of his personal friends; and was suspected of connivance with some of them in illicit trade with the enemy. As Cotton Mather wrote in 1706, a number of illicit traders, among whom was John Phillips, brother of the first Mrs. Mather, had been condemned by the General Court to pay heavy fines for their offence. It is certain that Dudley wrote to England in their behalf; and that the Privy Council ultimately ordered the fines to be repaid, on the ground that the General Court of Massachusetts had no cognizance of the offence. Before this decision, certain men of New England, mostly resident in London, had addressed to the Queen a formal petition for the removal of Dudley, for corruption, injustice, and oppression.

Harvard College,[23] meanwhile, had been proceeding under the charge of Vice President Willard, who had retained meantime his charge of the Old South Church, and seems to have given little more attention to academic duties than Increase Mather had given. Apparently, however, he was much less vigorously conservative in temper; and so far as records show made no particular efforts to secure a new charter. As we have seen, Dudley twice suggested that application be made for one to the Crown. But no notice was taken of these suggestions: the friends of the College, Quincy thinks, were convinced that no satisfactory charter could be secured from any more foreign source than their own elected Provincial legislature.

Willard's health was now failing. He managed to preside at Commencement, but gave the degrees so feebly that Sewall, who was not far off, could not hear a word he said. In the middle

[22] Book IV. Chapters VIII. to X.   [23] Quincy, Vol. I. Chapter VIII.

of August he went to Cambridge for the last time, where he found so few scholars that he returned home before prayer-time. And on the 12th of September, a friend informed Sewall that the President was very sick.

"I hoped it might go off," writes Sewall, "and went to Diñer; when I came there Mr. Pemberton[24] was at Prayer, near concluding, a pretty many in the Chamber. After Prayer, many went out, I staid and sat down: and in a few minutes saw my dear Pastor Expire: . . . just about two hours from his being taken. . . . The Doctors were in another room Consulting what to doe. . . . Tis thought cutting his finger, might bring on the tumultuous passion that carried him away. There was a dolefull cry in the house."

Three days later Mr. Willard was buried; both of the Mathers were among his bearers. And on the 2d of October, a fast day, the Mathers conducted afternoon exercises at the Old South.

The first business of the Corporation of Harvard College was to elect a President. Increase Mather was nearly sixty-nine years old. But Cotton Mather was only forty-four. His learning, his piety, his orthodoxy, and his devotion to the old principles of the College, made him, in his own opinion, the proper successor of Mr. Willard. There is reason to think that the want of deliberate judgment which naturally came from his overworked, over-wrought habits of life, led his hopes to run high. So what happened on the 28th of October must have stung him to the quick.

"The Fellows of Harvard College meet," writes Sewall, "and chuse Mr. Leverett President: He had eight votes, Dr. Increase Mather three, Mr. Cotton Mather one."

Within the week Sewall saw for the first time a document that gave rise to much excitement in Boston. This was "A Memorial of the Present Deplorable State of New England,"[25] lately published in London, and stating with great distinctness every charge against Dudley. These were supported by sundry affidavits, and by a long letter, evidently written by Cotton Mather. It is dated

---

[24] Willard's colleague at the Old South.
[25] Reprinted at the beginning of the second volume of Sewall's Diary, and summarized by Palfrey, Book IV. Chap. VIII. It is in a reply to this pamphlet that the scandalous story appeared which I lately cited, pages 153-54.

October 2, 1706:[26] it specifically mentions the proceedings against Phillips and the other illicit traders, and contains this passage:—

Our Present Governour is not without a number of those, whom he has by Promotions and Flatteries made his Friends; but this hinders not a much more considerable number, from wishing, that we had a Governour, who would put an end unto the horrid Reign of Bribery, in our Administration, and who would not infinitely incommode Her Majesty's Service, by keeping the People in continual Jealousies of his Plots, upon their most Valuable Interests.

On the 1st of November, the day when Sewall saw this pamphlet, the Governor produced in the Council a copy of the petition for his removal, and requested the Council to vote their abhorrence of it. Sewall pleaded for delay, but the vote was passed. The Deputies refused to concur in it. At a Conference of the Houses on the 20th,

Gov. made a long speech, begiñing from his father, who laid out a Thousand pounds in the first adventure, was Governour. He himself the first Magistrat born in New England . . . Took an opportunity to say, he heard some whisper'd as if the Council were not all of a mind: He with courage said that all the Council were of the same mind as to every word of the Vote. This gall'd me; yet I knew not how to contradict him before the Houses." At another conference next day, "the Govr. had the Extract of many of Mr. C. M. Letters read, of a later date than that in the printed book, . . . giving him a high character." On the 25th of November, "The Govr. read Mr. Cotton Mather's letter . . . in Council. . . . When the Govr. came to the *horrid Reign of Bribery:* His Excellency said, None but a Judge or Juror could be Brib'd, the Governour could not be bribed, sons of Belial brôt him no Gifts. Moved that [a committee] go to Mr. Cotton Mather with the Copy of his Letter, . . . and his Letters to the Govr., and speak to him about them: this was agreed to. I shew'd some backwardness, . . . hinting whether it might not be better for the Govr. to go to him himself: That seem'd to be Christ's Rule, except the Govr. would deal with him in a Civil way. . . . p. m. I desired the Governour's patience to speak a word: I said I had been concerned about the Vote pass'd Novr. I. 'At the Conference his Excellency was pleas'd to say, that every one of the Council remain'd steady to their vote, and every word of it: This Skrewing the Strings of your Lute to that height, has broken one of them; and I find my self under the Necessity of withdrawing my Vote; . . . and desire the Secretary may be directed to enter it in the Minutes of the Council.' And then I delivered my Reasons for it,[27] written and sign'd with my own Hand. . . . The Govr. directed that it should be kept privat: but I think Col. Lynde went away before the Charge was given. . . . Nov. 26 Mr. Secretary reports the Discourse with Mr. Cotton Mather favourably; It seems they stay'd there more than two Hours; and Dr. Mather was present. Mr. Mather neither denys nor owns the Letter: Think his Letters to the Govr. and that . . . not so inconsistent as they are represented. . . . The Council invited the Govr. to Diñer; . . . I drank to his Excellency, and presented my Duty to him. . . . In the evening by Candle-Light I fell asleep in the Council-Chamber: and when I waked was surprised to see the Govr. gone.[28]

On the 28th, Dudley wished the vote of November 1st published, to prevent the spreading of false reports.

"I said," writes Sewall, "I could not vote to it because I had withdrawn my vote. The Govr. said, I pray God judge between me and you! . . . Lord, do not depart from me, but pardon my sin; and fly to me in a way of favourable Protection."

On the 6th of December, there came before the Council a bill fixing the salary of the new President of Harvard College. To this was subjoined the following provision,[29] which we should now call a "rider":—

And inasmuch as the first foundation . . . of that House[30] . . . had its original from an act of the General Court, made and passed in the year one thousand six hundred and fifty, which has not been repealed or nulled; the President and Fellows of the said College are directed . . . to regulate themselves according to the rules of the constitution by that act prescribed.

Dudley and his Council approved this bill. The charter of 1650, thus revised, governs Harvard College to the present day. And thus it came about that Harvard College, in spite of all the labours and prayers of the Mathers, has become, for better or

[27] Borland, one of the convicted traders, had given Sewall to understand that the charges against Dudley were true; but subsequently denied Sewall's construction of his words. See Sewall's Diary, II. 215, 216.
[28] Sewall's Diary, II. 199-204.   [29] Quincy, I. 159.   [30] I. e. Harvard College.

worse, the perpetual nursery, not of priests, but of ever more earnest Protestants.

How the defeated party took this matter appears in a note of Sewall's for December 18th:—

Mr. Bridge[31] takes Job 15. 34.[32] for his Text; especially that clause, —Fire shall consume the tabernacle of Bribery: From which he preach'd an excellent sermon. . . . Dr. Mather not at Lecture. Governor . . . there.

In spite of sermons, Leverett was inaugurated on the 18th of January. The Mathers were not present. Sewall gives a minute account of the ceremony.

In the Library the Governour found a Meeting of the Overseers . . . according to the old charter of 1650. . . . Took the President by the hand and led him down into the Hall. The Books of the College Records, Charter, Seal and Keys were laid upon a Table running parallel with that next the Entry. The Govr. sat with his back against a Noble Fire; . . . President sat on the other side of the Table. . . . The Govr. read his Speech and (as he told me) mov'd the Books in token of their Delivery. Then the President made a short Latin Speech, importing the difficulties discouraging, and yet that he did Accept. . . . Had a very good Diñer upon 3 or 4 Tables. . . . Got home very well. *Laus Deo.*

On the 23d of January, Sewall attended a funeral. "When had gone a little way," he writes, "Mr. Cotton Mather came up and went with me." From the burying place they went to make a call, where they had some very pious talk.

"As went thence," continues Sewall, "told me of his Letter to the Govr. of the 20th Inst. and Lent me the Copy. . . . Dr. Mather it seems has also sent a Letter to the Govr. I wait with concern to see what the issue of this plain home-dealing will be!"

Palfrey[33] and Quincy[34] summarize these letters. Assuming all the spiritual authority of their ministry, the Mathers reiterate every charge that has been made against Dudley; and rebuke

---

[31] Minister of the First Church.

[32] "For the congregation of hypocrites shall be desolate, and fire shall consume the tabernacles of bribery"

[33] Vol. III. pp. 295, 296.   [34] Vol. I. pp. 201, 202.

him with every anathema of Puritanism. The letters are the agonizing death-cry of old New England.

Two or three more notes of Sewall's tell what this "plain home-dealing" seemed to the victors.

> Jany 31. Mr. Pemberton . . . talk'd to me very warmly about Mr. Cotton Mather's Letter to the Govr., seemed to resent it, and expect the Govr. should animadvert upon him. Said if he were as the Govr. he would humble him though it cost him his head; Speaking with great vehemency just as I parted with him at his Gate. The Lord apear for the Help of his people.—Feb. 2. . . . Somebody said, . . . That no man was admitted to be a Captain without giving the D. of Marlborough, or his Dutchess five hundred Guinys: the Govr. took it up, and said, What is that! Speaking in a favourable, diminutive way. And said that there had not been any admitted these thousand years but in a way like that; mentioning his own experience in the Isle of Wight. His Excellency seems hereby to justify himself against those who charge him with Bribery.—Febr. 5. Mr. Colman preaches the Lecture . . . from Gal. 5. 25. If we live in the Spirit, let we also Walk in the Spirit. Spake of Envy and Revenge as the Complexion and Condemnation of the Devil. . . . 'Tis reckoned he lash'd Dr. Mather and Mr. Cotton Mather and Mr. Bridge for what they have written, preach'd and pray'd about the present Contest with the Govr.

Next day, after a fortnight's waiting, Joseph Dudley sent his answer to the Mathers.[35] With Scriptures as good as theirs, he recommended self-scrutiny to them. And he went on thus:—

> Every one can see through the pretence, and is able to account for the spring of these letters, and how they would have been prevented, without easing any grievances you complain of. . . . I desire you will keep your station, and let fifty or sixty good ministers, your equals in the province, have a share in the government of the College . . . as well as yourselves. . . . I am an honest man, and have lived religiously these forty years to the satisfaction of the ministers in New England, and your wrath against me is cruel, and will not be justified. . . . The College must be disposed against the opinion of all the ministers in New England except yourselves, or the governor torn in pieces. This is the view I have of your inclination.

And this is the view posterity has accepted, with what justice the records I have quoted may help to show. While the Mathers

were reading this letter, Samuel Sewall, "in the up̄er Chamber
of the North-East end of the House, fastening the Shutters next
the Street," was holding a solemn fast. But though he prayed for
so many things that the record covers a closely printed page, I
found my eye caught chiefly by one passage:—

Save the Town, College, Province from Invasions of Enemies open,
Secret and from false Brethren: Defend the Purity of Worship. Save
Connecticut.[36]

[36] Diary, II. 217. 10 February, 1701-8.

XI. *Cotton Mather's Private Life to the Death of His Second Wife.*

$1707\text{-}1713$ For the next six years Joseph Dudley remained Governor of Massachusetts. His quarrel with the Mathers seems never to have been settled. Throughout these years, Cotton Mather was busier than ever in his pastoral work, and his endless plans for doing good in general; and Increase Mather, growing old, and not gaining buoyancy of temper, preached and prayed,—not a little about the good old time. With public offices and with the College, which prospered under the care of Leverett, neither seems to have had much to do. So the course of public affairs has little to do with us. In his relations with the General Court, Dudley seems, in his later days, to have been less aggressive. The war went on with varying success: Port Royal was taken in 1710, but there were disasters later, Indian massacres all along. In fifty years, Hutchinson estimated,[1] the population did not double: in 1709, Dudley estimated it at about fifty thousand, increasing at the rate of a thousand a year; Hutchinson thinks that from five to six thousand of the youth of the country fell in the wars which ended with the welcome peace of Utrecht in 1713. Meanwhile, according to Palfrey,[2] a new generation was growing up under the Provincial charter, far more loyal to the Crown than the old independent Dissenters of the Colony.

In this chapter our business will be to follow the private life of Cotton Mather until 1713.

Cotton Mather's diary for 1708 is not preserved. But in the collection of the American Antiquarian Society is a copy in his handwriting, with the date 1708, of Swift's burlesque prophecy of the death of Partridge, etc., which Cotton Mather seems to

[1] Palfrey, III. 303.　[2] Vol. III. p. 302.

have taken in sober earnest. In Sewall I find but one note worth
recording here. In June Mr. Bromfield received an anonymous
letter, "putting him upon enquiring after Debaucheries at North's,
the Exchange Tavern," and urging him to ask Sewall's advice.
Cotton Mather's constant eagerness to suppress disorder, his intimate relations with Bromfield and Sewall, and his frequent practice of "doing good" anonymously, make it not unlikely that this
letter came from him. I cannot refrain from citing one more note
of Sewall's, though—a little glimpse of manners: "Govr. calls and
smokes a pipe with my wife at night 9r. 1."

Sewall's diary for 1709 gives a few glimpses of the Mathers,
with whom his relations were now cordially intimate.

June 22. . . . Going to visit sick Mr. Gerrish . . . I met Dr.
Mather, who tells me that yesterday, he was 70 years old.—Octobr.
6. . . . Mr. C. Mather preaches from Prov. 14. 14. Backslider in
heart shall be filled with his own Ways. Mention'd the indulgence of
Adonijak; the prophet Micajah; not the prophet, but the King was
hurt by his estrangement.

There are glimpses of Dudley, too, giving no new traits; and
on January 28th, this note:—

The Govr. told me of News from Albany, as if the French of
Canaday were coming against us. The good Lord stop them!

Cotton Mather's diary for 1709 [3] is on the whole not noteworthy. On the 20th of June he makes an entry that is typical of
the year:—

I am so full of employments; and in such a happy way of continually every day doing a variety of services, which yett I do not
ask to have remembered, that I have not the Leisure, which else I
might have to replenish these memorials.

Little Sam had a fever. Another son, Nathaniel, was born to
him on the 16th of May, and died on the 24th of November. I
find but two other notes worth recording. In March, Mather was

"assaulted with Solicitations [from Hell] to look upon the whole
Christian Religion as—[I dare not mention what!]" but resolved to
"Beleeve Him wise and Just and good, and confess myself unable to
Judge of His Dispensations, but Refer all unto a Time when He shall

[3] In possession of the American Antiquarian Society.

please to entertain His people in another world with a Discovery of what He has done and meant in His former Dealings."

At this time Mather was very poor, he remarks,—literally in rags. In September, the other ministers dined with the "Wicked Governor."

"I," writes Cotton Mather, "have by my provoking plainness and Freedom in telling this Ahab of his wickedness procured myself to be left out of his Invitations. I rejoiced in my Liberty from the Temptations with which they were encumbred while they were eating of his dainties, and durst not reprove him. . . . And considering the power and malice of my enemies, I thought it proper for me to be this day Fasting in Secret before the Lord."

At the end of the diary is a long account of how he is accustomed on rising every morning to enter in a book "Good Devices" for the day: of them we shall hear more by and by. The volume closes, as usual, with notes of the course of his preaching for the year: among which is one telling how when his sermon was three quarters preached his meeting was broken up by a fire, and how when the congregation returned he began afresh and preached a brand-new sermon extempore.

His diary for 1710 is not preserved. Sewall tells a little of what happened to the Mathers. On the 3d of April there was difficulty in finding a minister to preach the election sermon: and though Mr. Pemberton finally agreed to do it, his temper—a very excitable one—was up. So when "word was brought that Dr. Mather was chosen to preach the Artillery Sermon, Mr. Pemberton said Must choose agen." Several notes of Sewall's this year show the infirmity of Pemberton's temper: the divine had an uncomfortable way of accosting his parishioner in public places and upbraiding him at the top of his voice.

Towards the end of the year Cotton Mather received from the University of Glasgow the degree of Doctor of Divinity. Even in Samuel Mather's lifeless book we can see how grateful the good man found this honour: for one thing he immediately began to wear a signet-ring bearing "a Tree with Psal. 1. 3⁴ written

---

⁴ "And he shall be like a tree planted by the rivers of water, that bringeth forth his fruit in his season; his leaf also shall not wither; and whatsoever he doeth shall prosper."

under it; and about it *Glascua Rigavit*.[5] The Cast of his Eye upon this, constantly provoked him to pray. . . . *O* GOD, *make me a very fruitful Tree*." [6] But he was not permitted to enjoy his title unmolested. One John Banister wrote thereupon the following verses.

"ON C. MR'S. DIPLOMA.

The mad enthusiast, thirsting after fame,
By endless volum'ns thought to raise a name.
With undigested trash he throngs the Press;
Thus striving to be greater, he's the less,
But he, in spite of infamy, writes on,
And draws new Cullies in to be undone.
Warm'd with paternal vanity, he trȳs
For new Subscriptions, while the Embryo [his
      two volumns] [7] lyes
Neglected—Parkhurst[8] says, *Satis fecisti*,
My belly's full of your Magnalia Christi.
Your crude Divinity, and History
Will not with a censorious age agree.
Daz'd with the stol'n title of his Sire,[9]
To be a Doctor he is all on fire;
Would after him the Sacrilege commit
But that the Keeper's [Leverett], care doth him
      affright.
To Britain's Northern Clime in haste he sends,
And begs an Independent boon from Presby-
      terian friends;
Rather than be without, he'd beg it of the
      Fiends.
Facetious George brought him this Libertie
To write C. Mather first and then D. D.[10]

On the 25th of November Increase Mather laid this libel before Sewall. On the 28th, Sewall had Banister and others before him

[5] Glasgow has watered it.   [6] See S. Mather's Life, pp. 74-77.
[7] "Biblia Americana."   [8] The publisher of the "Magnalia."
[9] Increase Mather, it will be remembered, was made Doctor of Divinity under the Harvard charter of 1692, subsequently disapproved by the King. See pages 98-100.
[10] Sewall's Letter-Book, I. 407. Cf. Diary, II. 290-95.

in consequence, and, in spite of a letter from Cotton Mather in
favor of Banister, imposed a fine on him. This greatly stirred up
Mr. Pemberton, who had lately been abused by a certain Captain Martin, against whom no proceedings had been taken.

"Mr. Pemberton," writes Sewall, "with extraordinary Vehemency
said, (capering with his feet) If the Mathers ordered it, I would
shoot him thorow. I told him he was in a passion. He said he was not
in a Passion. I said, it was so much the worse. . . . The truth is I
was surpris'd to see my self insulted with such extraordinary Fierce-
ness, by my Pastor, just when I had been vindicating two worthy
Embassadors of Christ (his own usual Phrase) from most villanous
Libels. . . . These Things made me pray Earnestly . . . that God
would vouchsafe to be my Shepherd, and . . . bring me safely to
his Heavenly Fold."

And the same evening Sewall visited Madam Pemberton, and
gave the nurse three shillings; which did not prevent Mr. Pemberton from giving out next Lord's day a most invidious psalm.[11]
The only other note of Sewall's I have recorded for this year
runs as follows:—

Mid-week, Jany. 31. Went and heard Mr. Bridge, and Dr. Cotton
Mather pray and preach, at the said Dr's House. . . . Dr. Mathers
[Text was] The whole world lyes in Wickedness. Had Cake and But-
ter and Cheese, with good Drinks, before parting.

In Sewall's diary for 1711, I find little that concerns us. The
Mathers were as busy as ever. On the 31st of May, Mr. Wadsworth gave a dinner for the Governor, to which he invited both
the Mathers: and both came,—a fact which throws a little fresh
light on Cotton Mather's secret fast in September, 1709.[12]
Cotton Mather's diary for 1711[13] is different from all the preceding ones. Those, as I have said, are not the original copies,
but abridgements made by himself; rather annual autobiogra-
phies than diaries proper. This volume and the six others that
remain are original copies, hastily written from day to day, and
little revised. They differ in character from the others, too. Instead of being records of what has happened, they are generally
daily entries of good devised for each day,—with the letters

[11] For all this matter, see Sewall's Diary, II. 290-95.
[12] See page 170.   [13] In possession of the American Antiquarian Society.

"G. D." prefixed. Now and then he inserts a passage that he thinks worth remembering. So we have now, for the years whose records are preserved, a daily note of what he means to do, and occasional notes of what has actually been done. One troublesome fact about the diary for 1711 is that he usually enters there only the days of the week, leaving the month to be calculated as best it may. The truth seems to be that, about this time, he concluded that he had wasted too much time on the records of his life: there were other things better worth doing.

His birthday note, with which this volume, like all the rest, begins, shows this state of mind. Hereafter he will keep no separate book of good devices: they shall be entered in his regular diary. He had devised a set of questions to ask himself each day: on Sunday, for example, he asked what he should do as a pastor; on Monday, what he should do for his family; and so on.

"There is no need of Repeating here," he writes, "The questions assigned for each day of the Week. My answer to each of them will be a Good Devised, for which a G. D. will be the Distinction in these Memorials."

Daily good devices fill the pages of this volume, which is twice as thick as any of the preceding ones. Perhaps his most curious note hereabouts is this:—

Having some Epistolar Conversation with Mr. De Foe I would in my letters unto him, excite him to apply himself unto the work of collecting and publishing an History of the persecutions which the Dissenters have undergone from the Ch. of E.—And give him some Directions about the work. It may be a work of manifold usefulness.

Somewhat later, curious reflections follow a fit of cholera morbus and a morning cough: the latter moves him to ejaculate, "Oh! that I may always cast up and throw off, whatever may be inimical to the Health of my Soul!" On the 2d of October there was a great fire in Boston, which aroused proper reflections in Cotton Mather; and which Increase Mather attributed to the growing profanation of the Sabbath. Later in the same month we find Cotton Mather writing to Sir Richard Blackmore and to Dr. Watts, whose hymns he greatly admired. At intervals through the year he mentions his cousin, Eunice Williams, a captive among the Indians, whose mode of life she ultimately adopted. At

Christmas he was greatly disturbed by some young people of both sexes belonging to his flock, who had "a Frolick, a Revelling Feast, and Ball, which discovers their corruption." And a month later he writes:—

Fast. . . . I took the catalogue of the Books which I have been the Author of. The Number in the Catalogue is Two hundred and five. On each of the Titles I made a pause. And I obliged Every one of them, to suggest unto me some Remarkable Article of Humiliation, which I thereupon with an Abased Soul mentioned before the Lord.

But the most interesting notes this year concern his family. Early in the year he notes a good device not to use his influence against a merchant who has injured him.

"No sooner had I written these words," he goes on, "but there was a pretty occurrence in the Family which carried with it a fine picture and Emblem . . . of the Disposition which I am Endeavoring. My little son Sammy did not carry it so kindly to his little sister Lizzy as I would have had him. I chid him for his crossness, and gave her a piece of *pome-citron*, but would give none to him, to punish him for being so cross to her. I had no sooner turned my back but the good-conditioned creature fell into Tears at this punishment of her little Brother, and gave to him a part of what I had bestowed upon her."

Somewhat later, he writes that his son Increase, now about twelve years old, is giving him trouble. Later still, he writes that the time is come for his daughters to be "fixed" in "the opificial and Beneficial mysteries wherein they should be well instructed." Katy, he decides, shall be taught medicine; the inclinations of Nibby and Nancy shall be consulted before he reaches a decision about them. Another daughter, Jerusha, was born this year. But towards the end of the year Increase is most in his mind.

"My Son Increase," he writes, "now being of Age for it, I would often call him into my Study, especially on the Lord's-day Evenings, and make him sitt with me, and hear from me such Documents of piety, and of Discretion, as I shall endeavor to suit him, and to shape him withal." A little later: "It may be of excellent consequence to my son *Increase* if he may turn into Latin, after the rate of one Question p. day, my *Supplies from the Tower of David*. It may also supply me with an Engine, which after my bestowing further Additions on it, may do inexpressible good in other Countreys." And his last daily note for the year runs thus: "G. D. Now my son Increase is arrived unto the exercise of making Themes, at the School, I would make this become an Engine of piety for him; and I would procure such subjects to be assigned unto him, as may most assist the study of goodness and virtue in him."

An active, busy year this seems to have been; less morbid than most. His final summary of it is perhaps worth recording:—

Thus I am come to the end of another year, overwhelmed with confusion, when I look back on the Sin and Sloth constantly attending me in it. It is true I have been helped by Heaven this year, To Lett not One Day pass, without Contriving and Recording, some Inventions to do Good; And those which have pass'd thro' my pen are but a few of the projections which I have had: . . . To lett not One Day pass, without actually expending something of my Revenues . . . on pious uses: To write some Illustrations for the most part Every Day; doubtless . . . I have this year added unto the *Biblia Americana* . . . more than a thousand: To preach many Sermons . . . : To publish near as many books as there have been Months in the year: . . . To make many hundreds of Visits; but never One, without some Explicit Essays or Desires to Do Good in it: To manage some scores of Correspondencies; and . . . to propose the Service of my Glorious Lord in every one of them: . . . To read over many Scores of Books, and gather into my Quotidiana from them: etc. etc. etc. But after all, o my dear Saviour, I stand in infinite need of thy Sacrifice. I have been a most unprofitable Servant. God be merciful to me a Sinner!

Mather's diary for 1712 is not preserved. In Sewall's I find nothing especial about him, except that he went to Commencement. From a note in Quincy,[14] it appears that a new Catalogue of the College was printed at this time, Leverett asked Dudley if Mather had ever apologized for the "undutiful" letter of 1707: if not, Leverett supposed Cotton Mather's new title had better not be recognized in the Catalogue. But Dudley told him not to leave out the title on any such account. And in Harvard Catalogues ever since Cotton Mather has been Doctor of Divinity. In the Mather Papers[15] are preserved some of his letters this year to John and to Wait Winthrop: they show him deeply interested in the European news of the day, which chiefly concerns the ap-

[14] Vol. I. p. 520.   [15] Pages 407-15.

proaching Peace of Utrecht. And Sibley names fifteen books published by Cotton Mather during the year.

So we come to his diary for 1713,[16] an eventful year in Cotton Mather's domestic life. At the very beginning of the year, we find him in much disturbance of mind because some of his flock had been inspired by Satan with the idea of starting a new meeting. He did his best to reason with them, but to little purpose. And towards the middle of March he writes:—

I ought to . . . grow in my Thankfulness to the glorious Lord, in that I have my mind preserved from Hypochondriac Maladies, which, considering my Studies and Sorrowes, tis a wonder, they have not utterly overwhelmed me. The view I have of some other men, unhinged and ruined that way, very much awakens my gratitude.

One of the other men in question was probably the Rev. Ebenezer Pemberton. But a note on the 24th of March shows trials nearer home:—

"Still my aged parent must be the object of my cares; To make him easy under his Resentments of the proceedings about the New Church; and to procure him Releefs against Bodily Distempers that somewhat incommode him; and to gett his mind raised unto the points of Resignation to God and Satisfaction in His Will, which become us in the Suburbs of the Heavenly World."—"God calls me," he writes a few days later, "in an extraordinary manner to be armed for the Trials which I may undergo in a church, breaking all to peeces, thro' the Impertinencies of a proud crew, that must have pues for their despicable Families."

So he prayed and fasted, and had his son Increase come in and pray too. Not long afterwards he realized that he was growing too impatient of slights, and resolved to govern his temper.

In April he was still in high excitement.

"There is one point in my Conversation," he writes, early in the month, "wherein I must press after much greater Sanctity and purity; and have my Behaviour in it more governed by that Reflexion, *The Eye of the Great God is now upon me!* . . . And I must go mourning to my grave, in the sense of the miscarriages, in this point, wherewith His Holy Eyes have seen me chargeable."

[16] In possession of the American Antiquarian Society.

A little later comes the vigil in which he begged to know the meaning of the descent from the invisible world so many years before.[17]

Education is the next thing in his mind. Increase, it is clear, must be "applied unto Saecular Business," and he must cry to Heaven thereabout. The tutors at the College must be reminded that they ought to "instill good principles into their pupils, and be concerned for their Orthodox and Religious, as well as Learned education." And a little later, he notes that he has "litt on a person" to restrain "profaneness in a considerable number of Unruly children on the Lord's day in our Congregation." About this time returned the hypochondriac notion that he was near his end, which often assailed him; he must select guardians for his children. A little later, he determined to write physicians "to obtain for me, as much as may be, of the knowledge of the Botanicks of the countrey: as also of rare cures or cases occurring to them." And a little later still comes this:—

"My poor son Increase! Oh! the Distress of mind with which I must lett fall my daily Admonitions upon him, even with a continual Dropping, especially on these Two points: Conversion to God, in a Sincere compliance with His Covenant: And, The Care of Spending Time so as to give a good Account of it."

Then the new church troubled him again:—

"When any persons . . . fall into errors and evils, and great miscarriages, I must keep a guard of meekness and wisdom on the expression of my zeal. . . . Violent, Boisterous, Intemperate Expressions . . . will not work the Righteousness of God. I am afraid lest I am sometimes too vehement." In answer to this resolution the Lord helped him to treat "the swarming Brethren" in an obliging manner,— "the best thing I can do to prevent the wiles of Satan." A few days later, "in a wicked book I readd a fling at clergymen, as a Revengeful generation of men, who never Forgive such as have offended them. I do not remember, for my own part, that ever I designed the Revenge of an Injury in my life. However, this Venemous Fling, shall quicken my Watchfulness, upon this Article."

Within a few days he had a chance to quicken it:—

[17] See page 90.

G. D. There are Knotts of Riotous Young Men in the Town. On
purpose to insult piety they will come under my Window in the
middle of the Night and sing profane and filthy Songs. The last night
they did so, and fell upon people with clubs taken off my wood-pile.
Tis high-time, to call in the help of the Government . . . for the . . .
suppressing of these disorders.

On the 1st of July, he took his son Increase to Commencement.[18] On the 4th, he held a vigil for the

Impurities which my life has been filled withal. . . . From the
Depths I cried unto the Lord, for his grace to be given unto my
children: particularly my son Increase.

The youth, now about fourteen, was beginning to show himself what he ultimately proved,—a sadly riotous young man. And
this may have been what prompted another good device, a few
weeks later.

I have shown too much Respect unto Wicked Men in my Conversation. . . . Though my Intention has been to show all Gentle-
ness to all men . . . yett I doubt, less Freedom with such Wretches,
less Familiarity with such Devils, would have been better.

So the year goes on, his family more and more on his mind. On
the birthdays of his children, he resolves, he will

not only discourse very proper and pungent things . . . relating to
their eternal Interests, but also oblige them to consider; *first, what is
their main Errand into the World;* and then, *what they have done of
that Errand.* And such of them as are old enough to Write, shall give
me some Written Thoughts upon these things.

His negro servant was best governed by reason: he would
assay to reason him into good behaviour.[19] His "aged parent"—
the phrase by which he names his father from this time on—was
out of order.

"I would persuade him to a frequent use of the *sal volatile,* which
God has blessed unto me for more than ordinary Benefit, and I would

[18] Sewall's Diary, II. 390.
[19] In the library of the American Antiquarian Society is an interesting memorandum of the conditions on which, a little later, this negro, Onesimus,
bought his freedom. He was to see that his place was properly supplied, and
to turn up every day accordingly.

prevent him with a Bottle of it." And when the remedy worked, he resolved "mightily to double my diligence, especially in Afternoon-Studies, for the Dispatch of those things I would fain finish before I Dy."

Meanwhile Increase was always on his mind: one day he made him read the life of a pious youth; again, while seeking a place for him, he would have him "preserve learning," and would daily inquire if he has made secret prayers; a little later, when the youth had blown up himself and his sister Lizzy with gunpowder,

"I would improve this occasion to inculcate Instructions of piety in them and the rest; Especially with Relation to their Danger of Eternal Burnings. Cressy[20] must also employ the leisure which this had occasioned for him, in the most profitable manner": there had been lately an opportunity "to gett . . . Increase cultivated with many points of polite conversation, in his Evening-Hours." Another note runs thus: "Oh! Why don't I in my Family more livelily keep up the Temper and Conduct of a parent expecting to be Speedily taken from his Family?" Another still: "My youngest little daughter[21] is a marvellous Witty, Ready, Forward Child": he would set the others to teaching her maxims of piety. Towards the end of September, the death of an "aged and pious Matron (the First-born of this Town) . . . affords me an opportunity to discourse with my mother, upon her preparation."

A little later, he was trying to get Increase a place with a religious merchant, in good business; and selecting guardians for his children; and praying to the Lord that He would return to them what their father had spent in charity.

I find but three other notes before October worth recording. The first runs thus:—

G. D. Perhaps by sending some Agreeable Things to the Author of the *Spectator,* and the *Guardian,* there may be brought forward some Services to the best Interests of the Nation.

The second expresses an intention to help an old man in the town, eighty-eight years old and needy, "who was a souldier in the Army of my admirable *Cromwel,* and actually present in the Battel of *Dunbar.*" The third is a resolution to counteract the

---

[20] Increase.   [21] Jerusha, born in 1711.

corruption spread by "filthy ballads," by having cheap hymns hawked about,—"some from the excellent Watts."

The rest of his story for this year is more notable in his personal history.

"12d. 8m.[22] This Day, in Ships arriving from London, I receive Letters from the Secretary of the Royal Society, who tells me, That my *Curiosa Americana* being Readd before that Society, they were greatly Satisfied therewith, and ordered the Thanks of the Society to be returned unto me; They also Signified their Desire and purpose to Admitt me as a Member of their Body. And, he assures me, that at their first lawful Meeting for such purposes, I shall be made a A FELLOW OF THE ROYAL SOCIETY. . . . This is a marvellous Favour of Heaven; . . . One that will much Encourage me . . . in my Essayes to Do Good: and add unto the Superiour Circumstances, wherein my Gracious Lord places me above the Contempt of Envious Men." So he cried to the Lord hereby to quicken his "Diligence in His Holy Service"; and resolved to improve his "Correspondence with the Secretary of the *Royal Society,* to sett afoot among the members thereof, such studies as may be for general Benefit, and have hitherto been but little prosecuted."

In less than a week he writes:—

A very deep storm . . . my family may expect in the common calamity of the spreading Measles.

Increase fell ill on the 18th: on the 30th, Katy and Nibby came down. The same day Mrs. Mather was brought to bed of twins, —a boy and a girl.

"The Glorious God," he writes, "in the Surprising Increase of my Family, rebukes my sinful Fears of having them all well-provided for. Thro' the Assistance of his Grace, I find my Soul rejoicing in the View of my having in my Family more Servants born unto my Saviour. . . . I must march against the least Tendencies of Unbelief."

On the 1st of November the twins were baptized: the girl was named for her maternal grandmother, Martha, which

signifying Doctrix may the better suit (as my Father said) a Doctor's Daughter. I then thought, who was *Martha's* brother; and that *Eleazar* was the same with Lazarus; and a priestly name; and the child must be led to look for the *Help of God,* which is the significa-

[22] October 12th.

tion of the Name. I also had an excellent uncle of that Name.[23] So I called them ELEAZAR and MARTHA.

In three days measles had attacked his wife, Nancy, Lizzy, Jerusha, and the maid.

"8. 9.[24] This Day, I entertained my Neighbourhood with a Discourse on Joh. xviii. 11.: *The cup which my Father has given me, shall not I drink it.* And lo, this Day, my Father is giving me a grievous and Bitter Cup, which I hop'd had pass'd from me. . . . When I saw my consort safely delivered, and very easy, and the Measles appearing with favourable symptoms upon her . . . I flattered myself that my Fear was all over. But this Day we are astonished at the surprising symptoms of Death upon her; after an Extreme want of Rest by Sleep, for Diverse whole Dayes and Nights together.—To part with so desirable . . . a companion—A Dam from such a Nest of young ones too!— . . . Tho' my dear Consort had been so long without sleep, yett she retained her understanding. I used my opportunities as well as I could, . . . with Discourses that night . . . to prepare her for what was now before us. It comforted her to see, that her children in Law, were as fond of her, as her own could be! God made her willing to Dy. . . . I prayed with her many Times, and left nothing undone, that I could . . . do for her consolation. On Monday, 9d. 9m., between three and four in the Afternoon, my dear, dear, dear Friend expired.—Whereupon, with another prayer in that Melancholy Chamber, I endeavoured the Resignation to which I am now called. . . . It comforts me to see how extremely Beloved and Lamented a Gentlewoman I now find her to be in the Neighbourhood."

"10. 9. In the midst of my Sorrowes . . . the Lord helped me to prepare no less than Two Sermons, for a public Thanksgiving, which is to be celebrated the day after tomorrow."

"11. 9. This day, I interred the Earthly part of my dear Consort. She had an Honourable Funeral."

And Sewall tells us that among her bearers were Pemberton and Colman.

14. 9. This morning, the first thing that entertains me, after my Rising, is, the Death of my Maid-Servant. . . . Tis a satisfaction to me, that tho' she had been a Wild, Vain, Airy Girl, yett since her coming into my Family, she became disposed unto serious Religion: . . .

[23] See page 20.
[24] November 8th.

and my poor Instructions were the means that God blessed for such happy purposes.

Next day Jerusha and the twins lay dying: Eleazar died at midnight on the 17th, Martha on the morning of the 20th.

21. 9. This Day I attended the Funeral of my Two—Eleazar and Martha. Betwixt 9 and 10 at night, my lovely Jerusha expired. She was Two years, and about Seven Months, old. Just before she died, she asked me to pray with her; which I did, with a Distressed, but Resigning Soul; And I gave her up unto the Lord. The minute that she died, she said, *That she would go to Jesus Christ*. She had lain speechless, many Hours. But in her last Moments, her speech returned a little to her. Lord, I am oppressed: undertake for me!

23. 9. This Day, I followed my dear Jerusha to the grave. But having a mind, full of Resignation, with Resolutions more than ever to glorify my dear Saviour; especially in what I may do for my own, and other children.

There were none in his family now, he remarked, under seven years old. Much might be done at table, then, for both their manners and their minds. A little later,

The Quiet and Easy and unhurried Condition which my Family (by sad things) is bro't unto, gives me now Opportunity to examine more Distinctly my children every night.

Along with religious books, he wrote and published a letter on the "Right Management of the Sick under the Distemper of the Measles."

Cressy was much on his mind: the boy must study fencing, music, geometry, navigation; "his genius stands much that way."

My two Younger Children,[25] shall before the psalm and prayer, answer a Quæstion in the catechism; and have their Leaves ready turned unto the proofs of the Answer in the Bible; which they shall distinctly read unto us, and show what they prove. This also will supply a fresh matter for the prayer that is to follow.

Late in January he wrote to a gentleman in Connecticut, urging him first to be good, and then to do good: by which it seems probable that he meant give money to the College that

[25] Elizabeth and Samuel, the latter just seven years old.

was soon to be called Yale. And his last note for the year runs
thus:—

I must in the Society for pure purposes, bring on an Enquiry,
what may be done for the suppression of some very wicked Houses,
that are the nests of much Impiety. I must also assist the Booksellers
in Addressing the Assembly, that their late Act Against pedlers, may
not hinder their Hawkers from carrying Books of piety about the
countrey. . . . And thus, the goodness, and mercy, of the glorious
Lord, has brought me to the end of another year. The Fifty-first year
of my age is terminated.

XII. *Cotton Mather's Private Life.*
—His Third Marriage.

1713-1718 The history of Massachusetts for the
next five years has little to do with our story. In brief what happened was this. In 1714, Queen Anne died; and on the 22d of
September, George I. was proclaimed at Boston. The commission of Joseph Dudley expired six months after the death of the
sovereign. Sewall's Diary[1] shows how reluctantly the first of the
Tories relinquished power; but relinquish he had to at last, and
retired to private life at Roxbury for the rest of his days. Next
year, a certain Colonel Burgess was appointed Governor: he was
unwelcome to the Province, whose agents paid him a round sum
to decline the office. Lieutenant Governor Tailer was at the head
of affairs until 1716. On October 4th, Samuel Shute, the new
Governor, arrived in Boston. The next two years passed in various
misunderstandings with the legislature, about which we need not
trouble ourselves.

Our business in this chapter is to follow Cotton Mather's life
to the close of 1718.

Cotton Mather's Diary for 1714 is not preserved; but in the
Mather Papers are several of his letters to the Winthrops during
that year. They show him interested in scientific and public matters. And one of them, of the 2d of March, contains a passage
worth quoting. For it shows that after all he might have been no
bad contributor to the "Spectator": he was not insensible to the
literary style of the new century.[2]

[1] Vol. III. pp. 35-39.
[2] His "Political Fables" of 1692-3, reprinted in the "Andros Tracts," are
another example of his lighter literary touch.

"There has been much Talk," it runs,[3] "about a Duel fought between the Duke *Hamilton,* and the Lord *Mohun.* . . . The former finding himself mortally wounded, made it an opportunity to thrust his Sword up to the Hilt in the unguarded body of the other. So both perished. . . . —I am now on a New side of the leaf, and so may take the Liberty to divert you with a short story; which therefore will not necessarily belong to anything in the t'other page. You knew old Major *Thompson.* He had a story, that a young Nobleman, travelling with his Tutor, visited a church in *Italy,* and viewing the Epitaphs, ask'd his Tutor to read one of them, which was not very legible. He read ποπυλοκολοθροπον [a word, whereof I am not learned enough to know the Etymology]. The Nobleman enquired what the English of it? And the Tutor answered, *The World is well rid of a Knave.* And so my old Major, was used, when he heard of the Death of certain persons, only to Lift up his hands, and say *Populokolothropon.* And others also, would quere Major *Thompson's* Greek, as they called it, on such occasions."

Sewall's Diary gives us a few more facts for this year. On the 4th of April, Mrs. Increase Mather died after fifty-two years of wedded life. One of her son's sixteen publications for this year was her funeral sermon. Before very long, the venerable widower married the widow of her nephew, John Cotton, of Hampton: she survived him. On the 20th of October, the "swarming brethren" gathered their New North Church, founded by "seventeen substantial mechanics"; and Increase Mather gave the charge, and Cotton Mather the right hand of fellowship, Pemberton joining them in laying on their hands. On the 24th of November, "a very cold day," one Mr. George, a merchant of Boston, was laid in Sewall's tomb, "till Madam George have an op̄ortunity to build one." Whether he was the "facetious George" who brought over Cotton Mather's diploma in 1710,[4] I know not: but of the widow we shall hear more. And on the 23d of December,

Dr. C. Mather preaches excellently from Ps. 37. Trust in the Lord, etc. only spake of the Sun being in the center of our System. I think it inconvenient to assert such problems.

[3] Mather Papers, 416. Lovers of "Henry Esmond" will find this task interesting.
[4] See page 171.

Sewall's Diary for 1715 gives a few glimpses of the Mathers. Early in the year, they were much interested in the discussions about Dudley's tenure of office, which was fast drawing to a close. On the 13th of April, they enjoyed a singular satisfaction: the Governor, on the verge of enforced retirement, dined with the ministers; and, as had happened at his first official feast in Boston,[5] Increase Mather craved a blessing, and Cotton Mather gave thanks. On the 2d of August there was a fast at Mr. Colman's about calling another minister; when in the afternoon

Mr. Pemberton pray'd, Dr. Cotton Mather preach'd from Isa. 5. 6. latter clause, I will command the clouds, etc.[6] Excellently: censur'd him that had reproach'd the Ministry; . . . call'd it a Satanick insult, twice over, and it found a kind Reception. . . . I could wish the extremity of the censure had been forborn—Lest we be devoured one of another.

A fortnight later, Mr. Pemberton vexed his parishioner by appearing in a "Flaxen Wigg." On the 26th of September, Mr. Bridge died,—apparently the most cordial ally of the Mathers in the Boston ministry.

"With him," writes Sewall, "much primitive Christianity is gone. . . . His Prayers and Sermons were many times Excellent; not always alike. It may be this Lethargick Malady might though unseen, be the cause of some Unevenness. . . . We may justly fear he is taken away from Evil to Come. Isa. 57."

For about this time trouble in England was expected. But a few days later came welcome news that all tumults were quelled; with which on the 7th of October Sewall visited "utrumque Doctorem." [7]

Cotton Mather's Diary for 1715 is not preserved. But in the collection of the American Antiquarian Society are three long memoranda in his handwriting which bear this date. The first is a copy of a letter to a lady, not named; the following extract will give a notion of its general character:—

[5] See page 139.
[6] "And I will lay it waste; it shall not be pruned, nor digged; but there shall come up briers and thorns: I will also command the clouds that they rain no rain upon it."
[7] "Both doctors"; that is, the Mathers.

"If he [who now addresses you] be One who Looks upon Love to his Neighbour, as a very essential Article of his Religion, and who so Loves every man, that the offer of an opportunity for the doing of Good unto any One, is the sweetest pleasure that can be given him, . . . it will be very Reasonably Inferred from hence, that the Gentlewoman who comes one day into the nearest Relation unto him, will be Lov'd by him, as much as can be wish'd by her." And he waxes warm about "Your bright Accomplishments, your shining piety, and your polite education, your superiour Capacity, and a most refined Sense, and incomparable Sweetness of Temper, together with a Constellation of all the perfections that he can desire to see related unto him."

This letter is very long indeed; the second memorandum is short enough to be quoted in full:—

21d. 1m.[8] 1715. In the Evening.—After some Words of decent Respect unto Mrs. G.—She said, she had thought fitt, to have one Interview alone with me, that I might fully know her mind, about the Matter I had proposed unto her. She remonstrated the Reproach that she had suffered in the Talk of people about that affair; and therefore she thought it time, to lett me know her Desire, that she might hear no more of it, and that I would Speak and Think no more of it. She said, There were other persons that would be more agreeable to me; and in whom the prayers of many good people for me, would be more likely to be answered. She gave me to understand, That if it were not for a Regard she had unto my Character as a Minister, she should forbid my ever making any more Visits unto her. She said, My Visits would have been a consolation and satisfaction unto her if I had mentioned nothing of this affair: But she peremptorily forbad my Writing any more Letters unto her. She many times insisted on it, That I would say to all persons, As for the Matter talk'd of, there is nothing in it. I offered that I would say to All persons, Tis a Matter which Madam is not at present disposed to hear of. She then said:—But people will say, Why does she Entertain him?—if she have no purpose hereafter to allow of his Intentions?—This she express'd herself desirous, that there should be no Occasion for. I represented unto her, some fatal consequences, likely to follow on this conduct. But she would not admitt any Apprehensions of them. The Conversation lasted for several Hours. On my part, it was as Calm, and as pertinent, and as obliging as my dull Witts could render it. With as full Answers as could be made unto the Things that were objected to me; and just

[8] March 21st.

Reasons for every step of my conduct. At last I said; *Madam, To give you a full Testimony of my Honour and Esteem for you, My Satisfaction shall be entirely sacrificed unto Yours.* She answered: *Say and Hold.*

The third memorandum is a copy of a very long letter to the Rev. Thomas Craighead, who had proposed that the pair have another interview. Mather thinks it undesirable for the moment, but begs Craighead

to assure that excellent person, that my Resolutions to keep out of Sight . . . oppress my own mind with Violence, which could be well borne, by none but One of my Age, and one so much used unto Sacrifices. . . . She may depend upon it, (tho', I know not, whether a Total Deliverance from me, would not make her yett more easy,) that I can by no means lay aside these Vast Respects. But must renew my endeavours one day to make her yett more sensible of them. However, to be free with you, I have strong Apprehensions that my Dying Hour will Intervene (which, Oh! join with me in my praises to our dear Saviour for it,) I often even long for, and hope it will be the best Hour that ever I saw.

Who Mrs. G. was must remain a conjecture. But the following passage from Samuel Mather's book[9] is suggestive:—

In his *fifty-third* year, July 5. 1715. he was married to his *third* Wife. She is the Daughter of the renowned and very learned Mr. SAMUEL LEE: She was the Widow of Mr. GEORGE, a worthy Merchant, when Dr. MATHER pay'd his Respects unto her in order to be Marry'd. She is a Lady of many and great Accomplishments, and is the *Doctor's* disconsolate Widow.[10] By this last Gentlewoman he had *no* issue.

Cotton Mather's Diary for 1716[11] begins with a birthday fast, in which his most remarkable petitions were for

the Good State of my Family; the Welfare of my Son abroad; the Rescue of my Daughter-in-Law from her unhappy Circumstances; the comfortable Disposal of my Daughters in the Married Life.

And amid such daily notes of good devised as fill his other diaries are occasional memoranda concerning his family affairs.

[9] Life, p. 13.   [10] Samuel Mather wrote in 1729.
[11] In the Library of the Congregational House, Boston.

Early in March he held a very ecstatic thanksgiving, in which, among other things, he writes,

I celebrated the Favours of Heaven to my Family, especially in the Excellent Mother that He has bestowed upon it.

A marginal note, evidently made later, throws painful light upon this: "Ah! Quam deceptus." [12] A glimpse of the beginning of his undeception comes in the middle of April:—

My Religious and Excellent Consort meets with some Exercises, which oblige me, (and, oh! how happy am I, in the conversation of so fine a Soul, and one so capable of soaring to the higher Flights of piety!) To treat her very much on the point of having a Soul, wherein God alone shall be enthroned, and all the Creatures that usurped his Throne Ejected.

Sammy at this time was ill of a fever; and Increase, the subject of constant prayers and letters, was off on a voyage.

Early in May, however, an edifying incident occurred.

"A Wondrous Thing is come to pass," he writes on the 6th. "My Consort's only Daughter has had an Husband, who has proved one of the Worst of men; a sorry, sordid, froward, and exceedingly wicked Fellow. His Life would have kill'd the Child: and have utterly confounded, not only her Temporal Interest, but my Wife's also. I was a Witness of their Anguish, And almost a year ago, I began to have some Irradiations on my mind, which I communicated unto them, that before a year came about, they should see a Deliverance. However, I could not bring about my purposes, to beseech the Lord Thrice until towards the Beginning of the Winter. But then, I kept *Three dayes of prayer,* in every one of which, a principal errand unto Heaven was, to putt over this Wicked Creature into the Hands of the Holy God, that in His Way, and in His Time, the poor child might be delivered from his Insupportable Tyrannies. But above all, that it might be by his becoming a New Creature, if that might be obtained. The Supplications were made on these, and on other Dayes, with a proper spirit of Charity towards the miserable Man, and with all possible Resignation to the Will of God. And my excellent Consort often went up with me to my Library, to make a Consort in them. Well: I had no sooner kept my *Third Day* but God smote the Wretch, with a Languishing Sickness, which no body ever knew what to make of.

[12] "How I was deceived!"

He was a Strong, Lively, Hearty Young Man; a Little above Thirty: But now, he Languished for *Six Months;* nor were any of the physicians tho' he successively employ'd no less than five of them, able to help him. In this while, our Faith, our Love, our patience, and our Submission to the Will of God, underwent many Trials more precious than Gold. But on the last *Wednesday,* the Glorious God putt a period unto the grievous Wayes of this Wicked Man.—Now what remains, is for me to make a very holy Improvement of these Dispensations. . . . *"O my God, I will call upon thee, as long as I live!"*

The gentleman whose death is thus narrated was named Howell. Cotton Mather was made administrator of his estate. Resulting complications, such as often attend the efforts of unpractised people to manage money matters, made him uncomfortable for years.

It was during this same month of May that Katharine Mather's consumptive symptoms became alarming. And Katharine was very dear to her father: she "understood *Latin,* and read *Hebrew* fluently." [13] But other matters were less depressing. On the 22d, Cotton Mather writes:—

This Day my son Increase returns to me: much polished, much improved, better than ever Disposed, with Articles of less Expense to me than I expected: And, which is wonderful, with an excellent Business prepared for him immediately to fall into. I am astonished at the Favours of the prayer-hearing Lord. Oh my Father, my Father, how good a thing it is to trust in thy Fatherly Care!—But Oh! What shall I now do to fix the returned Child for the Service of God!

A week later, discovering that Samuel had many play days, he had the happy thought of occupying the youth in turning into Latin some sentences about "the true and right Intent of play, and a good use of it."

June found Katharine worse; and Increase in evident need of "Proper Books, to employ him in the Intervals of Business . . . , and furnish his mind with valuable Treasures." The elder Increase Mather, too, was ailing.

"My parent just finishing seventy-seven," writes Cotton Mather, "I must now more than ever treat him, as one taking Wing immediately for the Heavenly World."

[13] S. Mather, *Life,* p. 14.

Harvard College, too, was employing far too much time in "*Ethicks* . . . a vile piece of paganism." But although his troubles were enhanced by the fact that Nibby fell ill of an ague, he had the satisfaction of accepting for her the proposals of a "hopeful young Gentleman, a merchant," whose intimacy with the Mathers had "brought him into a Business, which is likely to prove Superiour unto what any young Man in the Country pretends unto." So "that it may be to his Advantage, in regard to his Better part," Cotton Mather immediately began to administer to him "continual Admonitions and Inculcations of piety." And mid-July found the good man in a thankful mood:—

Except it be the Sickness of my Two Elder Daughters, I enjoy upon all accounts a most wonderful prosperity. A most wonderful prosperity! A valuable Consort! A comfortable Dwelling! A kind Neighbourhood. My son *Increase*, vastly to my mind—and Blessings without Number. Together with my own Health and Strength, strongly recruited. I must be solicitous to hear what the Holy One speaks to me in my prosperity.

On the 14th of August, an accident happened to him, which Sewall briefly notes with the remark that he "received no hurt." But Cotton Mather took it seriously.

"This day," he writes, "a Singular Thing befel me. My God, Help me to understand the meaning of it! I was prevailed withal, to do a thing, which I very rarely do; (not once in years.) I rode abroad with some Gentlemen, and Gentlewomen, to take the Country Air, and to divert ourselves, at a famous Fish-pond. In the Canoe, on the pond, my foot slipt, and I fell overboard into the pond. Had the Vessel been a little further from the Shore, I must have been drown'd. But I soon recovered the Shore, and going speedily into a Warm Bed, I received no sensible Harm. I returned well in the Evening; sollicitous to make all the Reflections of piety, on my Disaster, and on my Deliverance. But not yett able to penetrate into the Whole meaning of the occurrence. Am I quickly to go under the earth, as I have been under the Water!—My Consort had her mind, all the former part of the day, and the day before, full of Uneasy Impressions, that this little Journey, would have mischief attending it."

The state of things in September is expressed by his note for the 18th:—

Of my Two Elder Daughters, The one I am giving up to God, and preparing for the Finishing Stroke of the Sacrifice, which the Death of the dear creature puts me upon. . . . The other, I am giving away to an hopeful young Gentleman, who is tomorrow to become her Husband.

Next day Abigail was married to Mr. Daniel Willard. But Katharine grew steadily worse. Her temper, however, was serene.

"Death is become Easy," he writes, "yea, pleasant unto her: she rather chuses it, and has a contempt for this World, and a most satisfying Vision of the Heavenly World. It is very Strange to me; The child feels herself a dying: but has a strong and bright persuasion of her own Recovery. I have none. I expect the Speedy approaches of Death upon her.—I sett apart this Day, for prayer with Fasting in Secret, on the behalf of the Dying Child. And it was a Day of Inexpressible Enjoyments unto me. I obtained pardon for all the Sins, that may have had a share in procuring my present Sorrows. I resigned the Child unto the Lord: My Will was extinguished. I could say *My Father, kill my Child, if it be thy pleasure to do so.* But yett I interceded, that if it might be so, the cup of Death might pass from me."

Through October she grew gradually worse. But Cotton Mather was gladdened by the arrival of Governor Shute.

"Our New Governour," he writes on the 25th, "appears to have a Singular Goodness of Temper, with a Disposition to Do Good, Reigning in Him: He also favours me with singular Testimonies of Regard. Oh! Let me improve these unexpected opportunities to do good, in such a manner that God may have much Glory, and His people much Service from it."

In November there was little new. Displeased with some proceedings in the House of Representatives, he sent for the members to visit him at his house.

"I would endeavour," he writes, "their Illumination in the things of our peace. I would also Endeavour to reduce our own Frowards from the Error of their way."

The administration of the Howell estate, too, looked as if it were drawing to a close; and he determined to propose to his wife

what special Service for God and His Kingdome she will do, in case
the Administration be well finished, and she find any Estate remaining,
that may render her Capable of doing anything.

But the most remarkable thing that happened this month was
the merciless blotting, with a madly scrawling pen, of two long
passages of Good Devised.

"I could never learn," he writes in the margin, "How or Why these
Blotts were made."

Two years later he discovered.

Meanwhile Katharine had been steadily ailing. On the 16th
of December came the end:—

A little before 3h. A. M. My Lovely Daughter Katharine expired
gloriously. The Things which her dear Saviour has done to her and
for her, Afford a Wonderful Story. . . . Much of my Time, of Late,
has been spent in Sitting by her with Essayes to Strengthen her in her
Agonies, wherein God graciously assisted me. . . . I have been for
many months a dying in my feeling the dying circumstances of my
lovely *Katy.* and now, this Last Night, she is actually Dead: But how
triumphantly did she go away!

And he made many pious resolutions on this occasion, especially in regard to Creasy, whose conduct worried him again.
There was another thing to worry him, too:—

"The Health of my Lovely Consort, who is the greatest of my Temporal Blessings, is a particular matter of concern unto me."

The remaining two months of the year passed quietly. His son-
in-law, Mr. Willard, gratified him by joining the church. And on
the 3d of February he could write thus:—

My Heart is exceedingly affected with my most comfortable and
undeserved Enjoyments in my Domestic Circumstances. I can scarce
desire to be better off, than I am, upon all accounts. An amiable
consort, agreeable Children, most accommodated Habitation, a plen-
tiful Table, The Respects of Kind Neighbours, a flourishing Auditory.
—I am even distressed, That I may render unto the Lord, according
to the Benefits which I have received from Him. Full of Thoughts,
what shall I do in a way of extraordinary Thankfulness and Fruitful-
ness: Full of cries to Heaven, that I may be Directed, Quickened, Assisted unto a Right Behaviour.

It was during this year 1716 that Cotton Mather reduced to writing the affidavit, officially certified, of how an apparition appeared to Anne Griffin and Ruth Weeden. This admirable ghost-story, very like De Foe's "Mrs. Veal," is printed in the Mather Papers.[14] A note of Sewall's for the 13th of February will fitly close the year:—

Susan brings word that Mr. Pemberton had a good night. . . . Yet afternoon am sent for to him as aproaching his end. When came was finishing his Will. Then I went in to Him: He call'd me to sit down by him, held me by the hand and spake pertinently to me, though had some difficulty to hear him. Mr. Sewall [15] pray'd fervently, and quickly after he expired, bolstered up in his Bed, about ¾ past 3 after noon in the best Chamber. . . . My Son writ a Letter to Dr. Cotton Mather to preach for him, and before 'twas superscrib'd, he came in, which took as a Token for good.

Cotton Mather's diary for 1717[16] begins with his remarks about Pemberton:—

Yesterday in the Afternoon, there died the elder Minister of the Old South Church; . . . who was eight or nine years younger than myself. He was a Man of greater Abilities than many others; and, no doubt, a pious man; but a man of a strangely Choleric and Envious Temper, and one who had created unto me more Trials of my patience, and more clogs upon my Opportunities to Do Good, than almost any man in the world. The younger minister of that church, a dear son, and One of an Excellent Spirit, should have preach'd this Day; But in his Distress he flies unto me to take his place in the public Services. I cannot easily reckon up the opportunities to Do Good, which I find concurring, in this one Invitation to public performance, on such an Occasion. And the Glorious Lord helped me to glorify Him, in the speaking of many Things to serve the General Interests of Religion, as well as in the Testimony which I gave to what was Laudable in the character of the Departed Minister. Præliminary to my public performance, . . . I humbled myself before the Lord, bewayling all the Distempers which the Ill Carriage of the Deceased Neighbour may at any time have thrown me into, and admiring the

[14] Pages 421-24.
[15] Joseph, son of the Judge, and Mr. Pemberton's colleague at the Old South.
[16] In possession of the American Antiquarian Society.

Divine Goodness and patience which has given me to outlive so many of my younger Brethren.

The year goes on with no more notable matters than a good devise to "Read a Chapter of Egardus unto my Lovely Consort every morning before we Rise"; and a troublesome accusation of idolatry, based on the fact that he spoke civilly to a ship-carver who had made a figure of St. Michael for the French provinces.

"Our Excellent Governor," he remarks in May, "who has delivered the Country from a Flood of corruption, which was introduced by the selling of places, is to be encouraged."

And on the 3d of July:—

"This Day being the Commencement, as they call it; a Time of much Resort unto Cambridge, and sorrily enough thrown away, I chose to spend this time at home," and to pray that "the Colledge, which is on many accounts in a very Neglected and unhappy condition . . . may be restored unto better circumstances."

But all along come notes that show domestic trouble. His family is much on his mind. Finally, on the 14th of July, he writes thus:—

"Suppose that a child of my Singular Love and Hope should so fall into Sin, and be after wondrous meanes of Recovery so abandoned of God, . . . that there may be terrible cause to fear lest he prove a cast-away; . . . what should be my Behaviour?" He must guard himself against rebellion of spirit, adore the divine sovereignty, lament his own sins thus chastised, mourn for the sins of the child, and never give over crying unto the Lord.

"My Son Increase!" he writes on the 23d, "With what plainness, . . . but yett with what prudence must I dispense . . . my Admonitions unto him. I take him into my Library; There I renew my Importunities: I obtain from him expressions of Repentance, and fitt Answers to the Demands of piety. I pray with him there, and make him see I feel my Agonies for him. . . . Methinks I hear the Glorious One saying to me, *Concerning thy Son I hear thee!*"

Other things troubled him, as the months went on: "the Venome and malice" of the "Disaffected Rulers of our Colledge," for one thing; his daughter Abigail bore his first grandchild; his consort was ill; Sammy's education puzzled him. Finally, in the middle of October, he felt that he must sett apart Three Days [*Beseech the Lord thrice!*] to extraordinary supplications that [Increase] may not go on in a course of Impiety.

The same week Sewall gives us another glimpse of him. Mrs. Sewall was very ill.

Oct. 17. I asked my wife whether twere best for me to go to Lecture: She said, I can't tell: so I staid at home. put up a Note. It being my Son's Lecture, and I absent, twas taken much notice of.—Oct. 19. Call'd Dr. C. Mather to pray, which he did excellently in the Dining Room, having Suggested good Thoughts to my wife before he went down. . . . About a quarter of an hour past four, my dear Wife expired.—Oct. 20. I goe to public Worship forenoon and Afternoon. My Son has much adoe to read the Note I put up, being overwhelmed with tears.

A week later Cotton Mather preached Mrs. Sewall's funeral sermon.

Meanwhile he had been filled with unhappy forebodings. A few more notes tell the story.

[Nov. 5.] The Evil that I greatly feared is come upon me. I am within these few hours astonished with an Information, that an Harlot big with a Bastard, Accuses my poor Son Cressy, and Lays her Belly to him. The most sensible Judges, upon the strictest Enquiry, beleeve the youth to be Innocent. But yett, oh! the Humiliation!—Oh! Dreadful Case! O sorrow beyond any that I have mett withal! What shall I do now for the foolish Youth! What for my Afflicted and Abased Family! My God, look mercifully upon me.

19. My God has not heard me. . . . My poor Son has made a worse Exhibition of himself unto me this day than I have ever yett mett withal. Oh my God, what shall I do! What shall I do! I will not yett utterly cast off the wretched child. But I will still follow Thee with supplications for what nothing but an Almighty Arm can accomplish.

Dec. 22. The aspect that some occurrences have upon me tells me, that I have not sufficiently repented of some Former Iniquities. . . . My God, help me, help me, to conform unto Thy Dispensations, and ly in the Dust before Thee!

His wife was ill, too: and though Sammy was the best boy imaginable, his education was puzzling. Then his "transcendently wicked brother-in-law" died, and he had to console the widow. February found him a little more calm, determining to have a cold bath set up for fever-patients; and, entreating of his "Discreet Consort" that she would plainly discover to him any traits of his that she would have otherwise, he had the satisfaction to be told of nothing. For his own part, he thought himself too touchy,—

tho' I must be blind indeed if I do not see . . . that . . . I meet with very odd, absurd, and froward usage from some of the people.

But perhaps the most permanently notable of his good devices for the year—he made at least one every day—was that which he made on the 2d of January.

"What shall I do," he asked himself that morning, "for the welfare of the College at New-Haven? I am inclinable to write unto a wealthy East-India merchant at London, who may be disposed on Several Accounts, to do for that Society and Colony."

The College in question had been founded in 1700:[17] without any endowment to speak of, it had distinguished itself from Harvard by maintaining, in pristine austerity, the Calvinism of the fathers. So the Mathers, and Sewall, and all who felt the old time passing from Massachusetts, looked with growing fondness to New Haven. The letter which Cotton Mather projected on the 2d of January, he wrote on the 18th.[18] It was to Elihu Yale. And among other arguments he urged was this:—

Sir, though you have your felicities in your family, which I pray God continue and multiply, yet certainly if what is forming at New Haven might wear the name of YALE COLLEGE, it would be better than *a name of sons and daughters.* And your munificence might easily obtain for you such a commemoration.

Yale thought so too: he gave a handsome gift to the College; and ever since, thanks to Cotton Mather, the greatest nursery of New England priesthood has borne his name.

"Yale College," wrote Cotton Mather to Governor Saltonstall next June, "cannot fail of Mr. Yale's generous and growing bounty. I confess that it was a great and inexcusable presumption in me, to make myself so far the godfather of the beloved infant as to propose a name for it. . . . [But] when the servants of God meet at your Commence-

---

[17] Quincy, I. 197-200; Palfrey, III. 343-45.
[18] Quincy, I. 226-29, 524-27.

ment, I make no doubt, that under your Honour's influences and
encouragements they will make it an opportunity . . . to deliberate
upon projections to serve the great interests of education, and so of
religion, . . . and not suffer an interview of your best men to evaporate
such a senseless, useless, noisy impertinency as it uses to do with us at
Cambridge."

How things were going at Cambridge appears from a long note
of Sewall's[19] in the following November. At a meeting of the
Overseers, to consider an enlargement of the College buildings,
Sewall arose and said that there was an affair of greater moment:
he understood that exposition of the Scriptures in the Hall had
not been carried on; he asked the President "whether 'twere so
or no." Leverett was much displeased at Sewall's manner, but
admitted the charge. After a hot discussion, Mr. Wadsworth
moved that "the president should *as* frequently *as he could* entertain the students with Expositions of the Holy Scriptures."

"I mov'd," writes Sewall, "that *as he could* might be left out; and
it was so voted. Mr. President seem'd to say softly, it was not till now
the Business of the President to Expound in the Hall. I said I was
glad the Overseers had now the Honour of declaring it to be the
President's duty."

Next day Leverett repeated his view in private to Sewall.

"I said," writes the sturdy Puritan, "Twas a shame that a Law
should be needed: meaning *ex malis moribus bonae leges.*" [20]

In 1718, too, another matter showed how far the College had
strayed from the polity of the fathers. A graduate named Pier-
pont was refused the Master's degree on the ground that he had
contemned and insulted the government of the College. He sued
for it at law, with the encouragement of the Mathers. And Cotton Mather wrote a long letter in his behalf to Governor Shute.
It was of no avail. The courts held that the matter was wholly
within the jurisdiction of the College authorities.[21] And this is
why, in 1718, Cotton Mather again and again bewails "the
wretched condition of the College." On the 2d of July,

this being the Day of the senseless Diversion they call the Commencement at Cambridge, one of my special errands unto Heaven

[19] Diary, III. 202, 203.   [20] "Good laws spring from evil practices."
[21] Quincy, Vol. I. Chap. XI.

was to ask Blessings for the Colledge, and the Rescue of it from some
wretched circumstances in which it is now languishing.

And now and again he has words of counsel for the "good,
wise, generous Governor," who, Sewall tells, "gave occasional
balls, and went to a horse-race."

Cotton Mather's diary for 1718[22] contains good devices for
every day in the year. It shows his marvellous activity and rest-
lessness at its highest point. But what seems nearest to him is the
condition of his family. His aged parent was on his mind more
and more; he prayed and struggled for Increase with agonizing
efforts to achieve an assurance that after all the boy should be
saved; and now and again comes the single cry, "My God! My
God!" Once he writes,

Things appeared unto me, as if the Holy Ghost, were coming forth,
to take a terrible Vengeance on me for the sins which my life has
been filled withal; yea, and as if my Death being at hand I am to
Dy on Ill Terms with Heaven, and have the dreadful portion of the
Hypocrites assigned unto me.

There are one or two curious notes,—one showing his feeling
toward the mother country he never saw: he will write "home,"
he plans, about Jacobite troubles. And late in the year he projects
something he never executed,—an

Enchiridion of the Liberal Sciences . . . which might enable persons easily to attain them: and at the same time consecrate the whole
Erudition unto the Designs of piety.

But throughout the year one feels a growing trouble, and
knows not quite what it is. This note, written on the 18th of
November, is typical:—

My Family is in astonishing circumstances. O! the patience, the
prudence, the prayer that is called for. If it were not for my calling
of a glorious Christ into my mind continually, and the visits which He
graciously makes unto my poor, sinful, sickly soul, what, what would
become of me! I here leave this testimony to you, my children, or
whosever Hands these papers may fall into: That a glorious Christ
conversed withal, will be the life of the Soul that has Him dwelling
in it.

[22] In possession of the Massachusetts Historical Society.

On the 18th of January the volume suddenly breaks off, with
a resolution to read Thomas à Kempis,

a Book of piety, which tis observable, all Christians of all comunions
have approved and valued.

A little volume of seven leaves, entitled, "The Conclusion of
the LVI. Year," [23]—preserved quite separately from the rest,—
tells the secret.

"21d. xim. 1718. Wednesday," runs the first entry. "My Glorious
Lord has inflicted a New and a Sharp Chastisement upon me. The
consort in whom I flattered myself with the View and Hope of an
Uncommon Enjoyment, has dismally confirmed it unto me, that our
Idols must prove our *Sorrow*. Now and then, in some of the former
years I observed and suffered grievous outbreakings of her proud pas-
sions; but I quickly overcame them with my victorious Love, and in
the Methods of Meekness and Goodness. And, *O my SAVIOUR, I
ascribe unto thee all the glory of it, and I wondrously praise thee for
it:* I do not know, that I have to this Day spoke one Impatient or Unbecoming Word unto her; tho' my provocations have been unspeakable; and it may be few men in the World, would have borne them
as I have done. But this last Year has been full of her prodigious
paroxysms, which have made it a year of such Distresses unto me, as
I have never seen in my Life before. When the paroxysms are gone
off, she has treated me still with a Fondness, that it may be, few
Wives in the World have arrived unto. But in the Return of them
(which of late still grow more and more frequent) she has insulted
me with such Outrages, that I am at a loss, which I should ascribe
them to: Whether a Distraction which may be somewhat Hæredi-
tary,) or to a possession; (whereof the symptoms have been too dire-
ful to be mentioned.) In some other papers[24] I leave a more particular
Account of these Things. But what I have here to Relate is: That she
had expressed such a Venome, against my Reserved Memorials, of
experiences in, and projections for, the Kingdom of God, as has
obliged me to Lay the Memorials of this year, I thought, where she
would not find them. It has been a year wherein I have made more
Advances in piety, than in many former years. Perhaps, my Journey
thro' the Wilderness just expiring, I must ride more way in one year
now than in forty before. . . . For every Day I have noted, my purposes of Service for the Kingdom of God. For fear of what might

---

[23] In possession of the Massachusetts Historical Society.
[24] These papers I have not come across.

happen, I have not one disrespectful word of this proud woman, in all the papers. But this week, she has in her Indecent Romaging found them, and she not only detains them from me, but either she has destroy'd them, or she does protest, that I shall never see them any more. I have offered unto her, to blott out with her pen whatever she would not have to be there. But no loving Entreaties of Mine can prevail upon her to Restore them. Only, she gives me hope of Restoring some time or other, the papers of the Four or Five preceding years, which this ungentlewomanly woman has also stolen. . . . I have Lived for near a year in a continual Anguish of Expectation, that my poor Wife, by exposing her Madness, would bring a Ruine on my Ministry. But now it is Exposed, my Reputation is marvellously preserved among the people of God, and there is come such a General and Violent Blast upon her own, as I cannot but be greatly troubled at. I will now go on."

And go on he does, with good devices for every day until his next birth-day. But the secret was out. His wife was mad; and mad she remained all the rest of his life.

XIII. *Inoculation.*

1721   The history of Massachusetts during the ten remaining years of Cotton Mather's life concerns us little. In 1720,
Joseph Dudley died, in his last days weak as a child. Amid increasing troubles with the legislature, Shute remained Governor
until the death of George I.; but during the last years of
his office he was in England, and Lieutenant Governor Dum-
mer in charge of affairs at home. There were troubles with
Jesuits and Indians in Maine; there were financial difficulties,
and disputes about official salaries; there were squabbles about
the seizure of timber for the Royal Navy. George II.'s first Governor was William Burnet, still in office when Cotton Mather
died. Our business now is to follow Cotton Mather to his end.
In this chapter I shall tell of his life to the end of 1721.

His diaries for 1719 and 1720 are not preserved: nor do I find
any record of these years that shows him other than what we
have seen. Eternally busy with his preaching, his writing, his
reading, his scientific study, his endless projects to do what he
thought was good; perplexed with the growing infirmities of his
aged parent, with the periodic madness of his wife, with the constant misconduct of Increase, he passed through his fifty-seventh
and fifty-eighth years. And in 1721, like loyal sons of Harvard
since his time, he sent Sam to college there, with cordial letters
to a President of whom he heartily disapproved.

His diary for 1721[1] records one of the busiest and most useful
years of his life. The daily notes of good devices, for all manner
of things and people in all parts of the world, crowd the pages.

[1] In possession of the Massachusetts Historical Society.

But month by month there are notes of other matters. It may perhaps be best to glance at them month by month.

In March, busy as ever, he felt his family much on his mind; and one good device is worth remembering: new accomplishments for Cressy must be paid for,—"to render him a more finished gentleman [Oh! when, when shall I say Christian!]" So too is a note that recalls the death of Howell:[2] a "wicked party" had been raising trouble in the country, and Cotton Mather had prayed earnestly against them; this month one of their leaders was stricken with apoplexy.

"Methinks," writes the life-long foe of witchcraft, "I see a wonderful token for Good in this matter; and I go on with my Humble Supplications to the Lord."

Early in April, Increase was arrested for night-riot with "some detestable rakes in the Town."

"What, what shall I do!" writes his poor father. "How shall I glorify my Just, Wise, Dear Saviour on this deplorable occasion. And what is my Duty in relation to the Incorrigible prodigal."—"I must chase him out of my sight," he writes, a few days later, "forbid him to see me, until there appear sensible marks of repentance upon him. Nevertheless, I will entreat his Grandfather to take pains for his Recovery."—"I will write a tremendous letter to my wicked son Increase," comes still later; . . . "I will tell him that I will never . . . look on him, till the characters of a penitent are very conspicuous in him. . . . Lord, Tho' I am a Dog, yett cast out the Devil that has possession of the Child."—"Ah, poor Increase!" he writes at last, "Tho' I spake against him, yett I earnestly remember him, and my Bowels are troubled for him."

Nor was this the only trouble now: many of his flock were leaving for another church, which vexed him sorely. He comforted himself with this reflection:—

I shall enjoy a bright conformity to my Saviour, . . . if, just before my Death, I suffer a general withdrawal of my hearers from me.

But old Increase Mather was not so patient:—

My aged father laies to heart the withdrawal of a vain, proud, foolish people from him in his age.

[2] See page 189.

There is one charming note in May:—

> The Time of the year arrives for the glories of Nature to appear in my Garden. I will take my Walks there, on purpose to read the glories of my Saviour in them.

But that very week there was calamity abroad. His note for the 26th of May is probably the most memorable he ever made. He wrote good devices every day, we must remember. Hundreds of these and thousands came, for all we know, to nothing; but the one he made this day was of lasting good to humanity:—

> G. D. The grievous Calamity of the Small-pox has now entered the Town. The practice of conveying and suffering the Small-pox by Inoculation has never been used in America, nor indeed in the Nation. But how many lives might be saved by it, if it were practiced. I will . . . consult our physicians, and lay the matter before them.

The pestilence was very severe: it aroused the best activities of his nature. Nowhere else in his records does he show himself so free from morbid introspection, so active in self-forgetful altruism, as now. And in June, he laid before the physicians his suggestion of inoculation. He had read of it, I believe, in some papers of the Royal Society; and his early training as a physician gave him authority.[3] But the proposal was startling to many of the learned, and to all the vulgar. "It raised an horrid Clamour."

In July, this clamour was all about him. Quarrels with his stepchildren, the Howells, whose estate he had tried to administer, vexed him, at the same time; to meet their claims, he had even to sell some of his clothing. But what troubled him most was the panic of the plague-stricken town.

"The cursed clamour of a people strangely and fiercely possessed of the Devil will probably prevent my saving the Lives of my Two Children from the Small-pox in the way of Transplantation." And he prayed, "that God would requite me good for all the cursing of a people that have Satan filling of them; and yett appear, to rescue, and increase my opportunities to Do Good, which the great adversary is now making an Hellish Assault upon." He was assailed with "wild

---

[3] The American Antiquarian Society preserves a large manuscript of Cotton Mather's entitled the "Angel of Bethesda." Valueless to-day, this is said to be a good manual of contemporary medicine.

abuse . . . for nothing but instructing our base physicians, how to
save many precious lives"; but at the end of the month he could write
thus: "I must exceedingly Rejoice in my Conformity to my Admirable Saviour: who was thus, and worse Requited, when he . . . came
to save their Souls."

So came August. His son Samuel wished to be inoculated. But
if the boy should die, thought the father,

the people, who have Satan remarkably filling their hearts, . . . will
go on with infinite prejudices against me and my ministry. . . . His
Grandfather advises, That I keep the whole proceeding private, and
that I bring the Lad into this method of Safety. My God, I know not
what to do!
"It is the Hour . . . of Darkness on this Despicable Town," he
wrote later; but drew his pen through "Despicable" and wrote "miserable" instead.

In the middle of the month, he yielded to Sam's request, and
the lad was inoculated. He sickened so fast and so severely that
his father was seized with a dread that perhaps, before the inoculation, the poor boy had already contracted the disorder. And the
panic against inoculation rose so that the town became "almost
an Hell on Earth." Nancy came down with the pestilence, too;
and as the month went on, both grew worse. Yet in all his agony,
and with such execrations about him as even in his troublous life
he had hardly heard before, he resolved that he would write to
England, urging that they try inoculation there. So, with prayers,
and faith amid every doubt, he did his duty: and at the very end
of the month came relief. Opening his Bible for comfort, Cotton
Mather's eye fell on the words, "Go thy way, Thy Son liveth."
And that very day Sam was bled, and began to mend. Inoculation
had triumphed.

In September, both Sam and Nancy were convalescent; but
a new trial came. There was an interval of comfort; Cotton
Mather preached for the bereaved minister of the New North
Church,—the church of the "swarming brethren,"—thereby in-
troducing "a more peaceable condition of Things in our
Churches." But Increase began to misbehave again; and on the
19th, Abigail died in childbed. Cotton Mather's last prayer for the
month is typical of his mood:—

"That I may humble myself before the Lord," it runs, "for all the
Sins which the Death of my dear Nibby calls me to repentance for.
That I may obtain mercy for the Family that she has left behind her.
That Nancy may have a perfect recovery; Creasy be made a New
Creature; Liza have her life preserved in the Dangers of the Contagion;
and Sammy be bless'd in his Education. That I may be supported and
preserved in my daily Visits to the Sick Chambers that are so lothsome, and full of Malignity. That I may be directed, assisted, prospered in my whole Ministry. And have a particular Smile of Heaven
on the Essays I am now sending Beyond sea to serve the Kingdom of
God."

And this troubled month he gave no less than three publications to the press.

Early in October comes a different note. Three of his children
lived with him, and a kinswoman of his wife's.

Tho' I will have my Table Talk Facetious as well as Instructive,
. . . yett I will have the Exercise continually intermixed. I will sett
before them some sentence of the Bible, and make some useful Remarks upon it.

The pestilence was at its height, though: in one week 315
petitions for prayer were put up in the North Church; the next
week, 322. And Increase Mather, in his sorrowful old age, was
now "wholly Laid by from all public service." Cotton Mather
struggled hard. The petition for prayers fell to 180. But at the
end of the month he wrote:—

In my Remarks on the Folly and Baseness continually expressed by
our Absurd and wicked people, I do not always preserve that meekness of Wisdom, which would adorn the Doctrine of God my Saviour.
I will ask Wisdom of God for the cure of this Distemper.

What happened in November he shall tell for himself:—

My Kinsman, the Minister of *Roxbury*, being entertained at my
House, that he might there undergo the Small-pox *Inoculated,* and so
Return to the Service of his Flock, which have the contagion begun
among them: Towards Three a clock in the Night, as it grew towards
the Morning of this Day,[4] some unknown Hands, threw a Fired
Granado into the Chamber where my kinsman lay, and which uses
to be my Lodging-Room. The Weight of the Iron Ball alone, had it

[4] 14 November, 1721.

fallen upon his Head, would have been enough to have done part of
the Business designed. But the Granado was charged, the upper part
with dried powder, the lower part with Oil of Turpentine, and powder
and what else I know not, in such a manner that upon going off, it
must have splitt, and have probably killed the persons in the Room,
and certainly fired the Chamber, and speedily Laid the House in
Ashes. But, *this Night there stood by me the Angel of GOD, whose
I am and whom I serve;* and the Merciful providence of my SAVIOUR
so ordered it, that the Granado passing thro' the Window, had by
the Iron in the middle of the Casement, such a Turn given to it, that
in falling on the Floor, the fired wild-fire in the Fuse was violently
shaken out upon the Floor, without firing the Granado. When the
granado was taken up, there was found a paper so tied with string
about the fuse that it might out-live the breaking of the shell,—which
had these words in it:—*Cotton Mather, you Dog; Damn you: I'l
enoculate you with this, with a pox to you.*

Cotton Mather had read Foxe's Martyrs all his life. This attack
was such as had been made on the saints in Queen Mary's days,
and older still; he was almost a martyr.

"I would much rather Dy for my Conformity to the Blessed JESUS,"
he wrote, "in Essays to save the Lives of Men from the Destroyer,
than for some Truths, tho' precious ones, to which many Martyrs testified formerly in the Flames of Smithfield."

And he closed the month by publishing far and wide accounts
of inoculation,

by Which means, I hope, some hundreds of thousands of lives may
in a little while come to be preserved.

December brought lesser troubles. An enemy, to deride him,
named a troublesome slave "Cotton Mather"; but he placed his
hope in heaven, and prayed especially for "the welfare of the
unknown person, who sought my Death by the fired Granado."
And this month comes almost the last glimpse we have of the
riotous young Increase:—

My son Increase, by a violent and passionate Resentment of an In-
dignity, which a wicked Fellow offered unto me, has exposed himself
to much Danger, and me also to no little Trouble. I must employ this
occasion as much to his Advantage, especially in regard to piety, as I
can.

The month ended with reaction:—

By a dark and a faint Cloud striking over my Mind, I begin to feel some Hazards, lest my Troubles, whereof I have a greater share than any Minister in the Countrey, grow too hard for me, and unfit me and unhinge me for my Services.

And in January he told an assembly of ministers that his efforts to do good had brought obloquy on him and destroyed his usefulness. Hereafter he would follow good schemes, not propose them.

An Ingenious person in the company, Mr. Wm. Cooper, made the first and a quick Reply, . . . in these Words, *I hope the Devil don't hear you, Syr.*

The last note for the year fitly closes the record:—

The year being so finished, what can I do better than seriously peruse the memorials of it, and make the Reflections of piety that may be proper upon them.

XIV. *The Death of Increase Mather.*

1722-1723 In the year 1722, a startling thing happened at Yale College. The Rev. Timothy Cutler, who had been a successful President there for several years, announced his conversion to the Church of England. He was relieved of his office, and proceeded to England: whence by and by he came back as an Episcopal clergyman to Boston.

Whether this fact had anything to do with what went on at Harvard I cannot say. In the time that had intervened since Leverett had been made President, the course of things there had been wholly in the direction of the liberalism, which in growing and changing forms has constantly characterized the older College. As we have seen, the sympathy of whoever held faithfully to the old traditions of New England had been more and more directed to Yale. Quincy[1] shows good reason for supposing that Cotton Mather, without due openness, tried hard to divert thither at least a part of the benefactions of Thomas Hollis. This gentleman, a Baptist merchant of London, was in his time the most generous friend Harvard College had ever had. And the effort which the Orthodox clergy of Massachusetts made to confine the Professorship of Divinity that Hollis founded to their own creed—a creed distinctly different from his—is among the least admirable features of their hopeless struggle to maintain priestly authority in a state committed to constantly more advanced Protestantism.

The passage I cited from Sewall,[2] describing his controversy with Leverett in the Board of Overseers, relates one incident of a controversy that was going on at Harvard. Quincy[3] tells the

[1] Vol. I. Chapter XII.   [2] See page 198.   [3] Vol. I. Chapter XIII.

story in detail. The Corporation consisted chiefly of men in sympathy with Leverett; Colman, for example, was now a Fellow. Two tutors, apparently of more conservative temper, advanced a claim to seats in the Corporation. A fierce dispute broke out, of which the details need not concern us. One of its features, however, was an official inquiry into the actual state of the College, educational, religious, and moral. This was in progress throughout the year 1723: and Cotton Mather eagerly urged it on. His suggestions on points to be inquired into, Quincy prints in full. It seems possible that the state of the "beloved infant" Yale led him to hope for a return of grace to the mother Harvard.

In the beginning of this paper is a phrase which refers to the event of this year which meant most to Cotton Mather:—

The performances of a deceased person, and with what industry and fidelity the churches of New England were served in them, 'tis too late to inquire into.

The deceased person was Increase Mather. The old man had died on the 23d of August, 1723.

Cotton Mather gives a long account of his father's latter days;[4] of the constancy and method of his devotions and studies; of his benign charity,—a trait of which I find little trace elsewhere; of the grave civility of his carriage in all departments of life. His faults the pious son passes lightly: were it not for Sewall's diary, and the frequent allusions to "my aged parent" in Cotton Mather's own, we should not have the painful picture I can dimly see of the austere Puritan's sad old age. He had given the best energies of a life that had been among the most laborious of his time, to the Colony and the Province and the churches of Massachusetts. He had won for the people the Charter under which they lived less fettered, I believe, than any other colonists in the world. And his reward had been neglect. Political power, Harvard College, his very congregation, had one after the other been withdrawn from him. And plagued with the pains of pedantic old age, he had diffused about his last years, I fear, an atmosphere free from moral or spiritual exhilaration. The greatest of his trials, the most mysterious of all the dispensations he had to bear, was the disappointment of the greatest particular faith of his life. Again

[4] Parentator, XXXI., XXII.

and again, wrestling with the Lord, he had been assured that he should once more serve God in England. His son had shared his faith and his assurances. But they came to nothing. The College fell back to the old charter that fatally failed to secure it to the faith of the fathers. And what God meant, neither of the Mathers could ever guess. There is pathos in Cotton Mather's last note about the matter: after all, was not the faith perhaps fulfilled when, in 1715, an assembly of ministers asked Increase Mather to bear a formal address of congratulation to George I.?

A few of his last speeches Cotton Mather preserves. Of Boston he said,

"There is yet a number of Godly People in the town; they may be brought low, But the Town shall be yet preserved": of the times in general, "There will be no settled Good Times, I suppose, till the second coming of the Lord."

It was he who drew up a loyal address for the Ministers of Boston to King George, delivered from some Jacobite plot. And in the last year of his life he wrote a solemn paper, briefly asserting the old principles of New England, to maintain which the Colony and the College had been planted; and earnestly charging posterity with the duty of preserving them.

In his last days, grievously plagued with the stone, his spirit, like his father's before him, sank low.

In a deep Aybss of Humility, there was utterly Absorb'd with him all *Sense* of his *ever having done any good at all* in the World.

And he prayed, and begged those about him unceasingly to pray for the free grace of Christ. And hearing that Thomas Hollis had written to ask if he were yet in the land of the living, he bade his son write back:—

No, Tell him I am going to it; This Poor World is the Land of the Dying.

Late in July Sewall wrote thus:—

Fast at the Old North. As I went along towards Cambridge-Court, I called at the old Doctor's who was agonizing and Crying out, Pity me! Pity me! I told him God pity'd him, to which he assented and seemed pacify'd. He prayed God to be with me.[5]

---

[5] Diary, III. 325.

He lived three weeks longer. This is his son's account of his end:—

At last, he began to fall into the Torments of the *Wheel broken at the Cistern:* Which yet became not Intolerable, and forced no Ejaculation from him till about *Three Weeks before he Died.* Under these, about *Three Days* before his Expiration, coming out of a Dark Minute, he said, *It is now Revealed from Heaven to me, That I shall quickly, quickly, quickly be fetch'd away to Heaven, and that I shall Dy in the Arms of my Son.* After this, he kept very much calling for me; till *Friday, the Twenty-Third* of *August,* 1723, in the Morning perceiving the *Last Agonies* now come upon him, I did what I could after my poor manner, that he might be *Strengthened* by such *Quickening Words* as the *Lively Oracles* of our GOD have provided for such Occasions. As it grew towards Noon, I said unto him, *Syr, the Messenger is now come to tell you,* This Day thou shalt be in Paradise. *Do you Believe it, Syr, and Rejoice in the Views and Hopes of it?* He Replied, *I do! I do! I do!*—And upon these Words he *Dyed in my Arms.*

Posterity has inclined to deem him a cunning schemer, justly disappointed in such ambition as to-day not a few among us attribute to the priesthood of Rome. That he earnestly longed to see the temporal power of America at the feet of the spiritual, no man can doubt; nor yet that he saw in himself the man who should by right stand at the head of the spiritual power of his time and country. And there will always be men, and many, who cannot believe that such views can be held for any other reason than vulgar longing for human power. But whoever has followed the history of Harvard College, through Unitarianism, to that more shadowy heresy still which calls itself unsectarian religion, —even though he rejoice, as I do, in the unfettered spiritual freedom of the greatest stronghold of American Protestantism,—must know that the grim old man read the future right. If the faith from which he never swerved be true, then assuredly we of the later times are lost. And those who can train themselves to that sympathy without which no man can understand his fellows will not forget, when they sit to judge the greatest of the native Puritans, that not one of his efforts to preserve and strengthen his earthly authority was not also an effort to make their lives, and all the lives still to come, lives which should tread in the paths of salvation.

So, after nearly eighty-four busy, troubled years, he came to his peace. And so the son, who had never faltered in devotion, who for well on to forty years had shared every hope and grief with an affection as brotherly as it was filial, was left alone, to struggle with a world which all his life had been pressing onward from the station where his feet were planted. With a mad wife, with but four of his fifteen children left him, with his eldest son —and to the end his dearest—straying further and further towards perdition, with the New England churches ever straying further and further from the holy traditions they were founded to preserve, Cotton Mather was left alone.

XV. *The Last Diary of Cotton Mather.*

1724   The last of Cotton Mather's diaries preserved is
that for 1724.[1] The daily notes of good devices continue until
November, when a sharp fit of illness broke them off. And when
he grew better, and began to write once more, in a style whose
incoherence shows how his troubles had shaken him at last,
his first note tells that he will record his good devices no more;
in the little time left him on earth, there are other things that
call for every moment.

It was a troubled year, this 1724. Yet his first note is not a
troubled one. On his birthday he held a fast as ecstatic as any he
had known; and among his works for the day was the long Latin
epitaph with which he ended the life of his father,—the book
from which my picture of the old man has chiefly been drawn,
and the book which shows how firmly, even in his closing years,
Cotton Mather still held the faith which had governed his whole
life. And a little later he had a satisfaction: forty years before,
Increase Mather had preached against suicide a sermon insti-
gated by the act of one Taylor, father of the Lieutenant Governor to be, who had hanged himself with a snaffle-bridle. Another
notable suicide now occurring, Sewall sent to Cotton Mather,
asking whether the sermon were preserved. Cotton Mather found
it almost at once: Sewall had it published.[2] And so Increase
Mather though dead, still spoke to the people of New England.[3]
But there were many things to vex Cotton Mather, too: Increase
was gone to sea; the troubles about the administration of How-

[1] In possession of the Massachusetts Historical Society.
[2] Sewall's Diary, III. 331, 332.   [3] See page 21.

ell's estate went so far that writs against Mather were issued;[4]
and in his house was a niece of his wife,—

a very wicked Creature, and not only deaf to all proposals of piety,
but also a monstrous Liar, and a very mischievous person, and a Sower
of Discord, and a Monster of Ingratitude.

Nor did discord need to be sown in the unhappy house: Mrs.
Mather's paroxysms were worse than ever. Again and again this
year come Latin notes, telling under the thin veil of that learned
tongue what the horrors of his last marriage were.

Another matter which troubled him much he mentions thus:—

"I hear of strong Machinations and Expectations among the wicked
Church of England Men, to gett our Colledge into their hands; which
will be a most compendious way to bring Quick Ruine on our
Churches. I would apply myself with all proper Awakenings to the
men at Helm on this Occasion." And next day he would "sollicit for
Days of prayer . . . in the Colledge-Hall, on the Occasion of the
condition . . . it is . . . exposed unto."

The state of affairs was this. The Rev. Timothy Cutler, the
converted President of Yale, had come from England to Boston,
as Episcopal Rector of Christ Church,—the church from which
fifty years later, by a curious irony of fate, the lantern was shown
that sent Paul Revere galloping to Lexington and Concord. One
Mr. Myles was Rector of King's Chapel, the official place of
worship of the royal Governor. As "ministers of Boston," these
gentlemen claimed seats in the Board of Overseers of Harvard
College;[5] and though their claim was never allowed, it was urged
until after Cotton Mather was dead. And it had to be fought
hard.

It was this, among other things, which led Cotton Mather
to that day of meditation of which Upham has published the
greater part of the record.[6] He asked himself question after question about his earthly state, and gave answers; of which this is
an example:—

---

[4] The two Howells, who made all his trouble, were drowned, while skating
at the foot of Boston Common, Jan. 8, 1727-8. Sewall's Letter-Book, II.
307.
[5] Quincy, Vol. I. Chapter XVII.   [6] Salem Witchcraft, II. 503, *seq.*

What has a gracious God given me to do in *good offices* wherever I could find opportunities for the doing of them? I for ever entertained them with alacrity. . . . And yet I see no man for whom all are so loth to do good offices. . . . Often have I said, What would I give if there were any one man in the world to do for me what I am willing to do for every man!

But Upham thought irrelevant and not worth quoting the close of these meditations.

I have a clear and strong persuasion of a *Future State* . . . I do most freely . . . consent unto the condition of a *crucified man*, . . . without any prospect of any Outgate, but at and by the Dying Hour. Yea, Secondly, I have already received an abundant *Recompense of Christ*. . . . If I never had any other compensation for my Troubles, I have had so much, that I need not ask for any more.

Which words and others like them make the passage seem to me other than to Upham: he finds in it a confession of selfish wickedness which deliberately sacrificed human life in the witchcraft trials, two and thirty years before.

What Cotton Mather had to bear from his wife, these two notes tell:—

August 13. "This night my unaccountable Consort, had a prodigious return of her pangs upon her. . . . After a thousand unrepeatable Invectives, compelling me to Rise at Midnight, and retire to my Study that I might there pour out my Soul before the Lord; she also gott up in a horrid Rage, protesting that she would never Live or Stay with me; and calling up her wicked Niece and Maid, she went over to a Neighbour's House for a Lodging. . . . I, with my Son *Samuel*, and my daughter *Hannah*, retired up to my Library, where we together . . . poured out our Supplications. Towards the morning, I went unto my Bed, and enjoy'd some Repose. . . . What was pretended as the Introduction to the present, was, That, forsooth, for a Day or two, my Looks and Words were not so very kind as they had been."

August 23. "In the Evening, . . . my poor Wife, returning to a Right Mind, came to me in my Study, entreating that there might be Eternal Oblivion of every thing that had been out of point; . . . and that for the . . . further obtaining of this Felicity, I would now join with her in pouring out Supplications to the Lord. . . . I did accordingly. And the Tokens of the greatest Inamoration on her part ensued upon it."

Meanwhile another trial was in progress. On the 3d of May, John Leverett, President of Harvard College, was found dead in his bed. On the 6th, he was buried, and Cotton Mather was one of his bearers. Next day, Mather writes:—

"The sudden death of that unhappy man who sustained the place of president in our colledge, will open a Door for my doing of Singular Services to the Best of Interests. Indeed his being within a year of the same Age with myself loudly calls upon me to live in a daily expectation of my own call from hence. . . . I do not know that the care of the colledge will be now cast upon me: tho' I am told, it is what is most generally wished for. If it should, I shall be in abundance of Distress about it. But if it should not, I may do many things for the good of the colledge, more quietly and more hopefully than formerly. . . . Why may I not write unto the tutors . . . , and Sollicit . . . That they would exert their powers to make the Students, become indeed what they are called, and spend . . . their Time well; and therefore not content themselves with the daily Recitations (the matter of which also, ought to be further considered) but assign them suitable Books to read, and see that they Read them. That they encourage Sodalities among them; to meet every week for the Communications of their Acquisitions to one another. That they Countenance Industry, with distinguished Rewards . . . to the Meritorious. That they bring up the use of the Latin Tongue in Conversation among the Scholars. That above all things, they do what may be done for the Animation . . . of PIETY among the young men: . . . cast a kind Aspect on those who Associate for Devotions; and . . . establish them in the *Faith and Order of the Gospel*, in which the Churches of *New England* have their Beauty and their Safety."

August 12. "I am now informed that the Six Men who call themselves the Corporation of the Colledge mett, and contrary to the Epidemical Expectation of the Countrey, chose a modest young man, of whose piety (and little else) every one gives a laudable character. I always foretold these Two Things of the Corporation: First, That if it were possible for them to steer clear of me, they will do so. Secondly, That if it be possible for them to act Foolishly, they will do so. . . . It proves accordingly. Now, tho' the senseless Management of these men threatens little short of a Dissipation to the Colledge, yett I have personally unspeakably to admire the compassion of Heaven to me on this occasion. Tho' I have been a Man of Sorrows and acquainted with Griefs, yett none of the least Exercises I have met withal, was the Dread of what the Generality of sober people . . . desired: the Care of the Colledge. . . . I had a Dismal Apprehension of the Distresses, which a call to Cambridge would bring upon me. . . . But the Sleight and the Spite of my Six Friends, has produced for me an Eternal Deliverance. I doubt, I have expressed myself with a little too much Alacrity on this Occasion. Lord, help me to a wise Behaviour!"

Next day he wrote: "G. D. Hasten, Hasten, O Slothful Mather, in dispatching thy Treatise of Advice to the Candidates of the Ministry. Thou mayest thereby do more Good, than Twenty presidents of Colledges."

That very night was the one when his wife left his house.

A month later, he had another meditation about the College: Had the care of it come to him, it might have worried him to death; and who knows but the Lord, designing shortly to call him from earth, purposely delivered the College from a fresh inconvenience? Again, though as President he might have served God, the

Grace which I have already received in that kind, especially considering my prodigious unworthiness, may well be sufficient for me. . . . Finally, The preferring of a Child before me as my Superiour in Erudition, or in Capacity . . . to manage the Government of an Academy, or in piety and Gravity, This is what . . . it would be a Crime in me to be disturbed at.

The "Child" in question was Joseph Sewall, son of the Judge, and minister of the Old South Church. He declined the office. In November the Corporation met again.

"The Corporation of our Miserable Colledge," write Cotton Mather, "do again (upon a Fresh Opportunity) treat me with their accustomed Judgment and Malignity But Oh! may I take pleasure in the Opportunity I have to glorify my God and Saviour."

The choice of the Corporation fell on Colman, who also declined. It was not until June, 1725, that a President was finally found: it was Benjamin Wadsworth, who held office till after Cotton Mather died.

Meanwhile, in August, just when his wife was at her worst, had come a harder blow still. On the 20th he writes:—

While I am this morning, about projecting of Services for the Kingdom of GOD . . . I have sad Advice of His going on to pull down mine [House], with dreadful Dispensations. . . . My son *Increase* is Lost, is Dead, is Gone. The Ship wherein he was bound from *Barbadoes* to *St. Peter's,* had been out five Months . . . ; and some singular circumstances of the Vessel also . . . confirm the Apprehension that it is perished in the Sea. Ah! my Son Increase! My Son, My Son! My Head is Warm, and my Eyes are a Fountain of Tears. —I am overwhelmed!—And this at a Time when the Domestic Inhumanities and Diabolisms which I am treated withal, are so Insupportable!—Oh my God, I am oppressed: undertake for me.—But the Soul of the Child!—If the purposes which he left in my Hands were Sincere, and His Heart went with his pen,—All is well!—Would not my God not have me to hope so?—My Saviour yett affords me this Light in my Darkness, that He enables me, to offer up all the Sacrifices He calls me to.

In September came a rumour that, after all, the ship in which Increase sailed was safe; but a day or two later comes this note:—

"The Good News of poor Creasy's being Rescued and Releeved from Death is all come to nothing: Twas another Vessel. *O my Father, Thy Will be done.*"

Later still comes a supplication "with a special Regard unto the sad case of my son *Increase;* that I may have Light arise in Darkness to me under it; . . . and that the *Discourse,* which it has awakened me to prepare for the public may be published and prospered."

Late in November, as I have said, Cotton Mather fell very ill. For five weeks he was unable to make entries in his diary. As I have said, those he made when he grew better show him broken in health and mind as never before. I will cite but one: it is the last; and one, I think, with which he would have chosen to bid us farewell.

February 7. 1724-5. Lord's-Day. When I sitt alone in my Languishments, unable to Write or to Read, I often compose Little Hymns agreeable unto my present circumstances, and Sing them unto the Lord. Vast numbers have I had of these, which are immediately all Forgotten. But tho' none of them have been hitherto recorded, I will here insert one of them; inasmuch as I design to use it again, and often upon occasion. Having found my Mind for some time without such precious and Impressive Thoughts of God my SAVIOUR, as are the Life of my Spirit, I thus mourn'd and Sung unto the Lord:—

O glorious Christ of God! I Live
In Views of Thee Alone.
Life to my gasping Soul, Oh! Give!
Shine Thou, or I'm undone.

I cannot Live, my God, if Thou
Enliven'st not my Faith!
I'm Dead; I'm Lost; Oh! Save me now
From a Lamented Death.

For the Return of my Health I added:

My glorious Healer now Restore
My Health, and make me whole.
But this is what I most implore:
Oh, For an Healed Soul

XVI. *The Last Days of Cotton Mather.*

1724-1728 In this year, 1724, Cotton Mather's youngest surviving daughter, Elizabeth, had married one Edward Cooper. In this year, too, Benjamin Franklin saw him for the last time. In Franklin's Autobiography, the prince of self-made Yankees tells that one of the books that most influenced his youth was Cotton Mather's "Essays to Do Good," [1]—a work in which Mather insisted on a point that was always dear to him, the importance of combined, co-operative effort. In 1724, Franklin, better dressed than usual, came home for a few weeks from his first expedition to Philadelphia. Among other visits, the young man paid one to Cotton Mather, in the study where a placard bearing the words "Be Brief" warned visitors that they had to do with the busiest of men. When Franklin took leave, Mather showed him out through a dark passage, and, as the youth was walking ahead, suddenly called out, "Stoop!" Not understanding, Franklin took another step and bumped his head against a projecting beam. Whereupon Mather warned him that, throughout life, he would find judicious stooping a great means of avoiding trouble. So they parted. Years afterwards Franklin wrote Samuel Mather that he had never forgotten the useful counsel.

For the remaining three years of Cotton Mather's life, I find no record that shows him other than we have seen him. Between the beginning of 1725 and the end of 1728, Sibley shows that no less than fifty of his publications appeared,—sermons, books of good counsel, and so on. In general, one may say that his published work was historical, biographical, expository, and hortatory: its chief features are lives of good people, instructions as to how good may be done, explanations of Scripture and of various points

[1] See Sibley, III. 102, 103. The book was published in 1710.

of godliness, and such scientific instruction as appeared in his writings about inoculation. Considering how much he wrote and how actively he busied himself with public affairs, it is amazing that he left behind so little controversial writing. The fact is, I take it, that he was from the beginning so convinced of the essential authority of the clergy, that, except under very great provocation, argument of any kind seemed needless in one of his profession.

In August, 1726, his daughter Elizabeth died, leaving children. Of his own fifteen children only Samuel and Hannah survived him.

In December, 1727, he fell ill.[2]

"My *Last Enemy* is come," he said, "I would say my *Last Friend.*"

He lay ill five or six weeks. On Thursday, February 8th, he began to suffer with

an hard *Cough* and a suffocating *Asthma* with a *Fever;* but he felt no great Pain; he had the sweet *Composure* and *easy Departure,* for which he had entreated so *often* and *fervently* the sovereign Disposer of all Things.

On Sunday, writes Samuel Mather,

I asked him *what Sentence or Word . . . He would have me think on constantly,* for I ever desired to have him before me and hear him speaking to me. He said, "Remember only that one word *Fructuosus.*" [3]

On Tuesday, February 13th, 1728,—the day after his sixty-fifth birthday,—he died.

Sewall describes the last scene of all:—

Monday, Febr. 19. Dr. Cotton Mather is intombed: Bearers, The Rev'd. Mr. Colman, Mr. Thacher; Mr. Sewall, Prince; Mr. Webb, Cooper. The Church went before the Corps. First, the Rev'd Mr. Gee[4] in Mourning alone, then 3 Deacons, then Capt. Hutchinson, Adam Winthrop esqr. Col. Hutchinson—Went up Hull street. I went in a Coach. All the Council had gloves; I had a pair. It seems when the Mourners return'd to the House, Mr. Walter said, My Bror. had better Bearers: Mr. Prince answer'd They bore the better part.

[a] S. Mather, Life, VII. 3, 4.   [3] Fruitful.
[4] Cotton Mather's colleague at the North Church.

XVII. *Cotton Mather, the Puritan Priest.*

Before Cotton Mather's tomb was fairly closed, then, men who had known him best were whispering among themselves other than good things concerning the dead. Posterity has held them right. A subtle priest, self-seeking, vain, arrogant, inconsistent, mischievous in his eternal business, many have called him: even if honest, dreadfully deluded and grotesquely lacking in judgment, is what those mostly say who say the best. And if we had only public records to guide us, I should be disposed to assent.

The son of Increase Mather, the grandson of John Cotton and of Richard Mather, sprung of a race of chosen vessels of the Lord, himself a chosen vessel before his boyhood was fairly closed, intoxicated with such adulation as Urian Oakes spoke when, the youngest of Harvard graduates, he took his degree, he began his half-century of earthly work. Full of the traditions of the fathers, he pressed on, divinely authorized to lead the people of God in the path of salvation: whoever would not follow was godless. Then he saw his father's great work in England; and meanwhile did great work at home. He saw the tyranny of Andros fall: his prayers were answered. He saw Phipps come with the new Charter: New England was saved. Now he might lead on more confidently still. And he plunged into the horrors of witchcraft. And he saw theocracy fall with poor Sir William Phipps. And he saw Harvard College lost to the cause of the fathers. And he saw the very churches of Boston preaching new doctrines, full of delusion. For five and thirty years he saw the clergy of New England started on the course in which they still travel: from a position where the influence of the church was greater than anywhere else in the world, to one where the influence of the church has become almost imperceptible. And he fought against fate with every weapon he could clutch; and he believed his own advance-

ment was what God needed to restore His kingdom; and some of
the blows he struck—and for aught I know many of them—may
have been foul ones.

But before we can judge him aright, we must strive to see him
as he saw himself. This is what I have tried to do. I have told his
story perhaps too much in his own words. By no other means
could I show so simply what seems to me the truth: that with a
depth of human nature which makes him above most men who
have lived a brother man to all of us, he never ceased striving,
amid endless stumblings and errors, to do his duty.

It was his lot to possess a mind and a temperament more rest-
lessly active than most men ever know. With this nature, it was
his lot to live all his life in a petty provincial town, further re-
moved from the great current of contemporary life than any
spot to-day in the civilized world. And this he never realized;
nor have any of those realized who have sat to judge him. His
grandfathers, and the other founders of New England, came from
the midst of the seething England which was soon to dethrone
the Stuarts, full of the passion of a contest that had been to every
one of them the greatest of earthly realities. His father's life had
brought the elder man face to face with kings and bishops: Increase Mather had fought hard to preserve and to perpetuate a
Puritanism whose pristine freshness was still within his own
memory. But when Cotton Mather's time came, Puritanism—like
Anglicanism itself—was already not the great reality it had once
been: it had become a tradition. The world travels faster nowadays. The Civil War is already such a tradition to us.

This great tradition of Puritanism he fought so passionately
to defend had in it the seeds of a grim, untruthful formalism,
which has made it seem to many men of later times a gloomy
delusion, fruitful only of limitation and of cant. Those who see
in it only or chiefly this, forget what even to Cotton Mather himself was its greatest truth. Few human philosophies have been
more essentially ideal; few systems formulated by men have so
strenuously kept before the minds of those who accept them the
transitory unreality of those things which human beings can perceive, the eternal and infinite reality of the Divine universe that
lies beyond human ken. Once learn this, and nothing on this earth
is so great as to deserve a care, when we think of the infinite

realities beyond; nor anything on this earth so mean as not to be a manifestation of divine truth. At once contemptible and reverend, this earthly life of ours is but the fragment of an instant in the timeless eternities of God. But to the Puritans, it was an instant in which the infinite mercy of God, with free grace mitigating His infinite justice, gave every living man the chance and the hope of finding in himself the signs of eternal salvation. It is not every man who can rise to such heights of idealism as this: whoever cannot or will not so rise, whoever cannot feel beneath the austere pettiness of Puritanism the passionate enthusiasm that made things unseen—Hell and Heaven, the Devil, and the Angels, and God—greater realities than anything this side of eternity, can never even guess what Puritanism meant.

On its earthly side, however, Puritanism had a trait which has been more generally recognized, though not, perhaps, more fully understood. In its origin it was Protestant. It began, and it gained earthly strength, in a passionate revolt of human thought from those phases of ecclesiastical tradition which human experience had proved false and wicked. God's word contains God's truth, the first Protestants cried; we will read it for ourselves, none but God shall be our guide. So, Bible in hand, they led the way for who would follow; and when they were gone far enough to muster their forces, they would have cried halt. But what authority had they to stop the progress they had urged? God's world contains God's truth, cried those of their followers whose spirit came nearest to that of the leaders: let us read it there, and read it each for himself; none but God shall be our guide. And those who press ever onward, seeking God's truth each for himself, are Protestants of to-day. Protestantism can have no priesthood.

This truth Cotton Mather never guessed. To this day honest Protestant Christians are blind to it. Nor did he guess, either, some other truths which modern Protestant Christianity equally fails to recognize. The priestly office, let it derive its authority from Rome or Canterbury, Geneva or Utah, demands in those who exercise it even most fervently a trait which in its most obvious form the priests are the first to condemn,—histrionic insincerity. Placed before men as an accredited spiritual leader, the priest—whatever his mood or his character—must conduct himself, at least in his public functions, as if he were what no human being ever was or can be,—wholly given up to the service of God. And the adulation of the worshippers who see in him an ever present minister of God strengthens him year by year in the power in which applause strengthens the actor: the power of seeming at will to be what in the depths of his heart he is not. To gain this power, to strengthen it, is part of the priest's duty. And there is no way of strengthening it so certain as the way Cotton Mather took, like the saints of Rome before him. Day after day, week after week, month after month, year after year, he cast himself in the dust before the Lord; he strained his eyes for a fleeting glimpse of the robes and crowns of God's angels, his ears for the faintest echo of their celestial music. Pure in motive, noble in purpose, his whole life was one unending effort to strengthen in himself that phase of human nature whose inner token is a riot of mystical emotion, whose outward signs are un-witting manifestations of unfettered credulity and unmeant fraud.

Yet it is not as a sly and superstitious priest that I remember him to-day: any more than I think that slyness and superstition to-day make up the character of a Christian minister. In the first place, the passionate idealism to which he held with all his heart —like honest priests since the world began—coloured, and glorified, and made divine, even the meanest things in the petty earthly life he knew. A squatting dog brought him a message straight from the throne of God. In the second place, the life he lived—with all its grotesque pettiness—was the life which had in it the seeds of that great continental life in which lies the chief hope of the modern world. To understand the America of to-day, we must know the New England of the fathers; to know the first New England of the fathers, there is no better way than to study this man,—its last, its most typical incarnation. And as we study him, and then look back at the figure that emerges from the dusty books and manuscripts of two centuries ago, the final trait of him, that hides the rest, is this: strenuously, de-voutly, he did what he deemed his duty.

All about him he saw ever crescent disappointment and sorrow and earthly failure; but he never lost heart, not ever for a moment ceased effort, with word and deed alike, to do good to mankind. *Fructuosus*—be fruitful, do God's work here on earth—was his last command to his son. And the incessant training of his career in the art that in its meaner form he would have been the first to execrate,—the art of the actor, who can at will seem to be what in truth he is not,—made him what it makes good ministers to-day. More than other men they can sympathize with mankind: in agony, in sorrow, in sin, men turn to them for aid, for counsel, for charity in all its divinest forms. And this the saintly actors give as no other men can, thus doing good unspeakably reverend. The very weakness of their calling, so palpable to those who have not known their beneficence,—so fruitful of obloquy and execration in those who neither share their faith nor will let themselves sympathize,—makes them more blessed to mankind than a thousand of their more candid fellows. Out of evil God brings good: it is the histrionic insincerity of priesthood that brings to unhappy men the Divine sympathy of priests. And in his ministry Cotton Mather never faltered: with ever growing earnestness, he went through that grim and sorrowful old New England, in every deliberate thought and act ministering to the bodies and the souls of the people of God. *Fructuosus*—fruitful—is the final word for him.

And what fruit has his priesthood borne that is with us to-day? New England is far enough from the stern creed in which alone he saw hope of salvation. But not long ago an old friend, talking of the New England that both of us love, spoke a phrase I like to remember: "We have here," he said, "what the world has never seen before: we have devout free thought." It is the Protestantism of the fathers that has won us our freedom. But freedom alone were a curse. It is the faithful earnestness of the Puritan priesthood that has kept our freedom from straying into that pert irreverence which elsewhere than here has made so many who cast aside the false cast with it the true. And among the Puritan priests there was never one, I believe, more faithfully earnest than this Cotton Mather.

One hundred and sixty-three years have passed since he was laid in his father's tomb on Copp's Hill. And few of us to-day can believe that he is gone to such a little company of God's elect as would make the heaven he preached of. If he be, then, when by chance he looks back at the earth where he laboured, he must see a sight that for the instant should dim the joys of Paradise.

But there are not a few to-day who dream of a heaven in whose blessedness all the fetters of humanity are broken; where what is best in men waxes better than men can even dream, amid the ever-growing glories of eternal freedom from sin, and weakness, and sorrow. And if by chance his eyes have opened again in a heaven like this, and if from thence he looks back to an earth where his sins and errors have borne little fruit, but where the devoutness of the free thought of New England speaks still for what was best in his human life, he sees, I like to think, little that should disturb the great serenity of his peace.

Authorities.

The books I have cited are these:

ANDROS TRACTS, 3 vols. Boston: Prince Society, 1868-1874.

CALEF, Robert: *More Wonders of the Invisible World,* etc. Salem: Cushing and Appleton, 1823.

MASSACHUSETTS HISTORICAL SOCIETY: Collections:—
Fourth Series, Vol. VIII.: *The Mather Papers,* 1868.
Fifth Series, Vols. V.-VII.: *Sewall's Diary,* 1878-1882.
Sixth Series, Vols. I., II.: *Sewall's Letter-Book,* 1886-1888.

MATHER, Cotton: Manuscript diaries in possession of the Massachusetts Historical Society, Boston; of the American Antiquarian Society, Worcester, Mass.; and of the Congregational Library, Boston.

—— *Magnalia Christi Americana.* Hartford: Silas Andrus and Son. Vol. I., 1855; Vol. II., 1853.

—— *Parentator.* Boston: Nathaniel Belknap, 1724.

—— *Paterna* (manuscript), in possession of Mrs. Skinner of Chicago.

MATHER, Samuel: *Life of Cotton Mather.* Boston: Samuel Gerrish, 1729.

PALFREY, John Gorham: *Compendious History of New England,* 4 vols. Boston: J. R. Osgood & Co., 1884.

PEABODY, Wm. B. O.: *Life of Cotton Mather.* Sparks's American Biographies, Vol. VI. Boston: Hilliard, Gray, & Co., 1836.

QUINCY, Josiah: *History of Harvard University,* 2 vols. Cambridge: John Owen, 1840.

SIBLEY, John Langdon: *Harvard Graduates,* Vol. III. Cambridge: Charles William Sever, 1885.

UPHAM, Charles W.: *Salem Witchcraft,* 2 vols. Boston: Wiggin and Lunt, 1867.

The numerous standard books I have consulted I need not name. I may perhaps, however, mention the remarkable impression of Puritan ways of thought that may be obtained by reading the first two volumes of Stedman and Hutchinson's *Library of American Literature;* and the notable suggestiveness of Mr. Brooks Adams's *Emancipation of Massachusetts.*

Suggestions For Further Reading

(PUBLISHER GIVEN ONLY IF BOOK IS IN PRINT.)

I. MATHER AND PURITANISM

BEALL, Otho H., Jr., and Richard H. Shryock, *Cotton Mather: First Significant Figure in American Medicine*. Johns Hopkins, 1954. (Portions of the "Angel of Bethesda" and helpful assessment of Mather and eighteenth-century science.)

BOAS, Ralph, and Louise Boas, *Cotton Mather, Keeper of the Puritan Conscience*. 1928. (Seeks to "humanize" Mather; journalistic and eager to psychoanalyze.)

BURR, George L., ed., *Narratives of the Witchcraft Cases, 1648-1706*. "Original Narratives of Early American History" series, 1914; reprinted, Barnes and Noble, 1959. (Selections from Cotton and Increase Mather, Brattle, and Calef; Burr tends to excise from the texts the more interesting ideas.)

FORD, Worthington C., ed., *The Diary of Cotton Mather*. 2 vols., 1911-12; reprinted, Ungar, 1957. (The only major Mather text in print.)

HOLMES, Thomas H., *Cotton Mather: A Bibliography of His Works*. 3 vols., 1940. (Definitive critical comments by various hands concerning the major works.)

KITTREDGE, George Lyman, *Witchcraft in Old and New England*. 1929.

LUDWIG, Richard M., *Bibliographical Supplement to the Literary History of the United States*. Macmillan, 1959. (Expanded version of Vol. III, Spiller, *et al.*, *LHUS*, 1948; lists the major works of both Mathers and provides invaluable bibliography of reprints, articles, and monographs.)

MILLER, Perry, *The New England Mind: From Colony to Province*. Harvard, 1953, and Beacon.* (Intellectual history from the Synod of 1648 to the threshold of the Great Awakening; essential to an understanding of Mather and the issues he dealt with.)

——————, *The New England Mind: The Seventeenth Century*. Harvard, 1939, 1953, and Beacon.* (The contours of Puritan thought; the first premises inherited and modified by Mather.)

——————, *Orthodoxy in Massachusetts*. 1933; reprinted, Beacon.* ("Non-separating Congregationalism" from its Continental antecedents through the Cambridge Platform.)

* Available in a paperback edition.

——————, ed., *The American Puritans*. Anchor.* (Most useful anthology for the beginning student.)

——————, and Thomas H. Johnson, eds., *The Puritans*. 1938; rev. ed., Harper, 1963. (The landmark collection of primary materials, reissued with revised and enlarged bibliographies of writings by and about the Puritans. Editors' introductions constitute a cogent summary of Puritan thought.)

MORISON, Samuel Eliot, *Harvard College in the Seventeenth Century*. 2 vols., Harvard, 1936.

——————, *The Intellectual Life of Colonial New England*. Great Seal.* (First published in 1936 as *The Puritan Pronaos*; emphasizes "humanistic" range of Mather and New England culture.)

MURDOCK, Kenneth B., "The Colonial and Revolutionary Period," in Arthur H. Quinn, ed., *The Literature of the American People*. Appleton-Century-Crofts, 1951. (Succinct reassessment of the Mathers; bibliography of more important criticism.)

——————, *Increase Mather*. 1925. (Career to 1700; considers Cotton Mather's role in Revolution of 1689 and the witchcraft crisis.)

——————, *Literature and Theology in Colonial New England*. Harvard, 1949. (Measured analysis of place of sermons, poetry, history, and biography in Puritan life.)

——————, ed., *Selections from Cotton Mather*. 1926; reprinted, Hafner.* (Judicious excerpts and a cogent prefatory essay; the essential introduction to Mather.)

PARRINGTON, Vernon L., *Main Currents in American Thought. I. The Colonial Mind, 1620-1800*. 1926; reprinted, Harvest Books.*

SCHLATTER, Richard, "The Puritan Strain," in *The Reconstruction of American History*, ed. John Higham. Harper Torchbooks.* (Puritan historiography from J. T. Adams to the present; considers works of Morison, Murdock, and Miller "unsurpassed in the whole corpus of American historical scholarship.")

SCHNEIDER, Herbert W., *The Puritan Mind*. 1930; reprinted, Ann Arbor.* (Sketches basic themes against background of "social habitat," leaving "to others to dissect the theological bones of a once living religion.")

SIMPSON, Alan, *Puritanism in Old and New England*. Univ. of Chicago, 1955, and Phoenix.* (Excellent introduction to the broad spectrum of Puritan thought.)

II. WENDELL

BROOKS, Van Wyck, *New England: Indian Summer, 1865-1915*. 1940; reprinted, Everyman.

HOWE, M. A., DeWolfe, *Barrett Wendell and His Letters*. 1924. (Still the only full-length memoir. Extensive excerpts from correspondence, synopses of major writings, and a nearly complete listing of Wendell's publications, all of them out of print.)

* Available in a paperback edition.

JONES, Howard M., *The Theory of American Literature.* Cornell, 1948. (Remarks on Wendell's place in the development of American literary studies.)

MAY, Henry F., *The End of American Innocence.* Knopf, 1959. (The cultural scene, 1895-1915, with passing references to Wendell.)

Index

Adams, Brooks, his "Emancipation of Massachusetts," 230

Adultery, Cotton Mather's view of, 43, 120, 121, 123, 161

Afflations, 22, 105, 131, 138; Increase Mather's view of, 22

Allen, Rev. Mr., 44, 100

America, Cotton Mather's view of, 65, 67, 117, 119. *See also* England

Andros, Sir Edmund, Governor of New England: arrival, 33 ff., 51; life and character, 52; tyranny, 53, 56; deposed by Revolution, 56; subsequent career, 57; mentioned, 59, 60, 139, 223

"Andros Tracts," 54

Angels, Cotton Mather's view of, 39, 48, 59, 68, 84 ff., 106, 109, 110, 115, 119, 121, 123, 125, 129, 131, 136, 142 ff., 151, 207; vision of, 47

Anne, Queen, 139, 161, 184

Apostasy, Cotton Mather's view of, 51, 109 ff.; Increase Mather's view of, 103. *See also* Brattle Street Church

Assurances, of Cotton Mather, 37 ff., 46 ff., 62 ff., 68, 84, 87, 89, 102, 105, 108, 114, 119, 122, 127, 132, 136, 138, 141, 151, 154, 157, 195, 199, 205, 210, 216; of Increase Mather,

35, 53, 61, 99, 101, 211. *See also* Particular faiths; Premonitions; Presences of God

Atheism, temptations to, 19 ff., 60, 151, 169

Attention to divine services, Cotton Mather's, 41, 124

Banister, John, libels Cotton Mather, 171 ff.

Bellomont, Earl of, Governor of Massachusetts, 95, 102, 105, 110

Bishop, Bridget, hanged for witchcraft, 72, 80

Blackmore, Sir Richard, 173

Books, Cotton Mather favors hawking of, 41, 180, 183; gives away, 45, 62, 128, 131 ff., 155, 157 ff.; works with, despite devils, 82. *See also* Library; Writings of Cotton Mather

Boston, in Lincolnshire, 8 ff.; in Massachusetts, 9, 24, 41, 52, 56, 63, 73, 204, 211, 223

Bradstreet, Simon, Governor of Massachusetts, 31

Brattle, Thomas, treasurer of Harvard College, 105, 109

Brattle, Rev. William, of Cambridge, 54, 99, 103, 104, 105, 109, 148

Brattle Street Church (Fourth Church of Boston): origin, 103;

A 3
B 4
C 5
D 6
E 7
F 8
G 9
H 0
I 1
J 2